The Discourse of Wealth and Poverty in the Book of Proverbs

Biblical Interpretation Series

VOLUME 77

The Discourse of Wealth and Poverty in the Book of Proverbs

by

Timothy J. Sandoval

BRILL
LEIDEN • BOSTON
2006

This book is printed on acid-free paper.

Library of Congress Cataloging-in-Publication Data

Sandoval, Timothy J.
The discourse of wealth and poverty in the book of Proverbs / by Timothy J. Sandoval.
p. cm. — (Biblical interpretation series, ISSN 0928-0731 ; v. 77)
Includes bibliographical references and index.
ISBN 90-04-14492-7 (alk. paper)
1. Bible. O.T. Proverbs — Criticism, interpretation, etc. 2. Wealth — Biblical teaching. 3. Poverty — Biblical teaching. I. Title. II. Series.

BS1465.6.W35S36 2005
223'.706—dc22

2005050799

ISSN 0928-0731
ISBN 90 04 14492 7

PRINTED IN THE NETHERLANDS

For

Joanne Elizabeth Sandoval
and
Anthony Martin Sandoval

My first and best teachers

CONTENTS

ACKNOWLEDGMENTS

The Discourse and Wealth and Poverty in the Book of Proverbs is a slightly revised version of my 2004 Emory University dissertation of the same title. I am deeply grateful first and foremost to my advisor Carol Newsom who supported the project from the outset, encouraged me to make it truly my own, guided it through several important changes, and continually challenged me to refine my readings and arguments. Her exegetical and literary instincts, critical capacities, and intellectual acumen are matched by few. My gratitude also extends to the members of my dissertation committee. Martin Buss read my earliest musings on the question of wealth and poverty in Proverbs and provided helpful and timely insight throughout the process. Steve Kraftchick's keen analytical mind has instructed me on any number of occasions over the years and his critical response to especially the penultimate draft of the dissertation was indispensable to my completing the project. Whatever is of value in the present work is due in no small measure to these three individuals; for its shortcomings I alone am responsible.

Despite the long hours of solitary reading, study, and writing, the successful completion of this project would not have been possible without the support and encouragement of literally dozens of other individuals. In particular my thanks goes out to my other teachers at both Princeton Theological Seminary and Emory University. Choon-Leong Seow of Princeton first instructed me in Hebrew and instilled in me a love of the Hebrew Scriptures. At Emory Gene Tucker, Max Miller, Carl Holladay, Jon Gunnemann, and especially John Hayes offered their collegiality and taught me much more than I can name here. Likewise Neal Walls, now of Wake Forest University, though not directly involved in this project, over the years has been a true friend and academic mentor. Other friends from my Emory days, who now hold academic and other posts all over the country, include especially my Hebrew Bible classmates Carleen Mandolfo, Jacq Lapsley, Armin Siedlecki, Nickie Stipe, and Amy Merrill Willis; but also Graham Reside, Barbara McClure, Amy Cottrill, and Tim Verhey. I can scarcely imagine arriving at this point outside of their company.

I am also thankful to my faculty colleagues at Chicago Theological Seminary, both past and present, who over the last three years have supported and encouraged me as I struggled to finish the project. Ted Jennings has been a kind and prodding mentor. My colleagues in biblical studies, Ken Stone and Benny Liew, were especially helpful and encouraging as I explored various publishing options and strategies, as was Scott Haldeman. Bo Myung Seo, JoAnne Terrell, Laurel Schneider, Julia Speller, Robert Moore, Neil Gerdes, Lee Butler, Dow Edgerton, Thom Bower, and Janet Parker all had kind and encouraging words to offer along the way as well.

The friendship and support of many others during the years that I have worked on this project likewise needs to be acknowledged. Scattered across the United States and around the globe are: Sibylle Walker, Thomas Foell, Anne Regitze Skou, Chris Greenwald, Janice Tillman, David Nystrom and Karen Cox. Jeff Cox and Todd Cioffi, two of my oldest and closest friends, deserve special mention. I have been heartened by each in the inconspicuous but vital way that only confident friendship permits. Shannon Jackson, perhaps more than anyone over the years, shared the project's—and life's—successes and setbacks, and sweetened both. Parimal Patil was always willing to apply his extraordinary intellect to whatever issues from the project I might approach him with. More important, however, was his camaraderie when we were teaching colleagues at Emory University and his friendship, which like that of Emily Hudson, continues. In Chicago Esther Menn, Melody Knowles, John Knight, Cass Fisher, Mariana Fisher, Bill Wright, and Ajay Rao form for me an invaluable community of friendship, support, and intellectual curiosity.

I am grateful also to Professor Ellen van Wolde, who accepted the manuscript for Brill's Biblical Interpretation Series. Thanks are also due to Ivo Romein, Kim Fiona Plas, and Renee Otto from Brill who have overseen the publication process. My appreciation extends as well to the anonymous reader from Brill who provided me with helpful comments and suggestions. Greg Briggs provided invaluable assistance in preparing the Bibliography.

Over the years that I have been working on this project I have also been supported by two vibrant communities of faith: Oakhurst Presbyterian Church in Decatur, GA and Primera Iglesia Congregacional de Chicago. I am particularly grateful for the ministry of these two congregations and especially the leadership of Pastor Nibs Stroupe at Oakhurst and the Rev. José Rosa at Primera Iglesia. Likewise I have always been secure in the support and love of my family. My siblings Julia Bologna, Jeanne Cudworth, and Ted Sandoval, together with their families, through the occasional and curious inquiry of "are you done yet?" demonstrated this support and provided a further motivation to complete the project. The book, however, is dedicated to my parents, Joanne Elizabeth Sandoval and Anthony Martin Sandoval. I regret only that my father did not live long enough to see it appear in print.

Timothy J. Sandoval
Chicago, IL
April 2, 2005

ABBREVIATIONS

ABD	*Anchor Bible Dictionary*
BEO	Biblica et Orientalia
BET	Beiträge zur biblischen Exegese und Theologie
BHS	*Biblia Hebraica Stuttgartensia*, ed. K. Elliger and W. Rudolph (Stuttgart: Deutsche Bibelstiftung, 1977)
BTB	*Biblical Theology Bulletin*
BTS	Biblisch-Theologische Studien
BZAW	Beihefte zur Zeitschrift für die alttestamentliche Wissenschaft
DJD	Discoveries in the Judean Desert
ExpTim	*Expository Times*
GKC	Gesenius, Kautsch, and Coweley, Gensenius' Hebrew Grammar, 1910
HB	Hebrew Bible
HBI	History of Biblical Interpretation Series
IkathZ	*Internationale katholische Zeitschrift*
JANES	*Journal of the Ancient Near Eastern Society*
JBL	*Journal of Biblical Literature*
JNES	*Journal of Near Eastern Studies*
JSOT	*Journal for the Study of the Old Testament*
JSOTSup	Journal for the Study of the Old Testament Supplement Series
LAI	Library of Ancient Israel
LXX	Septuagint (Greek version of HB)
MH	Mishnaic Hebrew
MS(S)	Manuscript(s)
MT	Masoretic Text
NCBC	New Century Bible Commentary
NIB	*New Interpreter's Bible*
NJPS	New Jewish Publication Society Version
NRSV	New Revised Standard Version
OBO	Orbis Biblicus et Orientalis
OrAnt	*Oriens Antiquus*
OTL	Old Testament Library
RCT	Routledge Critical Thinkers

SBLDS	Society of Biblical Literature Dissertation Series
SBLSS	Society of Biblical Literature Semeia Studies
SNVAO	Skrifter utgitt av det Norske Videnskaps-Akademi i Oslo
SPAW	*Sitzungsberichte der Preussischen Akademie der Wissenschaften*
SPIB	Scripta Pontificii Instituti Biblici
STDJ	Studies on the Texts of the Desert of Judah
TBAT	Theologische Bücherei, Altes Testament
TDOT	*Theological Dictionary of the Old Testament*, Botterweck and Ringgren, 1974ff.
THAT	*Theologisches Handwörterbuch zum Alten Testament*
TrinJ	*Trinity Journal*
TS	*Theological Studies*
VT	*Vetus Testamentum*
VTSup	Supplements to Vetus Testamentum
WBC	Word Biblical Commentary
WMANT	Wissenschaftliche Monographien zum Alten und Neuen Testament
ZAW	*Zeitschrift für die alttestamentliche Wissenschaft*
ZBK	Zürcher Bibelkommentare

CHAPTER ONE

PROVERBS, METAPHOR, AND DISCOURSE

"Wealth and poverty" and "rich and poor" are terms that belong not only to the realm of economic discourse but to ethics as well. They involve a recognition of the unequal distribution of material goods in a society and so at the very least highlight issues of distributive justice, which is concerned with understanding why there are material inequalities in a particular society, how those inequalities are justified, ought to be justified, ought to be mitigated, or not. Yet matters of distribution are also intimately linked to the way a particular society structures its social relationships and corresponding social responsibilities—that is, how it answers the question of the appropriate ordering of human relationships. Discourses that have much to say about wealth and poverty reflect not only how problems surrounding the distribution of material goods are negotiated, but are part of a broader culture's creation of value, meaning, and significance—its entire moral universe. The practice of unfolding and explicating various discourses of wealth and poverty allows one to glimpse how such discourses are related to this wider context.

Although the discourse of wealth and poverty is not the only kind of moral discourse in the Hebrew Bible, it is one that exercised a particularly important role on the moral imagination of Israelite and Judean (Yehud) society. Such economic rhetoric is taken up in different ways in every division of the Hebrew Scriptures.[1] Ancient Israel's

[1] Note for instance the number of studies on the poor in the Psalms, which include Alfred Rahlfs, *ʿAni und ʿanaw in den Psalmen* (Göttingen: Dieterich, 1892); Harris Birkeland, *ʿAni und ʿanaw in den Psalmen* (SNVAO 4, Oslo, 1932); P. A. Munch, "Einige Bemerkungen zu den ʿanawim und den resaʾim in den Psalmen," *Le Monde Oriental* 30 (1936): 13–26, P. van den Berghe, "ʿAni und ʿanaw dans les Psaumes," in *Le Psautier* (ed. R. De Langhe; Louvain: Orientalia et Biblica Loveneinsia IV, 1962), 273–95; Susan Gillingham, "The Poor in the Psalms," *ExpTim* 100 (1988): 15–19. Often this literature is concerned with whether it is warranted to postulate at some point in ancient Israel's or Judah's (Yehud's) history the existence of a party of the "pious poor." See J. David Pleins, *The Social Visions of the Hebrew Bible: A Theological Introduction* (Louisville: WJK, 2001), 419–424.

wisdom literature is no exception.[2] The canonical (including deutero-canonical) wisdom books of Proverbs, Job, Ecclesiastes, Sirach, and Wisdom of Solomon—as well as certain extra-canonical works that exhibit a number of wisdom features such as the *Epistle of Enoch* and several Qumran texts—often thematize issues of wealth and poverty in important ways. It is, however, impossible in a single study to consider fully how the language of poverty and riches functions in

---

The prophetic concern with the poor and dispossessed is also a widely recognized and discussed theme, especially for those concerned with issues of liberation and social justice. See, for instance, Carol J. Dempsey, *The Prophets: A Liberation-Critical Reading* (Fortress: Minneapolis, 2000). A glance at the indices of Gustavo Gutierrez's *A Theology of Liberation* (New York: Orbis, 1973) and the volume edited by Norman K. Gottwald and Richard A. Horsley, *The Bible and Liberation* (rev.; New York: Orbis, 1993), however, is revealing. Gutierrez makes over eighty references to the prophets (versus eleven citations of wisdom texts). The Gottwald and Horsley volume reveals the same situation. One should note, however, that some liberationist thinkers have turned their attention to the biblical wisdom literature. See, for instance, Gustavo Gutierrez, *On Job: God Talk and the Suffering of the Innocent* (New York: Orbis, 1987); Diane Bergant, *Israel's Wisdom Literature: A Liberation-Critical Reading* (Minneapolis: Fortress, 1997); Anthony R. Ceresko, *Introduction to Old Testament Wisdom: A Spirituality for Liberation* (New York: Orbis, 1999); Elsa Tamez, *When the Horizons Close: Rereading Ecclesiastes* (New York: Orbis, 2000).

The rights of the poor in the pentateuchal legal codes have been examined by, among others, Norbert Lohfink, "Poverty in the Laws of the Ancient Near East and of the Bible," *TS* 52 (1991): 34–50, and Milton Schwantes, *Das Recht der Armen* (BET 4; Frankfurt: Lang, 1977)—though neither limit their study to the five books of Moses. On the question of social justice in the larger ancient Near Eastern context see Moshe Weinfeld, *Social Justice in Ancient Israel and in the Ancient Near East* (Jerusalem: Magnes, 1995). A number of older studies concerned more broadly with the question of the poor in the Bible include W. W. G. Baudissin, "Die alttestamentliche Religion und die Armen," *Preussische Jahrbücher* 149 (1912): 193–231; Antonin Causse, *Les "Pauvres" de'israël* (Strasbourg: Libraire Istra, 1922); Hans Bruppacher, *Die Beurteilung der Armut im Alten Testament* (Zürich: Verlag Seldwyla, 1924); and A. Kuschke, "Arm und Reich im Alten Testament mit besonderer Berücksichtigung der nachexilischen Zeit," *ZAW* 57 (1939): 31–57, whose work is noted by many. See further, Norbert Lohfink, "Gottes Reich und die Wirtschaft in der Bibel," *IKathZ* 15 (1986): 153–76, and *Option for the Poor* (Berkeley: Bibal, 1987).

[2] Only relatively recently, however, has intensive and extensive work having to do with matters of wealth and poverty in specifically wisdom texts begun. See, for instance, Harold C. Washington, *Wealth and Poverty in the Instruction of Amenemope and the Hebrew Proverbs* (SBLDS 142; Atlanta: Scholars Press, 1996); Raymond C. Van Leeuwen, "Wealth and Poverty: System and Contradiction in Proverbs," *Hebrew Studies* 33 (1992): 25–36; R. N. Whybray, *Wealth and Poverty in the Book of Proverbs* (Sheffield: JSOT, 1990); J. David Pleins, "Poverty in the Social World of the Wise," *JSOT* 37 (1987): 61–78; G. H. Wittenberg, "The Lexical Context of the Terminology for 'poor' in the Book of Proverbs," *Scriptura* 2 (1986): 40–85; Bruce V. Malchow, "Social Justice in the Wisdom Literature," *BTB* 12 (1982): 120–124. See too F. Charles Fensham, "Widow, Orphan, and the Poor in Ancient Near Eastern Legal and Wisdom Literature," *JNES* 21 (1962): 129–139.

all of these books.[3] Instead this project will detail and describe how the discourse of wealth and poverty is constructed and functions, not in every exemplar of ancient Israelite and Jewish wisdom literature, but specifically in the instructional book of Proverbs.[4]

The project is thus essentially an exercise in "biblical ethics"—a kind of sub-discipline of biblical studies that has as one of its goals

---

[3] The book of Job takes up the topics of wealth and poverty/rich and poor primarily as subsidiary arguments in the context of an exploration of issues that have been framed in other terms—namely the possibility of disinterested piety (cf. 1:9) and the adequacy of the moral framework shared by Job and his friends. See Carol A. Newsom, "The Book of Job: Introduction, Commentary, and Reflections," *NIB* 4:317–637, esp. 320–25; 627–32, and *The Book of Job: A Contest of Moral Imaginations* (New York: Oxford University Press, 2003). The economic rhetoric of Ecclesiastes is largely peculiar to this biblical book, though much of its language is known from the epigraphic material of the Levant from the Persian period on. On the largely commercial terminology of Ecclesiastes and the book generally, see C. L. Seow, *Ecclesiastes: A New Translation with Introduction and Commentary* (AB 18c; New York: Doubleday, 1997), esp. 21–35. Cf. Mitchell Dahood, "The Phoenician Background of Qoheleth," *Biblica* 47 (1966): 264–282. See too Michael V. Fox, *A Time to Tear Down and a Time to Build Up: A Rereading of Ecclesiastes* (Grand Rapids: Eerdmans, 1999), esp. 51–70, 97–107, 109–119. On the topic of wealth and poverty in Sirach, see Benjamin G. Wright III, "The Discourse of Riches and Poverty in Sirach," *SBL Seminar Papers*, 1998 (Atlanta: Scholars Press, 1998), 559–578. Wright has revised this paper with Claudia V. Camp. See, "Who Has Been Tested by Gold and Found Perfect? Ben Sira's Discourse of Riches and Poverty," *Henoch* 23 (2001): 153–74. Cf. Oda Wischmeyer, *Die Kultur des Buches Jesus Sirach* (Berlin: W. de Gruyter, 1994), esp. 51–69. On wealth and poverty in 1 Enoch see George W. E. Nickelsburg, "Revisiting the Rich and the Poor in 1 Enoch 92–105 and the Gospel of Luke," *SBL Seminar Papers*, 1998 (Atlanta: Scholars Press, 1998), 579–605. On the question of wealth and poverty in Qumran documents see Catherine M. Murphy, *Wealth in the Dead Sea Scrolls and in the Qumran Community* (STDJ 40; Leiden: Brill, 2002). The most significant wisdom text from Qumran, 4QInstruction, makes important use of especially poverty rhetoric. For a critical presentation of this text (with a commentary) see John Strugnell, Daniel J. Harrington, and Torlief Elgvin, in consultation with Joseph A. Fitzmyer, *Sapiential Texts, Part 2: Cave 4. XXIV* (DJD XXXIV; Oxford: Clarendon, 1999). On wealth and poverty in 4QInstruction see Matthew J. Goff, *The Worldly and Heavenly Wisdom of 4QInstruction* (STDJ 50; Leiden: Brill, 2003), 127–67; Murphy, *Wealth in the Dead Sea Scrolls*, 163–209.

[4] Though some would limit the designation "instruction" to Proverbs 1–9, these introductory chapters dictate how the rest of the book is read (see below) so that it is appropriate to consider the entire book to be "instructional" wisdom literature. Miriam Lichtheim similarly notes that although in Egyptian wisdom literature the designation instruction is technically limited to those works that are addressed from a father to a son, a number of other texts that do not strictly meet this criteria are well considered "instructional." See *Ancient Egyptian Literature: A Book of Readings* (vol. 1; Berkeley: University of California Press, 1973), 134. On the instruction genre and its appropriateness as a description of Proverbs 1–9 (but not the sentence material of later chapters), see William McKane, *Proverbs: A New Approach* (Philadelphia: Westminster, 1970), 1–10.

a full description of the moral contours of biblical and cognate texts.[5] However, in taking up this task the work will also shed light on the question of the social setting from which the text under consideration emerged. Hence this study of the discourse of wealth and poverty in Proverbs will also contribute to a more comprehensive understanding of the larger social landscapes of ancient Israel and Judah (Yehud) as these are refracted through the particular wisdom book of Proverbs.

1.1. Why This Text?

The book of the Proverbs is an ideal text in which to consider the discourse of wealth and poverty for it draws on wealth and poverty language more than any other book in the Hebrew Bible.[6] Forms derived from the root ר-ו-ש/ר-י-ש (e.g., "poor person," "poverty") appear no fewer than twenty-three times (twenty times in chs. 10–29; ten times paralleled to a form derived from the root ע-ש-ר; see below). Similarly the term דל ("poor, oppressed one") occurs fifteen times in Proverbs (all in chs. 10–29) while the lexeme מחסור ("lack," "poverty") is attested eight times (seven times in chs. 10–29). Less

[5] A more complete effort at "biblical ethics" would subsequently take up the question of what role the biblical witness might or ought to play in contemporary moral reflection. This study, however, is concerned primarily with the task of describing the moral world of a classical text. Two standard Christian handbooks or introductions to biblical ethics in English are Bruce C. Birch and Larry L. Rasmussen, *Bible and Ethics in the Christian Life* (exp. and rev; Minneapolis: Augsburg, 1989) and William C. Spohn, *What are They Saying About Scripture and Ethics* (rev.; New York: Paulist, 1995). See further Charles E. Curran and Richard A. McCormick, eds., *The Use of Scripture in Moral Theology* (Readings in Moral Theology 4; New York: Paulist, 1984); Thomas W. Ogletree, *The Use of the Bible in Christian Ethics* (Philadelphia: Fortress, 1983). Each of these rightly makes the distinction between the ethics of the Bible and the use of the Bible in ethics, and is primarily concerned with the latter. A number of other studies more concerned with the former aspect of "biblical ethics" include Waldemar Janzen, *Old Testament Ethics: A Paradigmatic Approach* (Louisville: WJK, 1994). Mary E. Mills considers the ethics of biblical narratives in *Biblical Morality: Moral Perspectives in Old Testament Narratives* (Aldershot, England: Ashgate, 2001). John Barton's *Understanding Old Testament Ethics: Approaches and Explorations* (Louisville: WJK, 2003) is concerned with the range of issues in biblical ethics. On the wisdom literature and Proverbs in particular, see Holger Delkurt, *Ethische Einsichten in der Alttestamentlichen Spruchweisheit* (BTS 21; Neukirchen-Vluyn: Neukirchener Verlag, 1993).

[6] Washington, *Wealth and Poverty*, 1.

frequent is עני ("poor, afflicted one"), which appears six to eight times (three times in chs. 10–29) depending on how one tallies the Ketiv-Qere עניים/ענוים. Likewise אביון ("poor one") is attested only four times (one time in chs. 10–29; three times in chs. 30–31). By contrast, the term עשיר ("rich person") appears nine times (all in chs. 10–29) while עשר ("riches") also is attested nine times (six times in chs. 10–29). Verbal forms of the root ע-ש-ר appear on at least five more occasions (all in chs. 10–29). The common term הון ("wealth"), too, is attested some eighteen times throughout Proverbs (twelve times in chs. 10–29).

Of course the discourse of wealth and poverty in Proverbs is not limited to the terms just noted. These simply are the primary lexemes the text employs and provide the organizational starting point of this study. An examination of other motifs and terminology, which might properly be understood as forming and informing the larger discourse of wealth and poverty, will necessarily be included as well—notably the rhetorics of desire and laziness, terms denoting precious metals, as well as the economic terminology of weights and measures, borrowing, lending, surety, money, and exchange.[7]

Furthermore, the discourse of wealth and poverty in Proverbs is also important to consider because this book is the template against which other biblical and early Jewish wisdom texts are read and judged.[8] Careful study of the economic rhetoric of Proverbs will provide a fuller framework for comparing the wealth and poverty language of these other wisdom works, which emerge from different social, economic, and political contexts.

Finally, a consideration of the discourse of wealth and poverty in Proverbs is appropriate because the precise nature of the book's treatment of this topic is something that has continually eluded interpreters. However, before considering this issue more fully in the following chapters, two further, but related, matters need to be considered. The first is the nature of metaphor, for metaphoric and figurative language, as I will show, plays an important role in the discourse of wealth and poverty in Proverbs. The second is the notion

---

[7] Cf. Whybray, *Wealth and Poverty*, 11–15 who offers an extensive listing of Hebrew terms that might be said to belong to the discourse of wealth and poverty in Proverbs.

[8] As Dianne Bergant (*Israel's Wisdom Literature*, 78) states: "The book of Proverbs is the basic source of the study of biblical wisdom."

of "discourse," for what a discourse is and what it might mean to analyze a discourse is not necessarily self-evident. Both discussions, however, constitute less a description of a method to be employed but represent more broadly a sketch of my methodological or literary-critical orientation.

1.2. Proverbs and Metaphorical Language

One of the most important characteristics of the discourse of wealth and poverty in Proverbs is its figurative or metaphoric quality. Without understanding something of the nature of this figurative language it is impossible to understand fully the book's talk about wealth and poverty. Indeed the book of Proverbs constructs for its readers a complicated symbolic moral world. In this symbolic construction, however, it is possible to discern aspects of the text's discourse of wealth and poverty that point to the appropriateness and necessity of considering the book's figurative imagination. Features internal to various proverbial sayings along with the book's programmatic prologue and the form of its short sentence sayings all point to the figurative quality of key aspects of the text.

1.2.a. *Paul Ricoeur and Metaphor*

Paul Ricoeur, as part of a larger intellectual project in which he seeks to preserve the truth value of literature and religious language—i.e., all forms of poetic discourse which are non-descriptive or do not attempt to refer immediately to the world of objects—has offered a powerful account of metaphor. Ricoeur's work is philosophically dense and sophisticated. However aspects of it are suggestive for studying the discourse of wealth and poverty in Proverbs. This is so not only because Ricoeur offers a helpful model of how metaphors themselves work, but also because of two further notions he puts forward. The first is his suggestion that a literary text opens up a view of a possible world that eclipses the tangible, objective world—a view that can be said to correspond to the patterns of value and meaning that might be discerned in a particular discourse. The second notion (which will be treated at the end of this chapter) has to do with his efforts to indicate how a text, which may not initially appear metaphorical, might reveal certain aspects of metaphoricity.

Ricoeur believes that when considering metaphor it is best to speak of metaphorical utterances rather than the metaphorical use of a word. For Ricoeur, metaphor takes place not at the level of the word, but on the level of the sentence; it has to do primarily with the semantics of the sentence rather than with the semantics of a word. A metaphor, for Ricoeur, is born out of the "tension" between all the terms in a metaphorical utterance.[9] Yet "the tension in a metaphorical utterance is really not something that occurs between two terms in the utterance, but rather between two opposed interpretations of the utterance."[10] It involves the difficulty or "absurdity" that arises when one attempts to interpret a metaphorical utterance literally—for example by understanding the terms in the utterance and their relationships only as they are regarded in lexically codified or common, ordinary usage.[11] As Ricoeur explains, "the metaphorical interpretation presupposes a literal interpretation which self-destructs in a significant contradiction."[12]

This contradiction, however, is resolved by means of what Ricoeur calls "resemblance"—the previously unnoticed "kinship" between two concepts that the metaphor awakens.[13] For Ricoeur, "what is at stake in a metaphorical statement is making a 'kinship' appear where ordinary vision perceives no mutual appropriateness at all."[14] Resemblance renders close that which was distant and the best metaphors "institute a resemblance" rather than merely register one.[15] Put otherwise, resemblance involves a kind of cognitive and affective mapping between two different conceptual domains, which one might call, in

---

[9] Paul Ricoeur, *Interpretation Theory: Discourse and the Surplus of Meaning* (Fort Worth: Texas Christian University Press, 1976), 49–50. Cf. Paul Ricoeur, "Biblical Hermeneutics," in *Paul Ricoeur on Biblical Hermeneutics* (Semeia 4; ed. John Dominic Crossan, Missoula, MT: Society of Biblical Literature, 1975), 77. Much of the following explication of Ricoeur's notions of metaphor draws on these two works. However, Ricoeur's discussions in *Interpretation Theory* and "Biblical Hermeneutics" are related to aspects of his major work, *The Rule of Metaphor: Multi-disciplinary Studies of the Creation of Meaning* (Toronto: University of Toronto Press, 1977); French original 1975. A brief and convenient introduction to Ricoeur's thought is Karl Simms' *Paul Ricoeur* (RCT; London: Routledge, 2003).

[10] Ricoeur, *Interpretation Theory*, 50, cf. "Biblical Hermeneutics," 77.

[11] Cf., for instance, Ricoeur, *The Rule of Metaphor*, 4, 63 and more generally chapters 1 and 2.

[12] Ricoeur, *Interpretation Theory*, 50; cf. "Biblical Hermeneutics," 77–78.

[13] Ricoeur, *Interpretation Theory*, 50; cf. "Biblical Hermeneutics," 78.

[14] Ricoeur, "Biblical Hermeneutics," 78–79.

[15] Ricoeur, "Biblical Hermeneutics," 79.

borrowing from I. A. Richards, the tenor and vehicle of the metaphor, or its focus and frame, to borrow from Max Black.[16] In the idiom of the cognitive metaphor theory of George Lakoff and Mark Turner, this is a mapping between a "source domain" and a "target domain."[17] For instance, the important metaphoric claim in Proverbs that WISDOM IS A WOMAN, which is not explicitly stated but implied through the personification of wisdom, involves the tension created in attempting to understand such a claim literally and subsequently the hermeneutical need for mapping aspects of a conception of woman (the source domain) onto wisdom (the target domain).[18]

Hence Ricoeur can speak of metaphorical utterances as signifying both what is and what is not. The metaphoric utterance "both is and is not" its literal interpretation. "The literal 'is' is overturned by the absurdity and surmounted by a metaphorical 'is' equivalent to 'is like.' "[19] Ricoeur recognizes, however, that with the metaphorical utterance "there are really not two significations, one literal and the other symbolic, but rather a single movement" which transfers the interpreter "from one level to another." The primary (literal) signification of an utterance is the path to the secondary (metaphorical) signification. The secondary signification comes "by means of, or through, the literal one."[20] In a broader discussion of "a metaphorical concept of truth," Ricoeur can even state that "there is no other way to do justice to the notion of metaphorical truth than to include the critical incision of the (literal) 'is not' within the ontological vehemence of the (metaphorical) 'is.' "[21]

This suggests the metaphoric process is essentially a "creation of meaning."[22] For Ricoeur, metaphorical language is not a mere ornament of discourse, as he argues certain post-Aristotelian representatives of classical rhetoric conceived it, but rather "says something

[16] Ricoeur discusses Richards and Black at some length on a number of occasions. See, for example, *The Rule of Metaphor*, esp. 65–100.

[17] George Lakoff and Mark Turner, *More Than Cool Reason: A Field Guide to Poetic Metaphor* (Chicago: University of Chicago Press, 1989); cf. George Lakoff and Mark Johnson, *Metaphors We Live By* (Chicago: University of Chicago Press, 1990).

[18] The practice of placing in capital letters all the terms of a particular metaphor that is being analyzed is adopted from Lakoff and Johnson, *Metaphors We Live By* and Lakoff and Johnson, *Cool Reason.*

[19] Ricoeur, *Interpretation Theory*, 68; cf. "Biblical Hermeneutics," 88.

[20] Ricoeur, *Interpretation Theory*, 55.

[21] Ricoeur, *The Rule of Metaphor*, 255.

[22] Ricoeur, *Interpretation Theory*, 52; cf. "Biblical Hermeneutics," 80.

new about reality."[23] This creation of meaning, however, has to do not simply with what a statement or discourse says literally, but with what Ricoeur calls its reference, "the sort of world which the work opens up *in front of* the text."[24] Metaphorical language is able to construct a new vision of reality, "one which is resisted by ordinary vision tied to the ordinary use of words." Distinguishing between first and second orders of reference, Ricoeur suggests metaphoric language, like poetic (i.e., non-descriptive) language in general, weakens the "first order reference of ordinary language" (tied to literal interpretation) so that the "second order reference" (tied to metaphorical interpretation) might be revealed.[25] As a species of poetic language, metaphor has the power "not to show us a world already there, as does descriptive or didactic language," but to eclipse "the objective, manipulable world" and "redescribe *what is* in a certain way."[26] Metaphorical utterances thus have what Ricoeur calls a denotative function. However, it is not the case that with the denotative aspects of a metaphorical utterance the brute facts of reality are somehow altered. Rather poetic, metaphorical language changes one's view of, or relationship to, reality.[27]

As I indicated earlier, Ricoeur's interest in metaphor is part of his larger project concerned with preserving the truth value of poetic utterances. In other writings Ricoeur moves away from describing this truth with the language of "reference" and questions the power of poetic language to transform life "by means of a kind of short-circuit operating between the 'seeing-as,' characteristic of the metaphorical utterance and 'being-as,' as its ontological correlate."[28] Rather he seems to become convinced of a need for what might be called, in the idiom of Hans-Georg Gadamer, a fusion between the horizon of the text and the horizon of the interpreter.[29] He becomes

[23] Ricoeur, "Biblical Hermeneutics," 76, 80; cf. *Interpretation Theory*, 46–48.

[24] Ricoeur, "Biblical Hermeneutics," 82; italics original. Cf. *Interpretation Theory*, 56–57; *The Rule of Metaphor*, 216–56.

[25] Ricoeur, "Biblical Hermeneutics," 84; cf. *Interpretation Theory*, 56–57.

[26] Ricoeur, "Biblical Hermeneutics," 87; italics original. Cf. *Interpretation Theory*, 60.

[27] Cf. Kirsten Nielsen, *There is Hope For a Tree: The Tree as Metaphor in Isaiah* (JSOTSup 65; Sheffield: Sheffield Academic Press, 1989), 55–56.

[28] Paul Ricoeur, *Time and Narrative*, vol. 3 (Chicago: University of Chicago Press, 1988), 159; cf. "Biblical Hermeneutics," 95–96.

[29] See Hans-Georg Gadamer, *Truth and Method* (2nd rev. edition; New York: Continuum, 1994), esp. 306–7; German original 1960. Cf. Joel C. Weinsheimer, *Gadamer's Hermeneutics: A Reading of Truth and Method* (New Haven: Yale University Press, 1985), esp. 183–84.

convinced that "the passage from configuration to refiguration required the confrontation between two worlds, the fictive world of the text and the real world of the reader."[30] Although this aspect of his thought is more fully articulated in later studies, Ricoeur nonetheless gestures toward the need for a kind of fusion of horizons in earlier works (such as those informing this discussion).[31] What is in any case clear early on and important for our purposes here, however, is Ricoeur's insistence on a text's ability to construct for a reader a symbolic world.

Ricoeur's considerations of metaphor are thus important for studying the wealth and poverty rhetoric in Proverbs because the book often deploys this sort of economic language in relation to wisdom and virtue in such a way that the utterances are often regarded as only, or primarily, literal language. However, as I just suggested, Ricoeur reminds us that a text or discourse may not only describe reality in a literal, or empirically verifiable and descriptive fashion, but it may actively create a (symbolic-textual) world. Indeed Ricoeur also suggests that in analyzing certain utterances it is not a matter of choosing between metaphorical or literal meanings, but is rather a matter of recognizing the possibility of both, of recognizing that metaphorical meaning is reached through the literal. To neglect attending to one or the other levels of meaning in a text, in which figurative language is deployed, is to under read. However, the difficulty with certain kinds of metaphorical utterances (including proverbial sayings) that are not always unambiguously marked by an absurdity when interpreted literally, is knowing when a metaphorical or figurative interpretation is warranted. Ricoeur's work, to which I will return below, is helpful in treating this question as well.

1.2.b. *Folk Proverbs and Metaphor*

One of the clearest signs in Proverbs that intimates at least aspects of the book's discourse might legitimately be viewed in metaphorical or figurative terms is the text's significant use of short, sentence sayings that formally resemble folk proverbs—the usually anonymous, brief, pithy, oral statements that are thought to represent the col-

[30] Ricoeur, *Time and Narrative*, vol. 3, 159.
[31] Cf. "Biblical Hermeneutics," 95–96. Already in 1971 in "From Existentialism

lective wisdom of a particular social formation. Paremiologists, scholars who are concerned with the study of the folk proverbs of different cultures and peoples, recognize the use of metaphoric language to be a staple of proverbial speech. Wolfgang Mieder, for instance, writes that "there is hardly any need for us to quote examples of proverbs containing metaphors" and cites several proverbs that employ metaphoric language, such as personification. "Clean brooms sweep clean" and "The pitcher goes to the well until it breaks at last."[32] Yet Mieder also mentions: "All that glitters is not gold" and "Don't look a gift horse in the mouth." These last two examples, however, can also make good sense when understood as literal utterances (Mieder's book actually includes a sketch of a man looking into the mouth of a horse, presumably an equine present). What Mieder thus seems to mean by his claim regarding metaphors and folk proverbs is not only that folk sayings employ metaphors, but also that folk sayings are regularly intended and understood metaphorically. There exists a commonplace recognition that even though a proverbial utterance may make perfect sense when taken literally, it should not be so understood because proverbs by their "nature" (i.e., their regular usage) are concerned to say something metaphorically about human beings, the world, or the ways and concerns of human beings in the world. More specifically, they are used to say something about the world and human beings in relation to quite particular contexts of human life.

Paremiologists like Mieder are keen to underscore the important role context and proverb performance plays in understanding what a proverb means metaphorically. Archie Taylor, perhaps the most celebrated modern student of proverbs, for instance, writes that proverbs "are not easily recognized as proverbial unless we have heard them applied to particular situations."[33] Similarly Ruth Finnegan

to the Philosophy of Language," *Criterion* 10, 3 (Spring 1971), which is re-printed as an appendix to the University of Toronto Press edition of *The Rule of Metaphor*, Ricoeur alludes to Gadamer's fusion of horizons (p. 319). See too *Interpretation Theory*, 93.

[32] Wolfgang Mieder, *Proverbs Are Never Out of Season* (New York: Oxford University Press, 1993), 9.

[33] Archie Taylor, "The Wisdom of Many and the Wit of One," in *The Wisdom of Many: Essays on the Proverb* (ed. Wolfgang Mieder and Alan Dundes; New York: Garland, 1981), 6. This essay is a reprint of the *Swathmore College Bulletin*, 54 (1962): 4–7.

states that "knowledge of the situations in which proverbs are cited may also be an essential part of understanding their implications." She cites an African Fante elder approvingly: "There is no proverb without the situation."[34] Barbara Kirshenblatt-Gimblett likewise avers that "a proverb's meaning and 'truth' are conditioned by the context."[35]

Paremiologists like those just cited, however, are often more adept at indicating that any particular folk proverb might mean different things when uttered in different particular contexts than they are at explaining how and why proverbs are metaphorical.[36] However, Peter Seitel, in his article, "Proverbs: A Social Use of Metaphor," not only underscores the importance of the context of proverbial performance for understanding folk proverbs, but seeks to offer an adequate model of how proverbs function metaphorically. He attempts to take into consideration the relationship between: 1) the speaker and hearer(s) of a proverb (e.g., questions of age, sex, status, etc.); 2) the "substantive terms of the proverb situation" (i.e., the relationship between terms in the proverb itself); and 3) the particular "social situation to which the proverb is applied."[37] Seitel both recognizes the possibility of metaphorical aspects within proverbial statements (i.e., what Ricoeur might call the absurdity or difficulty that a simple, literal interpretation creates), but also insists that the relationship expressed by the proverb's imagery needs to be mapped onto the human sphere. Seitel is concerned that one tends to the "metaphorical relationship between the imagined situation presented *in* the proverb *and* the social situation to which it refers."[38] One of the examples Seitel offers is: "If one finger brought oil, it soiled the others." To understand this proverb fully requires not only that one know something about fingers and oil. One also needs to understand the saying's cause and

[34] Ruth Finnegan, "Proverbs in Africa," in *The Wisdom of Many*, 19, 27; cf. 15, 23–24, 32. This essay is a reprint of Finnegan's *Oral Literature in Africa* (Oxford: Clarendon, 1970), 389–418.

[35] Barbara Kirshenblatt-Gimblett, "Toward a Theory of Proverb Meaning," in *The Wisdom of Many*, 115; cf. 119. This essay is a reprint of *Proverbium* 22 (1973): 821–827.

[36] Each of the scholars cited above likewise recognizes that broader forms of cultural knowledge (e.g., founding myths, etc.) might be vital for properly understanding forms of proverbial speech in any particular society.

[37] Peter Seitel, "Proverbs: A Social Use of Metaphor," in *The Wisdom of Many*, 126–128. This essay is a reprint of *Genre* 2 (1969): 143–161. Cf. Robert M. Harnish, "Communicating With Proverbs," *Communication & Cognition* 26 (1993): 265–290.

[38] Seitel, "Social Use of Metaphor," 126; italics added.

effect logic and the context in which it was uttered. Seitel reveals the last of these and notes that the proverb was spoken by a father to a son in order to encourage the son to choose companions wisely. Other paremiologists make similar, though usually less explicit, suggestions regarding a proverb's ability to speak to human existence and concerns.[39]

These notions regarding a proverb's metaphorical relationship to a specific social situation are similar to what Lakoff and Turner have to say about the metaphorical nature of proverbs. For Lakoff and Turner, proverbs "concern people, though they often look superficially as if they concern other things." Through the workings of a conglomeration of conceptual processes, proverbs offer us "ways of comprehending the complex faculties of human beings in terms of these other things."[40] They allow us "to comprehend general human character traits in terms of well-understood non-human attributes."[41] This connection between the images internal to a proverb and human life is essentially what Seitel is getting at when he speaks of "the social situation to which it [a proverb] refers." Hence for Lakoff and Turner, the implicit target domain of proverbs—that which the utterance desires to (re)describe—is regularly human life and behavior, even though this is not necessarily mentioned by the proverb itself.[42]

1.2.c. *Metaphoricity and the Gestalt of Proverbs*

As was intimated above, however, the problem with certain metaphorical statements, including a good deal of material in the book of Proverbs, is that a literal interpretation does not produce an immediate or unambiguous absurdity. In such instances the question becomes how one knows a particular utterance is to be understood not only literally, but also metaphorically; or, in Ricoeur's terms, how one knows to understand an utterance in terms of the metaphorical "is not" and not merely the literal "is." This question, however,

[39] See Taylor, "The Wisdom of Many," 5; Finnegan, "Proverbs in Africa," 17.

[40] Lakoff and Turner, *Cool Reason*, 166. Lakoff and Turner refer to the conglomeration of processes that enable proper understanding of folk proverbs as "the Great Chain Metaphor." See especially *Cool Reason*, 170–180.

[41] Lakoff and Turner (*Cool Reason*, 172) continue: "And conversely it allows us to comprehend less well-understood aspects of the nature of animals and objects in terms of better-understood human characteristics."

[42] Lakoff and Turner, *Cool Reason*, 174.

also gives way to a broader one. In Lakoff's and Turner's terms, how one knows a proverb is speaking not only of what it literally says, but of broader concerns of human life?

In regard to at least the second of these questions, paremiologists like Seitel and others cited above seem to assume that with folk proverbs one simply knows.[43] As I suggested, however, these writers, as well as Lakoff and Turner, each recognize the importance of context in this almost intuitive knowing. Hence Lakoff and Turner recognize that a proverb might, in fact, in certain instances be understood literally, as when the words "big thunder, little rain" are uttered by a person experiencing slight precipitation after having heard the loud crackling of an electrical storm. They recognize too that this proverb—"big thunder, little rain"—might not be used specifically to speak of human character, say ineffectual bragging, but to articulate something about perhaps even a vociferous dog, which is 'all bark and no bite.' Lakoff and Turner, however, also acknowledge that a proverb in a collection, i.e., divorced from a performance context, can nonetheless be understood—i.e., recognized as meaningful—because readers and hearers know proverbs normally function metaphorically to speak to the context of human life and the questions and concerns of human existence. That is, these readers can imagine or recall appropriate social contexts for the uttering of a particular saying and understand it in that light.[44]

Beyond simply recognizing the presence of metaphor in particular proverbs, Seitel and Lakoff and Turner are thus primarily concerned with the particular context of the proverb performance—the actual utterance of a proverb by a particular person in a particular social context and the ability of the proverb to speak appropriately and metaphorically to these sorts of particular contexts. Lakoff and Turner also appear to recognize that understanding a proverb in a collection is a somewhat more complicated act. This is significant for the study of Proverbs for it is precisely proverbs in a collection that one encounters in this book.

Although Ricoeur is concerned with a variety of types of literary speech, and not specifically the folk proverb, his understanding of

[43] Though again, through their notion of "the Great Chain Metaphor," Lakoff and Turner (*Cool Reason*, 170–180) attempt to describe *how* one knows.

[44] Lakoff and Turner, *Cool Reason*, 173–176.

other kinds of figurative utterances introduces an important further step for thinking about how one might best understand how proverbs in a collection, like those in the book of Proverbs, function. In speaking of the narratives of the parables of Jesus, for example, he notes that the clues they provide for a metaphorical understanding "are too implicit and elusive to be noticed beside the interference of the most important clues given by the [larger literary] context."[45] For instance Ricoeur suggests the figurative qualities of the parables are largely a result of their literary contexts, which often provide the reader with an explicit reading cue: "let those who have ears hear"![46]

This is significant, for at this point Ricoeur is moving more fully into the realm of hermeneutics and is concerned with the production of meaning at the level of discourse, here understood as the structure of a literary work as a whole. This structure—or what Ricoeur calls a text's "architecture" and what I call a text's Gestalt—provides a kind of interpretive lens through which to view both the various components of a discourse and the discourse as a whole.[47] This sort of hermeneutic move can be of help in developing a further response to each of the two questions posed at the beginning of this section—how does one know to interpret certain statements metaphorically and how does one know certain statements are metaphorically speaking to the concerns of human life. Importantly however, the architecture or Gestalt that Ricoeur has in mind "cannot be derived from that of the single sentences," because "the text as such has a kind of plurivocity, which is other than the polysemy of individual words, and other than the ambiguity of individual sentences." Discerning this Gestalt, however, is a kind of "guess" so that the "reconstruction of the text's architecture . . . takes the form of a circular process." As Ricoeur puts it, "the presupposition of a certain kind of whole is implied in the recognition of the parts. And reciprocally, it is in construing the details that we construe the whole."[48] The moral and literary architecture or Gestalt of the book of Proverbs, I will show, should prompt a reader first to understand

---

[45] Ricoeur, "Biblical Hermeneutics," 97.
[46] Ricoeur, "Biblical Hermeneutics," 98, 100.
[47] Ricoeur, *Interpretation Theory*, 77. Ricoeur (*The Rule of Metaphor*, 212–213) likewise uses the language of Gestalt in a related, though different, sense and context.
[48] Ricoeur, *Interpretation Theory*, 77.

a number of its wealth and poverty utterances not merely in terms of the literal "is," but in terms of the metaphorical "is not." Second it should assist the reader in recognizing these wealth and poverty proverbs to be contributing to an instruction that is more unified than a consideration of a single or small cluster of utterances might lead one to believe.

Despite his emphasis on the role of literary context, or the larger discourse, in recognizing metaphorical utterances, Ricoeur also offers other thoughts regarding how one might, apart from an explicit prompt from this context, discern "signs of metaphoricity" in a text. Although in his essay on biblical hermeneutics Ricoeur is concerned in particular with the narratives of the Gospel parables, some of his musings are suggestive for the discovery of such "extra-contextual" signs of metaphoricity in Proverbs.[49] Ricoeur, for instance, first notes the work of John Dominic Crossan. Crossan, according to Ricoeur, suggests that it is the "normalcy" of the parables that evokes metaphorical interpretation of them. The parable is "a case of understatement" which "means the most by saying the least;" it "should be interpreted metaphorically because it pretends to be plain and trivial."[50] If Crossan is correct, the characteristic of normalcy might likewise be said to be a potential sign of metaphoricity in the sentence sayings of Proverbs, which are also often described as 'plain and trivial.'

However, *pace* Crossan, Ricoeur himself suggests that rather than its normalcy, it is the "extravagance" of the parable, its mixing of the ordinary with the extra-ordinary, which serves as a sign of its metaphoricity. If Ricoeur is correct, in Proverbs one might consider the claims of what is commonly called the "act-consequence nexus," with its assertion that the wise and righteous will prosper and the wicked perish, as a kind of extravagance that signals the metaphorical aspects or possibilities of this book.[51] Indeed Ricoeur's extension of the notion of tension in metaphorical statements offers a potentially profitable approach to understanding how the extravagant claims of an act-consequence notion in Proverbs hint at the text's metaphorical possibilities. Ricoeur speaks not only of the tension between

[49] Ricoeur, "Biblical Hermeneutics," 97.
[50] Ricoeur, "Biblical Hermeneutics," 98.
[51] On the "act-consequence" notion in Proverbs, see below.

terms in a metaphor, or the tension in interpretation that arises when one attempts to understand a metaphorical utterance literally. He also speaks of a tension "at the level of reality itself between description and redescription."[52] This kind of tension is to be found in discourses (such as the Gospel parables) where there is little or no tension between terms in an utterance (i.e., between the tenor and vehicle) and little tension between literal and metaphorical interpretations of statements. The tension rather is between the world the text projects and normal perceptions of the world of objects. Put otherwise, the tension "obtains between the scene and everyday life and reality;" or "between the insight displayed by the fiction and our ordinary way of looking at things."[53] This tension, analogous to the tension that arises when one attempts to understand a metaphor literally, forces one to understand the world "of the text" as precisely that, a world the text figures and not some literal, empirically verifiable description of the world of objects.[54]

Although in the book of Proverbs the tension between the world the text projects through its act-consequence rhetoric and a reader's normal perceptions of the world of objects may constitute an "extra-contextual" clue that one should read this book with an eye to its more figurative interpretive possibilities, this combines with at least two clues from the literary context to elicit the reader's attention to the text's metaphorical qualities. A first literary cue is constituted by the fact that considerably more than half of the book is comprised of short, folk-like sayings, which as I suggested above, regularly function metaphorically to say something about human life and concerns. Although the sentence sayings in the book of Proverbs (see especially 10:1–22:16 and 25–29) are, in the form we now have them, the product of a scribal elite and so ultimately of a different order than the folk proverbs studied by paremiologists (see Chapter Two below), they are nevertheless related to and resemble such proverbs. These

[52] Ricoeur, "Biblical Hermeneutics," 95; cf. *The Rule of Metaphor*, 253–56.

[53] Ricoeur, "Biblical Hermeneutics," 94–95; cf. *Time and Narrative*, vol. 3, 159.

[54] At this point Ricoeur again appears to be moving toward conceptual formulations that will become clearer in his later work, namely the necessity of a fusion of horizons that I mentioned above, that "confrontation between two worlds, the fictive world of the text and the real world of the reader." For the later Ricoeur it is in, or by means of, this fusion or confrontation that the world of the text is able to transform or refigure the world of the reader.

formal similarities ought to attune a reader to the metaphorical interpretive possibilities of Proverbs' 'plain and trivial' discourse. Second, as I intimated above and will argue below in Chapter Two, the book's prologue (1:2–7) acts as a kind of hermeneutical guide for the reader and provides a strong, initial literary cue for recognizing the metaphorical aspects of the text. It is, in a sense, functionally equivalent to the parables' "let those who have ears, hear."

Together these two aspects of Proverbs' discourse—its programmatic prologue and its folk-like sentence sayings—combine with the "extra-contextual" tension between the world of the text and "everyday reality," as well as features internal to various proverbs, to lead to what, in Ricoeur's terms, can be called my initial "guess" about Proverbs: namely that one ought not to neglect the book's figurative or metaphorical aspects and that attending to the symbolic aspects of the book will produce a fuller, more robust, and more coherent interpretation of Proverbs' talk of wealth and poverty than has been offered previously. Of course, as Ricoeur also insists, it is necessary to move "from guessing to explaining" through "an investigation of the specific object of guessing."[55] As I intimated above, moreover, the movement from guessing to explaining constitutes an interpretive or hermeneutic circle. However this circle, as Ricoeur insists, need not be a vicious one. Certainly the architecture or Gestalt of a text might be viewed from many sides or angles so that "it is always possible to relate the same sentence in different ways to this or that other sentence considered as the cornerstone of the text."[56] Yet although there are always multiple ways to construe a text, for Ricoeur it is not true that all interpretations are equal. Any text will present "a limited field of possible constructions." Ricoeur grounds this position, that there are better and worse readings, through "the logic of subjective probability."[57] Whereas a logic of empirical verification seeks to demonstrate that a conclusion is true, a logic of probability intends to show that "an interpretation is more probable in light of what we know."[58] For this project, some consideration not only of metaphor (like that just undertaken), but also of the study

[55] Ricoeur, *Interpretation Theory*, 76.
[56] Ricoeur, *Interpretation Theory*, 77–78.
[57] Ricoeur, *Interpretation Theory*, 79.
[58] Ricoeur, *Interpretation Theory*, 78.

of discourse can help to flesh out concretely certain procedures that I will employ in seeking to articulate a reading of Proverbs' wealth and poverty rhetoric that is more probable than many previous and contemporary interpretations.

1.3. The Analysis of Discourse

A traditional or general meaning of discourse might be said to be "the ordered exposition in writing or speech of a particular subject."[59] Much of what follows will be an analysis of the discourse of wealth and poverty/rich and poor in Proverbs understood in this traditional sense—i.e., an analysis of the manner in which the wisdom text constructs and orders its "talk" about wealth and poverty.

However, definitions of "discourse," as a category of critical analysis, range widely and the term has taken on specialized senses in different disciplines and for different authors.[60] For Ricoeur, in the discussion above, discourse had primarily to do with the structure or architecture of a text as a whole, though Ricoeur's broader considerations of discourse are more complex.[61] Notions of discourse associated with the French philosopher Michel Foucault, who underscores the rules and possibilities of discourse, as well as the relationship of discourse to power, are perhaps the most celebrated recent considerations of the topic.[62] However, the approach of critics like

---

[59] Roger Fowler, "Discourse," in *A Dictionary of Modern Critical Terms* (ed. Roger Fowler; revised and expanded; London: Routledge and Kegan Paul, 1987), 62. Cf. Paul A. Bové, "Discourse," in *Critical Terms for Literary Study* (ed. Frank Lentricchia and Thomas McLaughlin; Chicago: University of Chicago Press, 1990), 50–65.

[60] For linguists, often a concern with discourse or discourse analysis signals: a) a concern with linguistic analysis above the level of the sentence; and b) a concern with the study of language in use. See, for example, Gillian Brown and George Yule, *Discourse Analysis* (CTL; Cambridge: Cambridge University Press, 1983); cf. Sara Mills, *Discourse* (New Critical Idiom; New York: Routledge, 1997), 9. For a sampling of the range of definitions for "discourse" see Adam Jaworski and Nikolas Coupland, eds., *The Discourse Reader* (London: Routledge: 1999), 1–3; Mills, *Discourse*, 2–6.

[61] See, for instance, Ricoeur, *Interpretation Theory*, esp. 1–23 and *The Rule of Metaphor*, 65–100.

[62] For Foucault, discourses (or discursive structures), as Roger Fowler explains, "consist in a certain regularity of statements which then define an object . . . and supply a set of concepts which can be used to analyse the object, to delimit what can and cannot be said about it, and to demarcate who can say it." See Fowler,

Roger Fowler and Norman Fairclough, whose textual analyses seek to combine the considerable theoretical insights of thinkers like Foucault with the practices and procedures of linguistics, most closely approximates my own. Hence, this project will examine Proverbs' wealth and poverty talk not primarily under the rubric of a Foucauldian notion of discourse but in a slightly different, and for some perhaps somewhat more mundane, manner—with "discourse," as Fowler has suggested, spoken with an Anglo-American rather than French accent.[63] This Anglo-American brand of "discourse" is one that is broadly concerned with "the whole complex process of people interacting with one another in live situations and within the structure of social forces"—i.e., with the entire elaborate system of "linguistic interaction between people uttering and comprehending texts."[64]

An important presupposition of the kind of discourse analysis and procedures adopted for this project, moreover, is the notion that the realm of language is a realm of social interaction, and even struggle, between contending ideological positions.[65] In Mikhail Bakhtin's terms, language is "dialogic." This Bakhtinian notion underscores the fact that utterances—words, and complexes of words—do not appear fresh or value free in a text, but carry traces of a previous life of

"Discourse," 64; cf. Mills, *Discourse*, 17. Foucault develops and applies his notion of discourse in a number of publications. Particularly important are: *The Archaeology of Knowledge* (London: Tavistock, 1972), esp. 21–131 and his 1970 lecture, "L'ordre du discourse" (Paris: Gallimard, 1971), which is translated as "The Discourse of Language" and placed as an appendix in the Tavistock publication of *The Archaeology of Knowledge* just cited. Significant as well are: *The Order of Things: An Archaeology of the Human Sciences* (New York: Random House, 1970); *Discipline and Punish: The Birth of the Prison* (Harmondsworth: Penguin, 1979); *The History of Sexuality, Volume 1: An Introduction* (Harmondsworth: Penguin, 1981).

[63] Fowler, "Discourse," 64.

[64] Fowler, *Linguistic Criticism*, 70, 86. Cf. Terry Eagleton, *Ideology: An Introduction* (London: Verso, 1991), 196, who, in speaking approvingly of this brand of discourse analysis, comments: "While sometimes solemnly labouring the obvious, wheeling up the big guns of linguistic analysis to dispatch the inconsiderable gnat of a dirty joke, this brand of investigation has opened up a new dimension in a theory of ideology traditionally concerned with 'consciousness' rather than linguistic performance, 'ideas' rather than social interaction."

[65] V. N. Voloshinov, who is sometimes called the "father of discourse analysis," underscores this point. See his *Marxism and the Philosophy of Language* (6th edition; Cambridge, Mass: Harvard University Press, 1996); Russian original 1929. Cf. Eagleton, *Ideology*, 193–196. For a brief summary of the relationship of Voloshinov and his writings to Mikhail Bakhtin and the "Bakhtin School," see Gary Saul Morson and Caryl Emerson, *Mikhail Bakhtin: Creation of a Poetics* (Stanford: Stanford University Press, 1990), 101–119.

use in particular social environments and remain charged with nuances from those contexts even when deployed in new contexts. "Each word" in a text "tastes of the context and contexts in which it has lived its socially charged life."[66] Utterances that make up a particular discourse always come preloaded and already inscribed with the experiences or traces of their usage in various social and historical contexts.[67] Hence, because a word or an utterance always has a history of use in a variety of concrete social contexts and is unable to loose itself entirely from those contexts, a multiplicity of social interests should be understood to have contributed to the construction of any particular discourse.[68] This means that although a specific voice or interest may dominate any particular discourse in a text, meanings previously imputed by various social interests remain with an utterance. At the same time, however, other, new social interests struggle to control, define, color, or inscribe it with a different ideological accent, to infuse it with new or different socially significant symbolic associations. Utterances are thus not "unitary," but as Green explains, "have struggles for meaning raging underneath their ostensibly unified verbal skin."[69]

Importantly, however, the symbolic coloring of an utterance in this Bakhtinian line of thinking also dialectically doubles back and serves to (re)construct the social world and agents from which it emerged. It is this "work on the world" that makes a claim to, or control of, the symbolic realm so important.[70] Wherever terms

[66] M. M. Bakhtin, "Discourse in the Novel," in *The Dialogic Imagination: Four Essays by M. M. Bakhtin* (ed. Michael Holquist; trans. Caryl Emerson and Michael Holquist; University of Texas Press Slavic Series 1; Austin: University of Texas Press, 1981), 293. Cf. Barbara Green, *Mikhail Bakhtin and Biblical Scholarship: An Introduction* (SBLSS 38; Atlanta: SBL, 2000), 47.

[67] Green, *Bakhtin*, 62.

[68] See M. M. Bakhtin, *Problems of Dostoevsky's Poetics* (ed. and trans. by Caryl Emerson; Theory and History of Literature 8; Minneapolis: University of Minnesota Press, 1984), 202. See further Green, *Bakhtin*, 47.

[69] Green, *Bakhtin*, 47.

[70] See Carol A. Newsom, "Knowing as Doing: The Social Symbolics of Knowledge at Qumran," *Semeia* 59 (1992): 139–153, esp. 141. She writes in a similar vein: "The way in which texts act in and on the world is distinct from an act of direct force because a text exists in the realm of the symbolic. As Jameson notes, the world is not simply a linguistic construct. The world, though, is not available to us in itself but only as we are able to textualize it, to bring it into the realm of the symbolic. Insofar as a text takes the world into itself as its subtext, the world can be acted upon in the symbolic work of the text." Cf. Carol A. Newsom, *The Self as Symbolic Space: Constructing Identity and Community at Qumran* (STDJ 52; Leiden: Brill, 2004), 15–17.

representing categories crucial to the structure of social life, such as "rich" and "poor" and "wealth" and "poverty," are prominent in a discourse, it is likely that there the effort of various social interests to control the symbolic shadings of such language is great. As I shall demonstrate, the discourse of wealth and poverty in the book of Proverbs is itself a site where powerful social voices, which compete with that of the text's instructing voice, are exposed and thwarted.

1.3.a. *Procedures*

Understanding discourse in this Anglo-American and Bakhtinian manner means that the analysis that follows will attend especially to at least two types of concerns. These two concerns might be called the textual and extra-textual elements of an utterance. On the one hand, to describe the discourse of wealth and poverty in Proverbs as fully as possible, one needs to attend to linguistic and grammatical matters. On the other hand, one also needs to discern the elements of discourse that are beyond or above the written text.

The Textual. An examination of the lexical, syntactic, grammatical and formal patterns of a text can reveal, in part, how different textual categories and figures are symbolically constituted. In Ricoeur's terms, it can reveal the world "in front of" the text. It can assist in discerning how a text constructs patterns of value regarding social relationships, identity, and values—its entire socially symbolic structure of meaning. In regard to lexical matters, for instance, tracing out patterns of value and usage associated with the various terms for wealth and poverty/rich and poor can prove a useful guide to a text's structure of meaning. As the study of linguistics has taught, words are always embedded within a web of other words and social contexts and it is only in relation to this web that any particular lexical item can be "defined."[71] Likewise, the status of particular character types (e.g., the rich and the poor) as grammatical subject or object, as well as the relationships of these types to various kinds of verbal forms (e.g., passive or active), also can provide clues as to

[71] The insight that etymological analysis is not a sufficient means to meaning has been mediated to biblical studies most prominently by James Barr. See *The Semantics of Biblical Language* (Oxford: Oxford University Press, 1961). For a self-consciously linguistic approach to the problem of wealth and poverty in Proverbs, see Wittenberg, "Lexical Context."

how a particular discourse creates its symbolic world. The same is true of a consideration of patterns of nominalization, personification, and especially metaphorical and literal usages of terms.

The Extra-Textual. The level of linguistic structure, however, is not the only level at which the symbolic work of a text can be traced. In any communicative act, extra-linguistic (or extra-textual) factors are also operative and they need to be inferred from context if a successful communication act is to occur. Any utterance is composed of what is actually articulated *and* what is tacitly assumed (by both the addressee and the one who addresses). Understanding an utterance thus entails that one actively grasp the context of communication in which it comes forth. It requires that one comprehend what is happening in the communicative act, including making a presumption regarding the aim or end of the utterance.[72] In the study of oral communication this means attending to a variety of matters. The work of Austin and Searle on "speech acts" has been of considerable significance in this regard. Words command and petition. They praise, pray, curse, and name—to mention just a few of the obvious functions of language.

Comprehending any utterance is thus at least in part a matter of understanding what it does, of grasping, in the idiom developed by Austin and Searle, its "illocutionary" force. However, the function of any particular utterance is not always straightforward or obvious. An utterance that looks like a question can, for instance, under certain circumstances function as an imperative, as when in a cold room one person "asks" another, "can you shut the window?" Likewise, what might appear as a simple observation of a particular situation can function in diverse ways depending when and where it is uttered, and by whom. In Israel's wisdom literature, for instance, commentators often recognize the didactic or admonitory function of certain proverbial sentence sayings that otherwise appear to make straightforward observations of social realities.

In dealing with biblical texts, however, we of course do not have to do with primary speech or conversation. Nonetheless a key insight from the study of speech acts—i.e., that language "does something," that an utterance carries a rhetorical force—is fundamental to the brand of discourse analysis that generates the kinds of questions to

[72] Cf. Green, *Bakhtin*, 53.

be put to the various proverbs and admonitions analyzed in the following pages.[73] For instance, recognizing the possibility in the book of Proverbs that indicative statements and "observations" might rhetorically be doing much more than they initially appear to be doing is an important interpretive supposition for my discernment of the nature of this text's discourse of wealth and poverty. More broadly speaking, as I shall indicate in the following chapters, the postulated social context of a particular wisdom utterance (e.g., in the royal court or agricultural village) also often plays a crucial role in how one identifies the way it is functioning.

Importantly with a book such as Proverbs, one can, and ironically must, look for clues to an extra-textual context by interrogating the text itself. As Green reminds in explaining Bakhtin's notion of dialogic utterances, even as they "bring to their new context a residue of their past adventures . . ., utterances in literature *must* be examined within the context of the work in which they appear."[74] Ricoeur would certainly concur. Often, attending to this most immediate, literary context is the key to discerning what kind of extra-textual context is most appropriately imagined for comprehending the rhetorical acts of Proverbs.

To understand a text like Proverbs it is thus not sufficient to recognize an utterance (or any complex of words) as forming a grammatically correct statement.[75] Nor is it enough simply to know to what particular words refer in a positivistic sense wherein the "meaningful use of language consists in the utterance of statements about the world which can be either confirmed or disconfirmed"—the (usually unacknowledged) philosophy of language or "lens" by which many in the past appear to have both read Proverbs and assumed

---

[73] See, for example, J. L. Austin, *How to do Things with Words* (Oxford: Oxford University Press, 1962); John R. Searle, *Speech Acts: An Essay in the Philosophy of Language* (London: Cambridge University Press, 1969). Cf. Fowler, "Discourse," 62–63; Brown and Yule, *Discourse Analysis*, 231–233; Jaworski and Coupland, *The Discourse Reader*, 14–19.

[74] Green, *Bakhtin*, 53; italics added. Among scholars of Israel's wisdom literature, especially Proverbs, the emphasis on discovering a concrete social context for the various wisdom forms (an extra-textual factor) coupled with a historicist bias (which gives priority to discerning the provenance of the wisdom utterances) has often led to the neglect of the primary (literary) context of the particular wisdom book itself (see Chapter Two).

[75] Cf. Fowler, "Discourse," 62.

the book was composed.[76] Rather, to understand the wealth and poverty language of Proverbs one must attend not only to the text's linguistic structures but *also* ask certain "pragmatic" questions, questions such as:[77] what exactly is this particular piece of language doing rhetorically? Or, at least, what is it trying to do? What is it highlighting or foregrounding? What is it obscuring and why? Why does the text employ this linguistic realization instead of another? And, what is the relationship of this particular utterance to the work as whole, i.e., to the text's architecture or Gestalt?[78]

When studying the discourse of wealth and poverty in Proverbs, if these types of procedures and questions are pursued and considered together, one can grasp something of the matrix of symbolic associations and patterns of value that the text generates regarding not only wealth and poverty, but such matters as social status, value, and identity. This in turn may illumine how the language of the text reflects and reinforces (or undermines and resists) patterns of social organization and value in the social environment out of which the discourse emerged. It thus provides a way to glimpse the text's moral vision, its creation of value and meaning vis-à-vis the particular social context in which it was produced.

Attending to the kinds of procedures and questions described above should thus produce a fuller and richer reading of Proverbs' discourse of wealth and poverty than has been offered previously. A reading that attends to such matters can also corroborate, to one degree or another, evidence for one or another hypothesis regarding the social context of the book formulated by other means of

[76] Fowler, "Discourse," 63. Cf. Eagleton, *Ideology*, 193–94.

[77] In linguistics, any analytic approach that involves contextual considerations can generally be categorized as "pragmatics." See Brown and Yule, *Discourse Analysis*, 26.

[78] As an example of how such a line of linguistic and pragmatic questioning can work and what it might reveal, Fowler offers for consideration the use of nominalization and personification in the statement: "The stock market had a good day today." He then presents "an alternative realization": "Today a number of stock brokers and speculators made a lot of money." The two phrases report, or one might say, "observe" the same situation. The first realization, however, obscures who immediately profits. The second does not. At an extra linguistic level one might imagine the evening news as a likely context for the first formulation, as its rhetorical force seems to be that of a simple reporting of facts. The second, however, is a much stronger statement that could conceivably be understood as a critique of a particular economic system and the persons and values associated with it. It would perhaps be more at home at a meeting of young socialists. See Fowler, "Discourse," 63–64.

inquiry (e.g., historical, archaeological). However, it will not necessarily be able to locate precisely, as some might hope, the status in real sociological terms of the "rich" and the "poor" in the socio-historical contexts from which the ancient text comes to us. The poems and sayings of Proverbs are both too diverse in origin and the book's economic imagery too general and symbolic to support highly specific claims regarding the social location of the real rich and poor that lie behind these textual figures.[79]

1.4. Conclusions

The fundamental structuring categories of rich and poor/wealth and poverty are categories of moral and not just economic discourse. Beyond denoting an unequal distribution of goods in a particular social formation, this language takes on a good deal of social symbolic value and carries out a good deal of social symbolic work. Discourses of wealth and poverty function to order, justify, and sometimes challenge social arrangements of distribution and economic practices. Yet they also can reveal much about how values, status, power, and identity more generally are distributed and maintained in a particular social milieu. In certain contemporary ethical-theological discourse(s), for example, the "rich" can be associated with rapaciousness, oppressiveness, and selfishness; or with industriousness, frugality, whiteness, entrepreneurship, divine favor, and liberty—to name just a few of the symbolic possibilities. The poor, on the other hand, can be associated with laziness, victimhood, and dark skin; or simplicity, dignity, piety, and—like the rich—divine favor. How these terms are filled out within the discourses that constitute the larger symbolic universe of a society can make a good deal of difference when the primary ethical questions surrounding distribution of material wealth and other social goods in that society are addressed. This would have been as true of ancient Israelite and Judean society as it is today.

This study of the discourse of wealth and poverty in Proverbs will thus consider the symbolic world the book constructs for its hearers

[79] For an attempt to describe somewhat more precisely the poor and poverty in real sociological terms see, for example, J. David Pleins, "Poor, Poverty," *ABD* 5:402–414.

or readers and will do so while taking seriously the text's figurative and rhetorical imagination. As an exercise in biblical ethics, the work will also offer a view of Proverbs' moral vision as this is revealed through its wealth and poverty language. The study will show the key role this rhetoric plays in the book's broader moral discourse and at the same insist that although the discourse of wealth and poverty in Proverbs is complex and by no means univocal, it is not as incoherent as is usually thought.

CHAPTER TWO

THE DISCOURSE OF WEALTH AND POVERTY IN PROVERBS

As I indicated at the outset of this study, the book of Proverbs draws on the language of wealth and poverty more than any other book in the Hebrew Scriptures. Yet the dominant scholarly consensus remains, in the words of Harold C. Washington, that this wisdom instruction, "gives no coherent view of the rich and the poor."[1] Proverbs, it appears, is a book that presents no consistent attitude or worldview when it comes to the poor and poverty and the rich and wealth.[2] Washington, however, has himself formulated the critical issue more appropriately than many when he notes that the book in fact "presents a complicated world of moral discourse."[3] It is within the context of this larger moral discourse that the book's use of the language of wealth and poverty/rich and poor must be understood. Though the discourse of wealth and poverty in Proverbs is complex and no doubt contains certain ambiguities, it is less equivocal than generally thought.

2.1. Proverbs, Wealth, and Poverty

At the beginning of the history of the modern critical study of Proverbs, most understood this anthology of wisdom sayings and poems to be the work of moralizing Jewish scribes of the later post-exilic period. Whybray, in his survey of the modern study of the book, in fact, speaks of a "virtual consensus" in this regard by about 1900.[4] C. H. Toy's 1899 commentary, which dates the earliest portions

---

[1] Harold C. Washington, *Wealth and Poverty in the Instruction of Amenemope and the Hebrew Proverbs* (SBLDS 142; Atlanta: Scholars Press, 1996), 1.

[2] Washington, *Wealth and Poverty*, 3.

[3] Washington, *Wealth and Poverty*, 1.

[4] R. N. Whybray, *The Book of Proverbs: A Survey of Modern Study* (HBI 1; Leiden: Brill, 1995), 1. Cf. Gerhard von Rad, *Wisdom in Israel* (London: SCM, 1972), 8–9; German original 1970.

of the book to ca. 300 BCE and speaks of "schools of moralists" and "a period of high moral culture," is representative of the trend.[5]

For much of the 20th century, however, the book of Proverbs—and what the book has to say about wealth and poverty—was believed to reflect a class ethic of the wealthy and powerful Israelite and Judean elite.[6] As the body of ancient Near Eastern comparative material became increasingly available, this perspective was reinforced by the notion that, on analogy with Egypt and Mesopotamia, Israel's wisdom literature found its home in or near the royal court, or schools associated with the court, early on in the period of monarchy.[7] An influential scholar like Gerhard von Rad in 1944, for instance, could write that the court of Solomon was "a centre of international wisdom-lore, as the Egyptian courts had been in an earlier age."[8]

Though few today would suggest the collections in Proverbs stem from an historical Solomon, assertions that Israelite wisdom (including Proverbs) finds its provenance among the political and economic elite remain common. Michael V. Fox, for instance, appears to tend toward this view when he writes that for the ancient Israelite and Judean scribes who produced Proverbs, "the court was the decisive locus of creativity."[9] However, an important minority of scholars

[5] C. H. Toy, *Proverbs: A Critical and Exegetical Commentary on the Book of Proverbs*, (rprt., Edinburgh: T&T Clark, 1988), xi, xxvi, and esp. xix–xxxi; 1899 original. Cf. Whybray, *Survey*, 1–5.

[6] R. N. Whybray similarly notes: "There has been a virtual consensus that Proverbs is the work solely of the upper class." See *Wealth and Poverty in the Book of Proverbs* (JSOTSup 99; Sheffield: JSOT Press, 1990), 45 n. 1.

[7] E. A. W. Budge's publications regarding the *Instruction of Amenemope* in 1923–1924 and Adolf Erman's "Eine ägyptische Quelle der 'Spruch Salomos,'" *SPAW* (1924): 86–93 were the watershed events as far as the study of Proverbs was concerned. For an overview, see Whybray, *Survey*, 18–22. Cf. Washington, *Wealth and Poverty*, 7–9.

[8] Gerhard von Rad, "The Beginnings of Historical Writing in Ancient Israel," in *The Problem of the Hexateuch and other Essays* (New York: McGraw-Hill, 1966); rprt. of "Der Anfang der Geschichtsschreibung im alten Israel," 1944. Von Rad speaks of "school wisdom in the early monarchy" in *Wisdom in Israel* as well. However he also recognizes the complexity of the matter. See *Wisdom in Israel*, 11–12 15–23. Cf. Brian W. Kovacs, "Is there a Class-Ethic in Proverbs?," in *Essays in Old Testament Ethics* (ed. James L. Crenshaw and John T. Willis; New York: KTAV, 1974). Kovacs' suggestion that Proverbs is the work of an "intelligentsia" is closer to my view (see below).

[9] Michael V. Fox, "The Social Location of the Book of Proverbs," in *Texts, Temples, and Traditions: A Tribute to Menahem Haran* (ed. Michael V. Fox et al.; Winona Lake, Ind.: Eisenbrauns, 1996), 227–239, esp. 236. Cf. J. David Pleins, "Poverty in

adopts an alternative approach. For these writers, at least the sentence material in Proverbs is best understood as originally and essentially the product of the agricultural, tribal, folk culture of Israel and Judah (Yehud) and should be interpreted against this background.[10]

2.1.a. *The Ambiguity of Wealth and Poverty in Proverbs*

Whether they locate the book and its traditions in the court or in folk culture, scholars nearly unanimously characterize the discourse of wealth and poverty in Proverbs (or the sages'/book's "worldview" or "attitude" toward wealth and poverty) as inconsistent or "ambiguous."[11] On the one hand, much of the wealth and poverty material in the book appears to adopt a critical attitude toward the poor and poverty, and a positive attitude toward wealth. Proverbs' frequent use of a cause and effect rhetoric, also seems to suggest the sages adopted a view of reality characterized by an underlying "act-consequence connection" (*Tun-Ergehen Zusammenhang*) where the wise

---

the Social World of the Wise," *JSOT* 37 (1987): 61–78. It is also sometimes postulated that scribes in ancient Israel would have been associated with a temple complex. Though the interests of palace and temple should not be collapsed, the two institutions would also have mutually undergirded one another.

[10] See, for example, Claus Westermann, "Weisheit im Sprichwort," in *Schalom. Studien zu Glaube und Geschichte Israels* (ed. K.-H. Bernhardt: Stuttgart: Calwer, 1971): 73–85, reprinted in *Forschung am Alten Testament. Gesammelte Studien II* (TBAT 55; Munich: Kaiser, 1974): 149–161. See further, Westermann, *Roots of Wisdom: The Oldest Proverbs of Israel and Other Peoples* (Louisville: WJK, 1995); German original, 1990; Whybray, *Wealth and Poverty*, Friedemann W. Golka, *The Leopard's Spots: Biblical and African Wisdom in Proverbs* (Edinburgh: T&T Clark, 1993), 36, 68. Washington in *Wealth and Poverty* makes similar claims about some of the sentence material. See also Fox ("Social Location," 228), who schematizes the history of research on the social context of Proverbs in a manner similar to the way I do here. Fox's rubrics, however, are "farm vs. school." Cf. von Rad (*Wisdom in Israel*, 17), who alludes to a third possible social context for the development of wisdom literature—that of middle class, rural land owners.

[11] See, for example, Washington, *Wealth and Poverty*, 3; Gerhard von Rad, *Wisdom in Israel*, 125–126; Roland E. Murphy, *Proverbs* (WBC 22; Nashville: Thomas Nelson, 1998), 261; Pleins, "Social World," 72; Bruce V. Malchow, "Social Justice in the Wisdom Literature," *BTB* 12 (1982): 120–124, esp. 121; Raymond Van Leeuwen, "Wealth and Poverty: System and Contradiction in Proverbs," *Hebrew Studies* 33 (1992): 25–36. See further Milton Schwantes, *Das Recht der Armen* (BET 4; Frankfurt am Main: Peter Lang, 1977), 260; Diane Bergant, *Israel's Wisdom Literature: A Liberation-Critical Reading* (Minneapolis: Fortress, 1997), 100. Claus Westermann (*Roots*, 21) also notes the variety of points of view in Proverbs regarding wealth and poverty. In his summary on page 73 of *Wealth and Poverty*, Whybray likewise alludes to a diversity of viewpoints in the book. This list could be easily expanded.

and righteous/foolish and wicked receive their just desserts—what I, in relation to the discourse of wealth and poverty, call a "wisdom prosperity axiom." On the other hand, other material in the book seems to call such a retributive axiom into question, or at least creates a tension in this regard, by commending compassion toward the poor and offering criticism of the rich.

Essentially all commentators address some of this apparent ambiguity in the book's wealth and poverty talk by separating out chapters 1–9 (as well as the so-called Amenemope material [22:17–24:22] and other minor collections in the book [e.g., chs. 30–31]), claiming this material emerged from a different social milieu than the formally distinct sentence proverbs of the rest of the book.[12] When considered in isolation the discourse of wealth and poverty in the "instructional material" of chapters 1–9 (and to an extent 22:17–24:22) does in fact seem to yield a higher degree of coherence than when it is read with the sentence material. Yet the diversity or ambiguity in the discourse of wealth and poverty, which I described above, is also apparent *within* the collections of sentence sayings that make up chapters 10:1–22:16 and chapters 25–29. This situation, however, is not so easily described or accounted for. If it is addressed at all, it is usually explained in one of two primary, but related ways.

On the one hand, it is sometimes suggested that those who produced Proverbs, including ultimately the central sentence collections of the book, held conflicting, or more persuasively, complex viewpoints based on their observations of complex reality.[13] Though the book adopts the "act-consequence connection" (or "wisdom prosperity axiom") whereby the poor are understood to be destitute because of laziness or other moral failings, and the rich wealthy because of uncommon industry or moral rectitude, the sages recognized, in Van Leeuwen's words, "exceptions to the general rules of life." Although "the basic teaching" of the book "is that right living

[12] See, for instance, Whybray, *Wealth and Poverty*, 9.

[13] See, for instance, Westermann (*Roots*, 21–22), who in a chapter entitled "Proverbs of Observation and Experience" insists that a good number of "statements about the rich and poor" in Proverbs (e.g., 14:4, 20; 22:2, 7; 15:15; 13:7–8; 18:23; 28:11; 19:6–7; etc.) "have sprung out of observations." Westermann, however, is most concerned with uncovering the origins of the sentence material and admits that those sayings are transformed in collections.

produces wealth and well being," the wise also realized some were poor for no fault of their own and recognized the rich could be unscrupulous.[14] The poor, for instance, might be poor as the result of oppression: "The field of the poor may yield much food, but it is swept away through injustice" (Prov 13:23; cf. 22:16).[15] Or, poverty may even be the result of the will of God: "Rich and poor have this in common, the Lord is maker of them all" (Prov 22:2; cf. 29:13).[16] For scholars like J. David Pleins, moreover, the sentiment of proverbs like 22:2 and 29:13 that, "both poverty and wealth are thought of as given by God or fate," is best understood as the ideological product of an urban economic and political elite.[17]

On the other hand, some scholars explain the perceived ambiguity in the discourse of wealth and poverty in Proverbs, and the sentence material in particular, in a somewhat different manner. These writers understand the book's wealth and poverty talk either: a) in terms of a historical development within what is again understood to be a relatively unified, "upper class" wisdom tradition; or b) via

[14] Raymond C. Van Leeuwen, "Proverbs: Introduction, Commentary, and Reflections," *NIB* 5:25. See further Walter C. Kaiser, Jr., "The Old Testament Promise of Material Blessings and the Contemporary Believer," *TrinJ* 9 (1998): 151–170; Malchow, "Social Justice," 121; Van Leeuwen, "System and Contradiction," 29; cf. von Rad, *Wisdom in Israel*, 125–26.

[15] This is one possible rendering and interpretation of רב־אכל ניר ראשים ויש נספה בלא משפט. Unless otherwise noted all translations of biblical texts are my own. The translations here of Prov 13:23 and 22:2 follow the NRSV.

[16] Cf. Kaiser ("The Old Testament Promise," 166), who suggests some proverbs promote the view that "it is only because of the providential will of God that . . . people are poor (Prov 20:12; 22:2; 29:13)." Of course like 13:23, Prov 22:2 (עשיר ורש נפגשו עשה כלם יהוה) also need not be interpreted only in this manner.

[17] Pleins, "Social World," 69; cf. Bergant (*Israel's Wisdom Literature*, 101), who seems to evaluate at least some of the material in Proverbs similarly. After speaking of the "pressures of the privileged" she writes: "There is a definite class bias behind much of this teaching." Norman K. Gottwald's suggestion that Proverbs' discourse of wealth and poverty reveals a class contradiction in a Marxist sense is a similar attempt at explaining the book's perceived ambiguities. He, however, is unfortunately unable to develop the suggestion in the context of his introductory textbook. See Norman K. Gottwald, *The Hebrew Bible: A Socio-Literary Introduction* (Philadelphia: Fortress, 1985), 571–575. Though Pleins does to some extent distinguish the sages of the wisdom literature from the ruling political and economic elite, he indicates that the former supported and reproduced the ideological biases of the latter. He writes: "It is to be expected, then, that the values and practices advocated in the wisdom tradition are in accord with the political and economic leanings of the ruling classes." See "Social World," 61–63. My view is somewhat different (see below).

an assertion that the various sayings emerged from very different socio-historical settings. The historical development explanation is perhaps most clearly articulated by James L. Crenshaw. In this view, the self-serving notions of the wisdom prosperity axiom is characteristic of early wisdom writers and is said to be reinterpreted or softened by the wisdom formulations of later sages once it became clear that the harsher, older act-consequence sayings no longer adequately described reality.[18] The view that different proverbial material originated in different social contexts holds that the harsher wealth and poverty sayings in Proverbs emerged from a rural, agricultural and tribal, folk milieu, but are softened or modified by material deriving from a quite different scribal context (perhaps, but not necessarily, at some remove chronologically). The harsher material is then explained as morally appropriate expressions for the social context that produced it. Washington's work is most notable in this regard. He suggests, for example, that the difficult sayings objectively describe the lot of the poor without passing moral judgment and state a "plain truth" that "labor is necessary." He contends that in "a relatively non-stratified village society" such sayings "are not as open to abuse as they would be in urban society" where they "could be misused to blame victims of oppression and exploitation." The Hebrew sages, however, tempered the folk wisdom that they passed on with "an equally august tradition"—which Washington associates with scribes in post-exilic Judea—"enjoining care for the poor."[19]

Whybray offers a variation on the perspective articulated by Washington. He too understands the largely instructional collections in the book (e.g., chs. 1–9) to reflect a different social perspective and context than the sentence sayings. Unlike Washington, however, he finds in the sentence material itself little ambiguity when it comes to the discourse of wealth and poverty and does not offer a theory of distinct social origins for different proverbs in the proverbial collections. Rather this material—which he insists reflects the precarious world of the small farmer—is both morally appropriate to the agrarian social context that produced it and largely coherent when it comes to matters of wealth and poverty. However, Whybray's posi-

[18] See especially, James L. Crenshaw, "Poverty and Punishment in the Book of Proverbs," *QR* 9 (1989): 30–43.

[19] Washington, *Wealth and Poverty*, 183–85.

tion requires some special pleading. The "variations," and "divergent views" in the proverbial material regarding wealth and poverty, which he recognizes in the otherwise "remarkably consistent" sentence literature, are "accounted for by changes of mood or circumstances. *Absolute logic* and consistency," he avers, "are hardly to be expected here."[20]

Both of these two main approaches to understanding wealth and poverty in Proverbs, together with their particular variations, share certain features. In each instance the interpreter appears to read the text's language of wealth and poverty and its cause and effect rhetoric in almost exclusively literal terms and discovers a wisdom prosperity axiom to be at work in many of the sayings. Subsequently, because not every wealth and poverty saying suggests such an axiom, an ambiguity in the discourse of wealth and poverty is discerned. This is followed by an attempt to explain that ambiguity by discovering the provenance of the material. Either Proverbs, including its discourse of wealth and poverty, is the work of a unified social group (e.g., upper class scribes associated with the royal court) who simply held contradictory opinions about the rich and poor (or different opinions at different times); or the book preserves sayings from one social context (e.g., the folk sayings of a small village, preliterate, tribal, agricultural society), which were modified or added to by scribes situated in, and responding to, a different socio-historical setting.

These attempts to explain a perceived ambiguity in the discourse of wealth and poverty in Proverbs by appeals to provenance are not unreasonable and have yielded some interesting and valuable results. Nevertheless such an approach is not without its shortcomings.

First, the appeal to an evolution in viewpoint in the work of upper class courtly sages is not wholly persuasive. If such scribes were responsible for the book from beginning until end, it is curious that Proverbs' discourse of wealth and poverty would in the first place appear so thoroughly ambiguous. Would we not expect a more unified perspective from such a cadre of elite, upper class bureaucrats? Similarly, if some of the material in Proverbs represents a subsequent modification or softening by scribes of viewpoints that emerged from other periods or contexts, one wonders both why the earlier

[20] Whybray, *Wealth and Poverty*, 11–74, esp. 62–63; italics original.

scribes were so obtuse and why the later scribes preserved the earlier impulses. Why did subsequent scribes not suppress more completely any understanding that contradicted their own?[21] Even if one accepts the not implausible notion that a multiplicity of material was preserved because the sages knew a multiplicity of experiences would demand different kinds of wise responses, the question of consistency (or inconsistency) in the moral principles and values underlying the material needs to be addressed. There is a difference between preserving a variety of particular responses to complex and changing phenomena (e.g., issues of wealth and poverty) and those responses preserving incompatible moral underpinnings. That Proverbs might preserve a variety of particular responses to issues of wealth and poverty is not problematic, it is even expected; but this diversity would not necessarily lead to an evaluation of the discourse of wealth and poverty as "ambiguous." That Proverbs preserves responses with incompatible moral underpinnings, however, if it is indeed the case and is in fact what produces an ambiguity in the sages discourse, needs to be more adequately elucidated. The appeal to historical development or multiple social contexts in discussions of the book is not sufficient to explain the level of diversity or ambiguity that is claimed to be present in Proverbs' presentation of wealth and poverty matters.

A shortcoming of the second position articulated above, that the text of Proverbs ought to be read against the context of a tribal, village culture, concerns the tradition processes that contributed to the development of the book. If a scribal group made use of traditional material in the formation of the collections of sentence sayings in Proverbs (as is likely; see below), there is unfortunately no way to be certain this proverbial material was preserved intact by those responsible for collecting it. There is therefore no way to be certain that the small agricultural village is the best context against which to read this material. The traditional utterances of tribal elders easily could have been modified by the sages who produced Proverbs; and if they were modified, there is no reliable way to extract the

[21] The questions in this section are, of course, to a large extent rhetorical. As I will suggest below it is likely that any socially recognizable scribal group in ancient Israel was probably more diverse than is often imagined. A more persuasive form of the argument that ancient scribes held diverse or contradictory views as regards wealth and poverty (or any topic) would fully articulate this.

traditional notions, motifs, etc., from the contribution of the scribe. There are no adequate criteria by which one can determine what in a particular proverb is of folk origin so that the saying, as presented in the text of Proverbs, can with reasonable certainty be said to be the product of an agricultural, tribal setting.[22] The fact that the proverbial material of contemporary, pre-literate, tribal cultures collected by modern anthropologists contains motifs and images similar to what is found in the Hebrew Proverbs does not warrant the claim that the two literatures—distinct historically, culturally, geographically—necessarily emerged from analogous social settings. It is also the case that, regardless of the context of its origin, once a particular sentence saying is grafted into the text of Proverbs its new primary context is the literary context of the book itself.

Fox, too, has called into question the adequacy of comparing the material in Proverbs with the proverbial sayings of contemporary pre-literate, tribal cultures and has leveled some important critiques against the assumptions of those who make such comparisons. He suggests, for example, that the comparative proverb material, rather than emerging from the world of a rural folk population, itself may be the product of courtiers. He asserts as well (in regard to the traditional proverbial material gathered by Golka) that, "the communities from which the parallels are taken were not preliterate—certainly not in the 20th century, when most of the sayings were recorded."[23] For Fox, even the impulse to locate the sentence material of Proverbs in a folk setting is problematic, for it is "not based on any real sociological data, or even . . . casual personal observation." Rather the tendency, which he associates with Golka, Westermann and Whybray, "reflects a romanticism that allows [one] to extract a communitarian ideal from proverbs (*some* proverbs) and then to spin a reality out of the ideal and identify *that* with life in a small, egalitarian village."[24]

[22] Von Rad's view is similar. Though referring to an earlier moment in the history of Proverbs interpretation, he writes: "The idea which used to be widespread, namely that its [the Solomonic book of Proverbs'] sentences are to be traced back to popular proverbs, can no longer be maintained." See *Wisdom in Israel*, 26.

[23] Fox also contends that it is only a strained argument that can insist that the so-called royal proverbs of the book of Proverbs be assigned to "simple folk," rather than "royal scribes." See "Social Location," 233–234; cf. Golka, *The Leopard's Spots*; Whybray, *Wealth and Poverty*, 45–58.

[24] Fox, "Social Location," 233–34 (italics original).

Moreover, if the comparative data from contemporary pre-literate peoples that is often drawn upon in these discussions is accurate, the book of Proverbs, it appears, actually contains very little material that furnishes strong parallels to that data. As Fox writes, those African proverbs marshaled by Golka for instance, "bear little resemblance to Israelite Proverbs."[25] Rather the book's programmatic and persistent deployment of moral and intellectual rubrics to structure its discourse (e.g., wicked/righteous, wisdom/folly, etc.), suggests a conscious, formal, didactic intent to the majority of the book's sayings and the collections as a whole. This tendency is something that is absent from the comparative material compiled by anthropologists and folklorists who are concerned to categorize and analyze their data within a conceptual framework developed within academic disciplines that emphasize proverb performance and usage.[26] By contrast, people in an ancient context whose compositional agendas and anthological strategies are not immediately or entirely clear to us, collected the materials in the book of Proverbs. As Fox puts it: "The redactors of Proverbs were not paremiolgists. They were close to authors or collage artists and they preserved proverbs that served their purpose."[27] Although the comparative proverbial material gathered by folklorists is important data, the insights it provides for understanding Proverbs are primarily heuristic. Its explanatory value is limited on the one hand to elucidating the "background," or perhaps better, the "lineage," of particular proverbial sayings and images

[25] Fox, "Social Location," 233–37. I would say the same for those African proverbs cited by Washington in *Wealth and Poverty*, esp. 180–85. The Mossi proverbs gathered by Naré likewise appear to have only a superficial similarity with Proverbs. Naré, however, is primarily concerned to compare the Mossi material with Proverbs 25–29. These chapters admittedly bear a somewhat closer resemblance to the proverbs of pre-literate, tribal cultures than others in the book of Proverbs. See Laurent Naré, *Proverbes salomoniens et proverbes mossi: etude comparative à partir d'un nouvelle analyse de Pr. 25–29* (Frankfurt am Main: Peter Lang, 1986).

[26] A convenient introduction to some of the issues in the broader study of proverbs, or "paremiology," is Wolfgang Mieder and Alan Dundes, eds., *The Wisdom of Many: Essays on the Proverb* (New York: Garland, 1981). See further Wolfgang Mieder, *Proverbs are Never Out of Season: Popular Wisdom in the Modern Age* (New York: Oxford University Press, 1993). Cf. further the section *Folk Proverbs and Metaphor* in Chapter One.

[27] Fox, "Social Location," 237. Furthermore, those responsible for the book of Proverbs certainly did not preserve the entire stock of proverbs in ancient Israel, as the appearance of isolated sayings elsewhere in the Bible attest. For these sayings, see Carole R. Fontaine, *Traditional Sayings in the Old Testament: A Contextual Study* (Sheffield: Almond, 1982).

and, on the other hand (as was suggested in Chapter One), to evoking the metaphorical nature of the book's moral discourse. For those concerned with understanding the Hebrew *book* of Proverbs—including its discourse of wealth and poverty—the collections as we have them in MT must be the locus of primary attention.

2.1.b. *The Scribes of Proverbs*

The material that makes up the book of Proverbs, including the sentence sayings, is thus best regarded as the product of a *scribal elite.* It is difficult to imagine the production (and use) of such didactic collections of proverbs, and certainly an anthology of such collections (a book), in anything other than an elite intellectual environment.[28] The fact that Proverbs is best regarded as the product of elite scribes, however, does not inevitably demand that the book—including all its talk about wealth and poverty—be understood as reflecting, reproducing, and undergirding the values and perspectives of the "rich" and/or politically powerful. Like jazz born out of the encounter of African traditions and rhythms with "New World" realities, languages, and instruments, what we have in Proverbs (and especially the sentence material) is a kind of literature that is something quite different from the traditional tribal, folk sources and courtly influences that spawned it. Although appropriate as instruction for youths and likely in part composed for all who were able to read, including probably some members of the political and economic elite, the book was written and compiled by (and primarily for) the literati.[29]

[28] As Philip R. Davies notes, even in modern western societies with literacy rates approaching 90% of the population, less than 1% write books. See *Scribes and Schools. The Canonization of the Hebrew Scriptures* (LAI; Louisville: WJK, 1998), 82.

[29] It is possible that scribes in ancient Israel might have been responsible for educating members of the royal household and political elites. However Proverbs—unlike several Egyptian instructions that are specifically addressed to future royal or high-ranking political functionaries—nowhere unequivocally alludes to such a function; cf. the fiction of the kings Merikare and Amenemhet I and the vizier Ptahhotep in instructing their sons and successors; cf. further von Rad, *Wisdom in Israel*, 83–84. Likewise, it is impossible to deny that at some point in Israelite and Judean history wealthy students (or their families) might have hired a wisdom sage to offer instruction in some kind of school setting. See, for example, the view of Leo G. Perdue in *Proverbs* (Interpretation; Louisville: John Knox, 2000), 69. It is sometimes thought, for instance, that Sirach 51:23's allusion to a "house of instruction" might suggest such a situation. See James L. Crenshaw, "Sirach: Introduction, Commentary, and Reflections," *NIB* 5:867.

The prerequisite for the emergence of a scribal class is simply a sufficiently complex economy and state apparatus for which record keeping and writing are necessary. It is thus reasonable to suppose that scribes in ancient Israel and Judah were initially a socially recognizable group of people employed by political sovereigns in order to record economic transactions and conduct diplomacy. It is important to remember, however, that such sages were not themselves rulers, but acted in the service of these political and economic elites. This is especially true where and when scribes functioned not merely or exclusively as high administrative officials (e.g., as the סופר of some biblical texts; 2 Sam 8:16–18; 20:23–25; 1 Kgs 4:1–6; 2 Chron 24:11–12; 2 Kgs 18:18, 37), but where the duties of such a professional caste were more stratified and entailed more bureaucratic, mundane types of activity—e.g., recording information in annals, writing up contracts, etc.[30] Although no biblical description of scribal training exists, Fox rightly notes that "the royal service would include clerks and officials of *high and low degree*."[31]

It would thus be "hardly surprising," as Philip R. Davies writes, that such an intellectual elite should "develop its own culture, distinct from the rural culture of the peasants and importantly, distinct from the ruling class that it served. Its stories, its values, and its skills will have differed" from those living in the villages, but also from those more fundamentally tied to central institutions such as the royal court, for the intellectual elites' "economic interests and intellectual horizons were different."[32] Certainly the scribes who produced the discourse of wealth and poverty in Proverbs "absorbed the culture of the regime that they served," as well as that of the rural population—probably drawing especially on the raw proverbial material of the latter. However, the "gift of writing" will have provided this scribal class (diverse in its own ranks due to the variety of functions and roles its members carried out) with a social identity distinct from

[30] See Michael Fishbane, *Biblical Interpretation in Ancient Israel* (Oxford: Clarendon, 1985), 25.

[31] Fox, "Social Location," 236; italics added. Fishbane likewise writes: "It may be assumed . . . that the skills taught in their various guild centres and schools (cf. 1 Chron 2:55) enabled these scribes to serve a variety of administrative and state functions." See *Biblical Interpretation*, 25. Cf. Christine Schams, *Jewish Scribes in the Second-Temple Period* (JSOTSup 291; Sheffield: Sheffield Academic Press, 1998), 36–71.

[32] Davies, *Scribes*, 18.

both the political and economic elite and the rural folk.[33] The character of this scribal caste would have been shaped, too, by the diversity of its particular members' participation in, and access to, other cultural and social formations—e.g., powerful or impotent families and clans, the cult, prophetic groups, etc.[34] The fusion of all these elements would have shaped a unique scribal ethos or culture, and it is this ethos and social context that is reflected in complex ways in the pages of Proverbs. Though traces of the history (or genealogy) of this scribal synthesis are evident in the different kinds of material Proverbs preserves (e.g., instruction vs. sentence sayings), to understand the book and its discourse of wealth and poverty fully, the "new work" of scribes—the finished book of Proverbs—must be distinguished from the sources that spawned it.

2.1.c. *The Date of Proverbs*

The book of Proverbs is notoriously difficult to date, and direct evidence for a pre-exilic scribal elite that would have been capable of producing the text (e.g., in schools or other institutions) is lacking. However, David W. Jamieson-Drake in his anthropological-archaeological study has suggested that it is not until some point in the 8th century BCE at the earliest that Israel's and Judah's economy and royal bureaucracy was sufficiently complex to support and require a small, moderately sophisticated scribal apparatus which (after 722/21) remained focused on Jerusalem.[35] It is thus not impossible that the collection and redaction-composition of some proverbial material began in this period, as Prov 25:1 may itself imply with its allusion to the labors of Hezekiah's men.[36] Yet the process certainly continued into the Persian era and it is likely the different collections in

[33] Davies, *Scribes*, 19.

[34] Von Rad also alludes to a rich diversity within scribal ranks and at points speaks of Proverbs' "middle class" ethic. See *Wisdom in Israel*, 18, 21, 82, 84. On the range of diversity in scribal ranks in especially the later Second Temple period see Carol A. Newsom, *The Self as Symbolic Space: Constructing Identity and Community at Qumran* (STDJ 52; Leiden: Brill, 2004), 29–68.

[35] David W. Jamieson-Drake, *Scribes and Schools in Monarchic Judah: A Socio-Archeological Approach* (Sheffield: Almond, 1991), esp. 137–138, 147–149; cf. Davies, *Scribes*, 77.

[36] The mention of Hezekiah is routinely taken as historical. Von Rad (*Wisdom in Israel*, 15), for example, notes that the superscription of 25:1 "is hardly ever doubted now." Similarly Van Leeuwen writes: "Although questions have been raised about the historicity of the heading, there seems no reason to doubt it" (*NIB* 5:217). Van

Proverbs took a shape close to their final form in this period.[37] The Hebrew version of the book was drawn together as a whole in the late Persian period at the earliest, though some scholars would put this consolidation in the Hellenistic period.[38]

The version of scribal work on Proverbs just offered carries considerable explanatory value when considering the text's discourse of wealth and poverty. It accounts, on the one hand, for some of the *complexity* of this discourse, to which the quotation from Washington at the beginning of this chapter alludes. On the other hand, it can also account for the *coherency* (vs. ambiguity) that can be discerned in the book as a whole and its wealth and poverty talk in particular. The text's complexity is primarily due, as I intimated in Chapter One, to the fact that the material in the various sections of the book carries traces of a life and usage in at least two social formations, the court and the rural village, which ought to be distinguished from the scribal culture that finally produced the book. However, this complexity, is also in part a result of the fact that the collections emerged in different periods in the history of ancient Israel and

Leeuwen cites Michael Carasik, "Who Were the 'Men of Hezekiah'" (Proverbs xxv 1)?" *VT* 44 (1994): 289–300, as one who questions the historicity of the note. See too Hans F. Fuhs, *Das Buch der Sprichwörter: Ein Kommentar* (Forschung zur Bibel 95; Würzburg: Echter Verlag, 2001), 339–40. In my view, taken together the note of 25:1 and the archaeological data like that gathered by Jamieson-Drake warrant the modest inference that the redactional-compositional process of the book of Proverbs began in the pre-exilic period.

[37] There is a good deal of evidence that the kind economic activity Proverbs assumes was prevalent during the Persian period. On the economic activity of the Persian period, see C. L. Seow, *Ecclesiastes: A New Translation with Introduction and Commentary* (AB 18c; New York: Doubleday, 1997), 21–36. Christine Roy Yoder has marshaled the same kind of evidence vis-à-vis the instructional material of Proverbs 1–9 (and 31:10–31). See her *Wisdom as a Woman of Substance: A Socio-Economic Reading of Proverbs 1–9 and 31:10–31* (BZAW 304; Berlin: W. de Gruyter, 2001), 39–72.

[38] Washington (*Wealth and Poverty*, 111–133) reviews the evidence and favors a Persian period date. So too Yoder, *Woman of Substance*, 15–18. Michael V. Fox writes: "A Persian or early Hellenistic dating is likely for the latest strata of the book." See *Proverbs 1–9: A New Translation with Introduction and Commentary* (AB 18a; New York: Doubleday, 2000), 6. Claudia V. Camp suggests a somewhat later date is appropriate. See "What's So Strange about the Strange Woman?" in *The Bible and the Politics of Exegesis* (ed. David Jobling et al.; Cleveland: Pilgrim, 1991), 17–31. Toy (*Proverbs*, xix–xxxi) likewise dates the book to the Hellenistic period. At least in its Greek form, the shape of the book of Proverbs as a whole (and to a lesser extent the individual collections and sayings) continued to be negotiated by different communities into the Hellenistic period, as the order and content of the collections in LXX attests.

Judah (Yehud). The book's coherency in outlook is due largely to the fact that each collection in Proverbs, whether emerging and finalized in pre-exilic or post-exilic times, is the work of an educated, elite, scribal caste and embodies their perspectives and ethos.

2.2. The Instruction of Proverbs 1–9 and 10–31

Above I suggested that for those concerned with understanding the discourse of wealth and poverty in the Hebrew book of Proverbs the locus of attention should be the final form of the proverbial collections as they have been handed down in MT. However, because the sayings that comprise the various collections that make up Proverbs, as well as the collections themselves, likely emerged in different historical periods and no doubt underwent different histories of transmission, one of the first questions that must be asked in studying the book's discourse of wealth and poverty is whether one should examine chapters 1–9 and the formally distinct collections of chapters 10–31 independently; or, whether there is warrant for considering the book as a whole.

It has been typical for scholars to examine the major sections of the book separately. The sentence sayings in chapters 10:1–22:16 together with chapters 25–29 have been the focus of much attention. Though it is not necessarily explicitly stated, the tendency to examine the major sections of the text independently seems due primarily to the formal similarities the later chapters share with one another over and against the wisdom poems of chapters 1–9.[39] The generic and stylistic differences between collections in the book hence serve as warrant for examining the major sections of the text separately. A further implicit motivation in such procedures, as I intimated earlier, appears to be a belief that the sentence material

[39] For example, the studies of Van Leeuwen ("System and Contradiction") and Pleins ("Social World") are almost exclusively concerned with the material found in chapters 10–29. The studies of Westermann, Holger Delkurt, and Jutta Hausmann, though not exclusively concerned with wealth and poverty in Proverbs, also limit their studies, including treatment of this topic, to the sentence material of the later chapters of the book. See Westermann, *Roots*; Holger Delkurt, *Ethische Einsichten in der Alttestamentlichen Spruchweisheit* (BTS 21; Neukirchen-Vluyn: Neukirchener, 1993) and Jutta Hausmann, *Studien zum Menschenbild der älteren Weisheit* (Tübingen: J. C. B. Mohr, 1995).

originated in a particular socio-historical setting (e.g., a rural, tribal culture) distinct from the environment that produced the poems of chapters 1–9. A corollary assumption seems to be that a focus on provenance is the best way of explaining differences in the book's discourse of wealth and poverty.

Although there are obvious disparities between the material in Proverbs 1–9 and that which is found in the remainder of the book, this study will consider the discourse of wealth and poverty as it emerges throughout the entire book of Proverbs. This, however, will not mean neglecting the generic and stylistic differences between major sections of the text, but rather understanding their significance in the context of the book's overall structure and instructional purpose. The canonical shape of the text, of course, encourages reading the book in this kind of undivided manner. The evidence for a certain amount of editorial unity to Proverbs, as well as literary integrity to its different collections, that scholars increasingly recognize also suggests some merit to this approach.[40] However, it is not simply a commitment to a particular canonical or literary methodology, which insists on examining the "final form" of the text that lies behind my choice to consider the discourse of wealth and poverty in the book of Proverbs as a whole. Rather, as I will show, it is a recognition that the wealth and poverty talk in Proverbs 1–9 functions in ways similar to the wealth and poverty language of subsequent chapters.

[40] As Bergant writes (*Israel's Wisdom Literature*, 78), there appears to be in the book "a definite structural framework that bespeaks editorial intentionality." Cf. R. B. Y. Scott, *Proverbs and Ecclesiastes* (AB 18; Garden City, N. Y.: Doubleday, 1965), 22; Fuhs, *Das Buch der Sprichwörter*, 172–73. Note further Van Leeuwen's structuralist and semantic study of chapters 25–27 in which he discerns several "proverb poems." See Raymond C. Van Leeuwen, *Context and Meaning in Proverbs 25–27* (Atlanta: Scholars Press, 1988). See further Knut Martin Heim, *Like Grapes of Gold Set in Silver: An Interpretation of Proverbial Clusters in Proverbs 10:1–22:16* (BZAW; Berlin: W. de Gruyter, 2001); Claudia V. Camp, *Wisdom and the Feminine in the Book of Proverbs* (Sheffield: Almond, 1985). For an overview of the modern discussion surrounding the structure of the book, see Whybray, *Survey*, 34–61 and R. N. Whybray, *Proverbs* (NCBC; Grand Rapids: Eerdman's, 1994), 15–17. Whybray's own statement regarding the structure of the text is *The Composition of the Book of Proverbs* (JSOTSup 168; Sheffield: JSOT, 1994).

2.2.a. *The Prologue's Virtues*

Although there is unanimous agreement that Proverbs is concerned with offering the reader some kind of instruction, there can be legitimate disagreement as to exactly what the book's educational or instructional task is and how the various collections carry out this task rhetorically. It is often maintained, for instance, that Proverbs (especially the sentence material) primarily offers a kind of practical wisdom or instruction based on experience and observation of the world (social and natural) designed to help the hearer succeed or prosper in a variety of spheres of life, including the economic realm.[41] Such a formulation is not so much wrong, but like the proverbial notion of an act-consequence nexus, it is in need of nuance (see below). It is best to regard the material in the book of Proverbs to be doing significantly more than offering the hearer a guide to worldly or material success.

A consideration of the book's prologue, which is widely regarded as articulating the purpose not only of chapters 1–9 but Proverbs as a whole, makes clear the instruction intends to do more than offer a simple guide to prosperity.[42] The text of Proverbs 1:2–7 reads:

(2) לדעת חכמה ומוסר להבין אמרי בינה
(3) לקחת מוסר השכל צדק ומשפט ומישרים
(4) לתת לפתאים ערמה לנער דעת ומזמה

[41] See, for example, Whybray, *Proverbs*, 4; Perdue, *Proverbs*, 5–6; Richard J. Clifford, "Introduction to Wisdom Literature," *NIB* 5:9, 11; Toy, *Proverbs*, xiv; Arndt Meinhold, *Die Sprüche* (2 vols.; ZBK; Zürich: Theologische Verlag, 1991), 1:38–39; Otto Plöger, *Sprüche Salomos (Proverbia)* (Neukirchen-Vluyn: Neukirchener, 1984), xxxiv; Scott, *Proverbs and Ecclesiastes*, 23; von Rad, *Wisdom in Israel*, 4–5, 85; Roland E. Murphy, *The Tree of Life* (Grand Rapids: Eerdmans, 1990), 7–11, 17; Yoder, *Woman of Substance*, 103–04; Bergant, *Israel's Wisdom Literature*, 86. Fox's evaluation that the book sets forth "guidelines for securing a life of well-being, decency, and dignity" is somewhat more nuanced. However, in a vein similar to many others, he also writes: "To be sure, wisdom will also bring exterior rewards—life, health, wealth, favor, and well being." See his *Proverbs 1–9*, 3, 75.

[42] See Ploger (*Spruche Salomos*, 8), who notes that together with v. 1, lines 2–6 serve as an "introduction" (*Einführung*) for the entire book. Van Leeuwen ("Proverbs," *NIB* 5.32) likewise writes: "These verses [the prologue] state the pedigree, essence, and purpose of the book called Proverbs." Similarly Murphy (*Proverbs*, 3) states: "These verses [the prologue] are clearly composed as a kind of preface to the book." Whybray (*Proverbs*, 31) believes that an original form of the prologue (vv. 1–4, 6) introduced only chs. 1–9 but that in its current form the lines introduce the entire book. Cf. William McKane, *Proverbs: A New Approach* (Philadelphia: Westminster, 1970), 262; Clifford, *Proverbs* (OTL: Louisville: WJK, 1999), 32.

(5) ישמע חכם ויוסף לקח ונבון תחבלות יקנה
(6) להבין משל ומליצה דברי חכמים וחידתם
(7) יראת יהוה ראשית דעת חכמה ומוסר אוילים בזו

2) For knowing wise instruction, for understanding words of insight;
3) For gaining instruction in wise dealing: righteousness, justice, and equity.[43]
4) For giving to the simple cunning; to the youth, knowledge of shrewdness.[44]
5) Let the wise person hear and gain learning and let the understanding person acquire skill,[45]
6) To understand a trope and figure, the words of the wise and their riddles.[46]
7) Fear of the Lord is the beginning of knowledge; fools despise wisdom and instruction.

The prologue makes clear that Proverbs intends to present to its addressee a complex view of wisdom. Although ancient writers and audiences may not have made such distinctions, according to the text's opening lines, the book's vision of wisdom is one where intellectual virtues ("wise instruction" and words of insight; v. 2), practical virtues (cunning and "knowledge of shrewdness;" v. 4), and especially the social virtues of צדק, משפט, and מישרים (righteousness, justice, equity; v. 3), which stand at the pinnacle of the opening poem, are highly valued.[47]

The structure of the prologue can be outlined as follows:

I. The Purpose of Proverbs (vv. 2–4)
  A. To instill intellectual virtues (v. 2)
    – *for (ל) knowing wise instruction,*
    – *for (ל) understanding words of insight*

---

[43] The rendering of v. 4 follows the NRSV.

[44] The translation of both חכמה ומוסר (v. 2) and דעת ומזמה (v. 4) as *hendiadys* ("wise instruction" and "knowledge of shrewdness" respectively) follows Fox. See *Proverbs 1–9*, 58–67.

[45] That the prefixed verbal forms here are jussive is clear from *wĕyôsep*. Cf. Fox, *Proverbs 1–9*, 62. Fuhs, *Das Buch der Sprichwörter*, 37, however, prefers to read indicative forms.

[46] On the rendering of משל as "trope" and the proverbial *hapax* מליצה (cf. Hab 2:6) as "figure," see Fox, *Proverbs 1–9*, 54–56, 63–64, and below.

[47] Cf. especially William P. Brown, *Character in Crisis: A Fresh Approach to the Wisdom Literature of the Old Testament* (Grand Rapids: Eerdmans, 1996), 23–30 who likewise recognizes that the social virtues, which he calls "moral, communal virtues," stand at the pinnacle of the prologue. Brown, however, understands the structure of the opening poem in manner somewhat different than I—i.e., he understands vv. 5–6 as sketching part of the book's purpose. For my view, see below.

B. To instill social virtues (v. 3)
  – *for* (ל) *gaining instruction in wise dealing:*
  – *righteousness, justice, and equity.*

C. To instill practical virtues (v. 4)
  – *for* (ל) *giving to* (ל) *the simple cunning,*
  – *to* (ל) *the youth, knowledge of shrewdness*[48]

II. The Invitation
  A. The call (in the jussive) to assume the position of the wise person (v. 5)
  B. The tasks of the one who assumes this position (v. 6)

III. The Motto
  A. Fear of the Lord

The relationship in Proverbs of these sets of virtues to each other as well as to a broader notion of wisdom and a vision of a good and flourishing human life is complex. What seems clear, however, is that "wisdom" in Proverbs is best conceived as a comprehensive virtue, a kind of "meta-virtue," which includes all other virtues in itself.

By closely associating the intellectual, practical, and social realms and subsequently inviting the hearer to take up the task of attaining to these virtues and values, to *choose* the way of wisdom (vv. 5–6), the structure of the prologue suggests much. It reveals that Proverbs is concerned to shape the whole character of the hearer for the whole of life.[49] The book is concerned to create a particular kind of person who can be characterized by the virtues it values—what it would call a wise person. The text intends to function not just normatively by providing the hearer specific commands, but formatively, shaping the addressee's character through its promotion of particular virtues.[50] In this regard the infinitive absolute השכל in 1:3, the

[48] Although the second word of the first half of v. 4 also is prefixed with *lamed*, one of the important points of the outline is to illustrate that each half-verse of lines 2–4, with the exception of 3b, begins with *lamed* (see below).

[49] See, too, Brown's description of the *ethos* of the instruction in *Character in Crisis*, 30–36. Cf. Clifford, *Proverbs*, 20; Fuhs, *Das Buch der Sprichwörter*, 12–15. Whybray (*Proverbs*, 4) begins to point to the kind of understanding I am suggesting, but in my view still privileges the practical advantages of wisdom too strongly. For him, even though "intrinsically good," morality and religion "are presented as essential features of the pursuit of wisdom *because* they lead to prosperity"; italics added.

[50] Cf. Fox, *Proverbs 1–9*, 75, 92–93.

verse that structurally marks the pinnacle of the prologue's articulation of the book's purpose, is appropriately rendered by the NRSV as "wise dealing" and not something like "success" (Clifford; NJPS).[51] The latter rendering, though possible, appears to reflect an interpretive point of view that regards the book largely as a guide to worldly and material success; the former translation underscores a perspective that understands Proverbs more fully as didactic, moral literature.

Certainly the sages recognized a degree of material prosperity (along with the acquisition of other goods such as the satisfaction of erotic desires or the attainment of social status) to be an important aspect of human flourishing. Yet absent here in the important initial formulation of Proverbs' vision of the end of wisdom, or what one might call the "good" human life, is any mention of the role of material riches. Nor is there any indication that one of the purposes of the way of wisdom is the attainment of material prosperity. The book, if the prologue can serve as a guide, is most concerned to promote a life of virtue, characterized by the virtues it highlights. As I will argue, for Proverbs, the acquisition of material wealth and other goods is never to be equated or confused with the attainment of the good life itself, namely the realization of wisdom's virtues.

The sages, however, recognize that the great mistake of many is to *believe* that the attainment of wealth (or another lesser good) is, in fact, the key to human flourishing. A consequence of these sorts of false beliefs is that humans will begin to overvalue lesser goods, a situation that produces passionate desire for them. Hence a large part of the book's task is essentially to structure (or re-structure) its hearer's desires by undermining one set of beliefs and putting new beliefs in their place.[52] Although material riches (and other lesser goods) may well be aspects of a good and flourishing life, for Proverbs these do not in themselves constitute or produce that life. Rather, the virtues that belong to wisdom's way, as articulated most clearly in the prologue, are what lead to genuine human flourishing. It is

---

[51] Clifford, *Proverbs*, 33.

[52] Proverbs thus belongs, at least in part, to that strand of moral thinking that recognizes the passions and desires to be intimately linked with beliefs. On this type of thinking in ancient Greek, particularly Hellenistic, philosophy, see Martha C. Nussbaum, *The Therapy of Desire: Theory and Practice in Hellenistic Ethics* (Princeton: Princeton University Press, 1994).

this that the hearer of Proverbs needs to believe, and if he does, he will recognize the value of wisdom's virtuous way and desire this as passionately as one might desire wealth or some other lesser good.

Proverbs' own discourse, however, must compete precisely against the message of other discourses, or perhaps better stated, a kind of broad, implicit, but real social script, which perennially overvalues lesser goods such as material riches, sexual satisfaction, and the attainment of social status.[53] Hence one of the primary rhetorical strategies Proverbs deploys (though certainly not the only one) is to value the way of wisdom via images of precisely these generally over-valued and over-desired lesser goods, especially wealth. Yet as its prologue anticipates, Proverbs permits little, if any, trade off between the life of virtue or the way of wisdom and other goods when reckoning the value of each. As I will show, in contrast to wisdom's virtues, the lesser goods for Proverbs, because they must to some extent remain external to a person, are considered undependable, unstable, fleeting and therefore ultimately not terribly valuable or desirable. They cannot bring the security and well being that humans seek in striving after them. Only the virtues of wisdom's way—which are internal to a person's character and so reliable and enduring, and hence valuable and desirable—can do this. Moreover, as I will suggest, Proverbs insists via its act-consequence rhetoric that virtue belongs to the genuine structure of the cosmos.

By deploying images of the lesser goods and accenting these images in a way that points to the value of the life of virtue Proverbs not only encourages a hearer to choose wisdom. The book also thereby undermines and thwarts that broad social script that places too much worth on lesser goods.

2.2.b. *The Prologue as Hermeneutical Cue*

Proverbs 1:2–6 (7) is regularly regarded as articulating the purpose of the book through a string of infinitive constructs in vv. 2a, 2b, 3a, 4a, and 6a, which are dependent on v. 1 but which, curiously,

[53] The language of "social script" here is deployed to suggest that Proverbs' wealth and poverty language may be responding to a more general anxiety concerning economic matters and value rather than a genuinely articulated discourse, such as might be revealed through a study of, for example, the Tobiad narratives of the Hellenistic period.

are interrupted by the finite verbs of v. 5.[54] Though some (e.g., Toy, Whybray) believe v. 5 is an interpolation, Fox (and others) are right to see the line as "a logical continuation of the grand promises of the Prologue."[55] As many have noted, moreover, v. 5 can be read to suggest that the book is designed to instruct not only the young and the simple, but also to "advance the education of those already learned."[56]

I differ from most others, however, in understanding lines 2–4 and 5–6 to be functioning more fully and intentionally as an introductory unit. Verses 2–4 of Proverbs' prologue alone sketch the educational "purpose" of the book, as the outline above indicates. Verses 5–6 subsequently exhort the hearer to engage this purpose, to choose the way of wisdom. These lines not only suggest that the prologue envisions two potential groups of readers, the wise and foolish youth; they serve as an "invitation" to any hearer or reader who *would be* wise or understanding to continue reading, to strive to comprehend the book's tropes and figures and to learn how to interpret the enigmatic words of the wise. Verse 7 with its emphasis on the fear of YHWH can be regarded as the book's "motto."[57]

---

[54] See Murphy, *Proverbs*, 3–4; Clifford, *Proverbs*, 35; McKane, *Proverbs*, 263; Fox, *Proverbs 1–9*, 58; Plöger, *Sprüche Salomos*, 9; L. Alonso Schöckel and J. Vichel Lindez, *Proverbios* (Nueva Biblia Española, Sapienciales I; Madrid: Ediciones Cristiandad, 1984), 154. Fuhs, *Das Buch der Sprichwörter*, 37, however, understands the infinitives of the prologue to be dependent on the finite clause of v. 5.

[55] Fox, *Proverbs 1–9*, 62; Toy, *Proverbs*, 8; Whybray, *Proverbs*, 33.

[56] Fox, *Proverbs 1–9*, 62.

[57] Such a designation is customary. See, for example, Fox, *Proverbs 1–9*, 67; Plöger, *Sprüche Salomos*, 13; Van Leeuwen, "Proverbs," *NIB* 5:33; Murphy, *Proverbs*, 4; Toy, *Proverbs*, 10. Alonso Schöckel and Vichel Lindez, *Proverbios*, 158, call v. 7 "the great principle" (*el gran principio*); Fuhs (*Das Buch der Sprichwörter*, 42) declares it the book's "thesis" (*These*). Though not properly part of the prologue, v. 7's location at the beginning of the book sets the text's moral instruction within a religious framework and underscores the importance of the virtue of "fear of the Lord" for Proverbs. Its status is on a par with the various virtues articulated in the prologue proper. The "fear of the Lord" in Proverbs connotes, at least, a kind of reverence that permits and drives one to engage seriously the demands and ethical norms the book presents as grounded in, and in accord with, the deity's will. Cf. André Leliévre and Alphonse Maillot, *Commentaire des Proverbes, t. III, Chapitres 1–9* (Lectio Divina Commentaires 8; Paris: Éditions du Cerf, 2000), 24–28. For other views on this concept, see, for example, Clifford, *Proverbs*, 45–46 and esp. Fox, *Proverbs 1–9*, 69–71. In connection with the phrase "fear of the Lord" one should also recall that scholars have often debated to what degree Proverbs represents "secular" or Yahwistic wisdom. See, for instance, the perspectives and arguments of McKane, *Proverbs*; Von Rad, *Wisdom in Israel*.

This understanding of the prologue's structure dispenses with any need to explain via literary-historical arguments why v. 5 disrupts the prologue's supposed chain of infinitive constructs, each beginning with *lamed*, and makes sense of this verse's deployment of jussive verbal forms.[58] Each stich of vv. 2–4 (with the exception of the second stich of v. 3) does begin with a *lamed* (though not necessarily in an infinitive construction), and these lines, with their infinitives, do articulate the purpose of the book. However, it is the formal, aesthetic observation that each half-verse in lines 2–4 begins with a *lamed* that is most significant.[59] The absence of the *lamed* in the second stich of v. 3 is anomalous and marks or highlights the social virtues spoken of in this stich as particularly important to wisdom's project. The use of jussives in v. 5, instead of some other verb forms, such as the imperfect, expresses the volitional aspect of the prologue—its command or invitation to the hearer to continue reading and to embark upon the task of attaining wisdom.

As I intimated already, the prologue, moreover, is not necessarily imagining only, or simply, two distinct audiences, the foolish youth and the wise sage returning for a refresher course.[60] On the one hand, vv. 5–6 encourage any anticipated reader rhetorically to begin occupying the subject position of the wise (חכם) and understanding (נבון) person he in fact will become—if he stays the course and strives

[58] For such a literary historical endeavor see Whybray, *Proverbs*, 31. These efforts appear in any case misguided. The passage's first two infinitive constructions with *lamed* introduce half verses (vv. 2a and 2b). The third, by contrast, introduces all of line three (v. 3a). That is, unlike verse two where both halves of the verse begin with an infinitive with *lamed*, the second stich of verse three (v. 3b) begins with neither a *lamed* nor an infinitive. The prologue's fourth infinitive construction with *lamed*, in verse four, again introduces a half verse (v. 4a), but the *lamed* that introduces the second stich of this verse (v. 4b) is not part of an infinitive construction. The infinitive of v. 6 again begins an entire line. Even if one considers v. 5 secondary and intrusive, this is hardly a tightly structured infinitive based introduction.

[59] Cf. n. 58.

[60] Yoder (*Woman of Substance*, 3) similarly writes: "'The instructional goals of Proverbs 1–9 and, arguably, the entire book are broadly defined at the outset (1:2–7): to teach the inexperienced (פתאים; 1:4) how to live wisely (1:2–4, 6), to further educate the mature sage (1:5–6), and *to remind everyone* that knowledge begins with the 'fear of the Lord'" (italics added). Cf. Fuhs, *Das Buch der Sprichwörter*, 38; Plöger, *Sprüche Salomos*, 10; Perdue, *Proverbs*, 69; Clifford, *Proverbs*, 35; Van Leeuwen, "Proverbs," *NIB* 5:32; Alonso Schöckel and Vilchez Lindez, *Proverbios*, 157.

to understand Proverbs' wisdom. On the other hand, certainly the language of "simple youth" in v. 4 suggests the book does have in mind young males, perhaps in a classroom setting, as one potential audience. As Claudia V. Camp has noted, however, the poetic nature of much of Proverbs "suggests a context rather less constrained than that of the classroom."[61] Indeed in subsequent pages, Proverbs imagines as its addressee a male who is potentially physically able to rob and murder (e.g., 1:10–19); who understands the value of material wealth (e.g., 3:14–15); who might go surety for a neighbor (e.g., 6:1–5); who possesses strong sexual appetites and is of marriageable age (e.g., 6:24–35). Although one might argue that such teaching could be addressed to young boys in anticipation of their coming of age, it seems most appropriate to older males—those who have at least reached adolescence. The language of נער ("youth") in v. 4 is also somewhat ambiguous. In the Hebrew Bible it can occasionally clearly refer to quite young people. However, as H. Fabry points out, the upper age boundary varies: 20 (e.g., Ex 30:14), 25 (Nu 8:24), 30 (Nu 4:3, 23; I Chron 23:3).[62] The Midrash on Prov 1:4 likewise "states that one is a *naʿar* until age 25 (R. Meir), 30 (R. Akiba), or 20 (R. Ishmael), because from the age of 20 one is held accountable for one's sins."[63] The 'simple youth' of Proverbs' prologue hence are probably best considered young men and the text's rhetoric as designed to communicate to such an audience.

But even if this is the case, the prologue's language of "simple youth" (פתאים, נער), like the rhetoric of the wise, understanding person, encourages the reader or hearer to assume a particular subject position: one who is in need of instruction. The prologue's rhetoric thus simultaneously urges any who read the book to assume the position both of a young seeker and of a wise and understanding person (a חכם and נבון) and to begin eagerly to discern the tropes (משל), figures (מליצה), riddles (חידת; sg. חידה) and other sayings of the sages, i.e., precisely those things of which the book itself is comprised.

Indeed, these three terms in the prologue—משל, מליצה, and חידת (sg. חידה)—are especially significant. Although translated in various ways, commentators (e.g., Whybray, Toy, Fox) nearly always con-

[61] Claudia V. Camp, *Wisdom and the Feminine*, 58.
[62] H. Fabry, *TDOT* 9:480.
[63] H. Fabry, *TDOT* 9:480.

sider them to connote cryptic or opaque and obscure utterances in need of interpretation.[64] However, this insight rarely carries interpretive weight and is often dismissed. Murphy, for instance, writes: "The riddle . . . and the puzzle [i.e., מליצה and חידה], if these are correctly translated, are hardly in evidence in the collections."[65] Though Fox recognizes that the rhetoric of the prologue pushes the reader toward a reinterpretation of the book as a *literary* text, he does not seem fully to follow through with this insight. Rather he seems to opt for tradition-historical reading the book (or at least chapters 1–9) as oral literature. He states that although in Proverbs one must seek wisdom, this means "to assimilate the values of the teachings and to be wise, not to work hard to get at their message. Basically the father's words of wisdom need only be heard and obeyed, not probed and interpreted."[66]

Although it may be that the particular literary forms of the riddle or puzzle are not easily discerned in Proverbs, in my view commentators too quickly dismiss the import of the presence of such rhetoric at the book's outset. The difficult terms in the prologue, which connote opaque speech, serve an important purpose that ought not to be ignored. They function as a kind of hermeneutical cue

---

[64] Whybray (*Proverbs*, 34) notes מליצה may refer to a "saying needing interpretation"; he likewise states that משל may in the prologue refer to "an obscure saying." Toy calls מליצה a "figurative saying, one that looks toward another sense." He notes too that חידה "signifies some sort of deflected discourse." Among the range of meanings he cites for נוש' is "an enigmatical saying." See *Proverbs*, 4, 8. Fox recognizes in the range of meanings of משל, "trope," which as such "may be a symbol" or "enigma." For him מליצה is best rendered as "epigram," though following Toy he also recognizes the term may point to a "figurative saying" or "trope." Though חידה can be a "riddle," he suggests it is most fundamentally, "an enigmatic, difficult saying that requires skilled interpretation." See Fox, *Proverbs 1–9*, 54, 63–65. Cf. Leliévre and Maillot, *Commentaire*, 23–24.

[65] Murphy, *Proverbs*, 5. Fox (*Proverbs 1–9*, 65–67) and others similarly point out that there is likely no example of a true "riddle" (חידה) in Proverbs. It is thus perhaps best to understand the mention of riddles as Van Leeuwen does—i.e., as a reference "to any puzzling, thought-provoking utterance and to the mental effort required to use proverbs rightly." See "Proverbs," *NIB* 5:33. However, I would emend Van Leeuwen's comment and capitalize the word "proverbs," since the prologue, as he himself notes, is articulating the purpose of the entire book, which includes both "proverbs" or sentence sayings and longer wisdom poems, etc. Although Toy (*Proverbs*, 6) understands that the terms in v. 6 point to certain cryptic utterances, he nonetheless confidently writes that the line does not in the least refer to "esoteric teaching."

[66] Fox, *Proverbs* 1–9, 76.

and point to the book's figurative qualities.[67] The wise but 'seeking' reader of Proverbs that the prologue imagines knows how to look beneath the surface of the book. He knows how to interpret the meanings to which the text's tropes and figures point and to consider the interaction of this figurative language throughout the book. This general orientation is manifest in the way the discourse of wealth and poverty works as well.

This conclusion is not all that surprising. Each of the interpreters cited above is right to point to the fact that the key terms of 1:6 connote some sort of opaque speech. Although the usage of משל in HB suggests a range of meanings for the term ("by-word," "saying," "proverb"), that the term can connote a sort of figurative speech is clear from its usage in Ezek 17:2 and 24:3. In both of these passages, Ezekiel's cryptic oracle is introduced as a משל. In Ezek 17:2 the term is paralleled with חידה, a word that in the Samson tale in Judges (see esp. Judg 14:12–19) likewise plainly alludes to enigmatic speech.[68] The term מליצה is a *hapax* in Proverbs and otherwise appears in HB only at Hab 2:6 in conjunction with משל and חידה. Habakkuk 2:6 is difficult, but the association of מליצה with two other terms connoting cryptic speech suggests it carries similar nuances. The fact that the *hiphil* of the root ליץ can be used to express mocking or ridiculing speech, and the participle מליץ can mean something like "interpreter," underscores the likelihood that מליצה refers as well to some sort of deflected discourse that requires interpretation.

Although not alluding to the prologue specifically, others also acknowledge more broadly the figurative aspects of the book of Proverbs. Von Rad, for instance, notes that proverbial statements "always have a characteristic openness, something that points beyond themselves, an element which leaves room for all kinds of associations and, indeed, in certain circumstances, even permits of a figurative

---

[67] Cf. n. 42 above.

[68] In HB riddles can be associated with sexuality, the case of Samson being the most celebrated. Given the significant rhetoric of sexuality that Proverbs employs (e.g., especially in regard to the strange/foreign woman and Woman Wisdom in chs. 1–9), the mention of riddles in the prologue, despite the relative absence of this literary form in the text, is perhaps not as anomalous as it may initially appear. The reader in a sense needs to figure out the "riddle of the women"—what each represents, etc.—as well as any other provocative rhetoric Proverbs makes use of. On the enigmatic nature of metaphorical speech generally, see the words of Ricoeur cited below.

interpretation."[69] Cross-culturally there is also evidence that proverbial speech sometimes is cryptic speech. Ruth Finnegan, for instance, mentions several African cultures where different forms of proverbial utterance have esoteric functions.[70] Further, as I intimated in Chapter One, the proverbial speech of folk proverbs is generally understood by paremiologists as metaphorical speech. As Paul Ricoeur has suggested, moreover, metaphorical language actually works like "the active resolution of an enigma," an activity which in part appears to be what the prologue is asking the reader of Proverbs to undertake.[71]

Since not all who stumble across the pages of Proverbs will be able to act like a חכם and נבון, however, the prologue thus reveals what might be called a slyly subtle esoteric bias to the book's wisdom instruction—a bias which becomes more evident as one recognizes the manner in which Proverbs divides the world into "insiders" and "outsiders," the wise and foolish, the righteous and the wicked. Yet Proverbs is not a genuinely esoteric text and so perhaps the use of such a term should be avoided. The prologue, however, does appear to suggest that a degree of literary expertise may indeed be required of the book's reader.[72] In sum, although much in Proverbs might be appropriate for the instruction of younger males, the prologue indicates as well that the book often requires—as a trope or a figure does—a more sophisticated reading beneath the surface or literal meaning. In short, the prologue is an important hermeneutical cue directing the reader's interpretive strategies.[73]

---

[69] Von Rad, *Wisdom in Israel*, 31.

[70] Ruth Finnegan, "Proverbs in Africa," in *The Wisdom of Many: Essays on the Proverb* (ed. Wolfgang Mieder and Alan Dundes; New York: Garland, 1981), 30. This essay is a reprint of Finnegan's *Oral Literature in Africa* (Oxford: Clarendon, 1970), 389–418.

[71] Paul Ricoeur, "Biblical Hermeneutics," in *Paul Ricoeur on Biblical Hermeneutics* (Semeia 4, ed. John Dominic Crossan; Missoula, MT: Society of Biblical Literature, 1975), 79; cf. *The Rule of Metaphor*, 25–27.

[72] See too Sirach 39.2–3, which similarly describes the sage as one with sophisticated literary skills. Ben Sira's scribe is one who "penetrates the subtleties of parables," and who "seeks out the hidden meanings of proverbs and is at home with the obscurities of parables" (NRSV). Cf. Newsom, *The Self as Symbolic Space*, 39–41.

[73] Murphy (*The Tree of Life*, 16) likewise states that "the hermeneutical key to the entire work" is found in chapter one's prologue. Similarly, Fuhs, *Das Buch der Sprichwörter*, 12, 37, calls the prologue the "hermeneutical key" (*hermeneutische Schlüssel*) to understanding the book. In my view, however, neither of these authors present readings of Proverbs that sufficiently follow through on this insight.

2.2.c. *The Two Ways as Hermeneutical Orientation*

I suggested above that the book of Proverbs is concerned primarily to construct for its addressee a particular moral self or identity characterized by the broad virtues articulated in the prologue, virtues which ought to permit a hearer to enjoy a good and flourishing life. I also just suggested that the prologue's invitation to attend to the book's figurative and metaphorical qualities is an important hermeneutical cue for any reader of the text who would seek to discern the book's moral message. A further important way the book carries out its task of character formation is by dividing the world up into "two ways": the way of the wisdom, understanding, and righteousness that leads to life, and the way of folly and wickedness that leads to death. The authoritative voice of the patriarch or teacher (subsequently identified with the voice of Wisdom and grounded in the divine; cf. 1:20; 3:19) adopts this strategy early on in chapters 1–9 in an attempt to win the addressee's allegiance to the path of wisdom.

The moral metaphor of the way, which is prominent in chapters 1–9, continues on into chapters 10–31 and is one of the important images that unite the book.[74] Together with the prologue's cue to read wisely, this two ways rhetoric in chapters 1–9 serves the reader as an important hermeneutical guide. Whatever values, virtues, or conduct the book positively values and recommends carry the rhetorical force that these belong to the way of wisdom and righteousness. They also bear with them the promise of "life" (a strong symbol of what endures and hence possesses value) as well as the authority of the teacher or parent. The opposite is true as well. Whatever the text disavows carries the rhetorical force that it belongs to the way of folly and wickedness and is a rejection of the parent or teacher. More threateningly this path leads to "death" (a strong symbol of the fleetingness of what possesses little value).

The sentence sayings of Prov 10:1–22:16 and 25–29, however, do not always directly instruct the hearer regarding the way of wisdom

[74] Note the distribution of three important terms for "way" or "path" in Proverbs: דרך, נתיבה, ארח. In chapters 1–9: 1:15 (two), 19; 2:8 (two), 12, 13 (two), 15, 19, 20 (two), 25; 3:6 (two), 17 (three), 23, 31; 4:11, 14 (two), 18, 19, 26; 5:6, 8, 21; 6:6, 23; 7:8, 19, 25 (two), 27; 8:2 (two), 13, 20 (two), 22, 32; 9:6, 15 (two). In chapters 10–31: 10:9, 17; 11:5, 20, 29; 12:15, 26, 28 (three); 13:6, 15; 14:2, 8, 12 (two), 14; 15: 9, 10, 19, 24; 16:2, 7, 9, 17, 25 (two), 29, 31; 17:23; 19:3, 16; 20:24; 21:2, 8, 16, 29; 22:5, 6; 23:19, 26; 26:13; 28:6, 10, 18; 29:27; 30:19 (four), 20.

and folly as explicitly as the rhetoric of chapters 1–9 does. They are generally anonymous proverbs that often take the form of indicative statements and sometimes appear to offer simple observations of the world. Yet, as I intimated in Chapter One, the form of a sentence and its intent may not be the same. As I will show, in the context of the book of Proverbs, observations may implicitly critique social arrangements or carry the force of an admonition. Together with the evidence of literary integrity to the book that scholars are increasingly recognizing, this fact suggests that the sayings of the second half of the book ought to be read in light of chapters 1–9.[75] Hence, like the book's initial instruction in chapters 1–9, the later material of chapters 10–31 is also to be related to the formation of virtue.

The text of Proverbs thus expects a certain "literary competence" and sophistication from its readers or hearers.[76] It expects at least some of its readers or hearers, in the language of the prologue, not only to begin to discern the tropes, figures, and enigmatic words it employs. It expects them also to recognize the rhetorical force of its various utterances and to perceive which virtues and vices are being highlighted when, and whether they belong to folly's path or wisdom's way. Proverbs, in sum, expects certain readers to be able to recognize its figurative and rhetorical dimensions and thereby distinguish the moral vision that its discourse, including its discourse of wealth and poverty, is constructing.

2.2.d. *Wealth as Motivational Symbol*

In Proverbs, as I will demonstrate, wealth imagery is a potent symbol of the desirable. It is often associated specifically with wisdom

[75] Cf. Van Leeuwen ("Proverbs," *NIB* 5:24), who states that chapters 1–9, together with chapters 30–31, form "an interpretive 'frame' through which to view the small wisdom utterances they enclose." Fox, too, speaks of chapters 1–9 as an "introduction" to the rest of the book. See *Proverbs 1–9*, 325. Carole R. Fontaine states that these chapters "act as a theological and literary prologue to the proverb collections that follow." See her "Proverbs" in the *Women's Bible Commentary* (ed. Carol A. Newsom and Sharon H. Ringe; expanded edition; Louisville: WJK, 1998), 154.

[76] I borrow the phrase "literary competence" from Jonathan Culler. See his *Structuralist Poetics: Structuralism, Linguistics and the Study of Literature* (Ithaca: Cornell University Press, 1975), 113–130.

and other virtues and represents, in Ricoeur's terms, both what it literally says and also symbolically or metaphorically all that the text imagines its hearer might find to be desirable. Given the persistent and intimate linkage of wisdom terms with terms for wealth, it is clear on the one hand that for Proverbs material wealth, as a good and desirable thing, must be properly ordered under the rubric, or within the framework, of wisdom. On the other hand, the close and regular association of the two sorts of terminology (wisdom and wealth) intimates as well that the symbol of wealth in Proverbs also plays the most important role of any of the text's tropes in the book's effort to persuade the hearer of Wisdom's value. It serves, in other words, as the text's most important rhetorical motivation.

Wealth imagery in proverbs is thus what Kenneth Burke might call a "god term." For Burke, a god term represents the ultimate in a series of dialectical movements and the pinnacle in a hierarchy of related terms.[77] As Burke explains, god terms are representative both of themselves and "the family or class substance" with which they are identified.[78] They do not merely stand for something other than themselves. But neither do they represent only what they literally say. This type of symbol thus works in a manner similar to Ricoeur's understanding of metaphor (see Chapter One); and for Ricoeur, the two, metaphor and symbol, are indeed closely related.[79] For Burke it is the conclusion of a dialectic, like that achieved in god terms, that produces an ultimate rhetorical motive. It is the peculiarly human penchant, or need, to realize or resolve a dialectic movement in the pinnacle of a hierarchy that provides the most fundamental basis of persuasion.

However Burke, whose writing is somewhat esoteric and opaque to the uninitiated, also speaks of the "factor of advantage" as a likewise important, if penultimately significant, form of rhetorical motivation.[80] This aspect of Burke's thought (rather than the resolution

---

[77] Kenneth Burke, *A Rhetoric of Motives* (Berkeley: University of California Press, 1969), 276; first printing 1950, Prentice-Hall.

[78] Burke, *Rhetoric*, 277.

[79] Paul Ricoeur, *Interpretation Theory: Discourse and the Surplus of Meaning* (Fort Worth: Texas Christian University Press, 1976), 45–69.

[80] Burke himself (*Rhetoric*, 276) is clear that he does not wish this aspect of rhetorical motivation to be neglected, even as he warns of the "fallacy of overly materialistic interpretations which would slight dialectic as a factor."

of dialectic) is more helpful in understanding how wealth imagery functions as a potent symbol of the desirable in Proverbs, especially since the high rhetorical status of wealth is ultimately eclipsed or superceded by the image of wisdom, the book's truest god term.

For Burke, "the ultimate form of persuasion is composed of three elements (speaker, speech, and spoken-to)." However, this form of persuasion might only be maintained "insofar as the plea" in the act of persuasion remains "unanswered." For an act of persuasion "to go on eternally" it "could not be directed merely towards attainable advantages." That is, as Burke quips, "a persuasion that succeeds dies." Subsequently if the advantages offered in a particular act of persuasion are obtainable, the act of persuasion can be maintained only by what Burke calls "interference"—a not-getting of sorts, some intervention that perpetuates the act of persuasion by re-introducing or reinstating an aspect of unattainability.[81]

The image of wealth, however, comes with a kind of built-in mechanism of interference. To the extent that wealth, say in the form of money, is attainable, its usefulness as a rhetorical motivation has a clear limit. Yet there is a widely shared sense that although one may acquire property or currency, the more abstract notion of "wealth" or "riches" is something one can never be assured of having attained, or of having attained enough of. There is a sense that a full attainment of wealth is impossible. (The same is true of social status or honor, another important symbol of the desirable in Proverbs.) Because one can never be assured of having attained wealth (or honor) exhaustively, it must always be pursued. Consequently wealth (along with honor), is an ideal trope to be used in conjunction with wisdom. The text's association of wealth with wisdom perpetually motivates the quest for wisdom. It intimates that for Proverbs wisdom, like wealth, is something that needs to be continually sought. Proverbs 30:15–16 suggests the sages in fact understood something of the unattainable nature of wealth. The NJPS renders the lines thus:

> The leech has two daughters, "Give!" and "Give!"
> Three things are insatiable;
> Four never say, "Enough!":
> Sheol, a barren womb,

[81] Burke, *Rhetoric*, 274.

Earth that cannot get enough water,
And fire which never says, "Enough!"[82]

The leech, Sheol, a barren womb, parched earth, and fire are depicted as things with appetites that can never be fully satisfied or appeased. That which they desire they can never "get enough" of. This is significant, for the Hebrew term that is translated by NJPS as "enough" is the common term for wealth, הון. This is the only instance in Proverbs where commentators insist on rendering the term in an adverbial sense, e.g., as something like "sufficiency."[83] This is no doubt a legitimate translation. The important point for this study, however, is that Proverbs speaks of the strong and perpetually unfilled desires of Sheol for humans, a barren woman for children, parched land for water, and fire for fuel, as the "wealth" these things seek, but can never claim to have achieved.

Yet as I suggested earlier, for Proverbs it is only wisdom that can bring humans real benefit. By contrast, wealth and honor (or rather the quest for these), belong to what Burke calls "the frenzied human cult of advantage, the quest of many things that cannot bring real advantage, yet are obtainable."[84] Sexual fulfillment, another important symbol of the desirable in Proverbs, likewise might be said to belong to this cult of advantage, at least as far as Proverbs is concerned. As a rhetorical motivation, however, sex works somewhat differently than wealth and honor; it possesses a slightly different instrument of interference. Wealth and social status each comes with a built-in mechanism of interference that preserves its effectiveness as a motivation: namely, the sense that one never really attains it or possesses enough of it. Sexual desires, however, can be satisfied in a way that the desire for wealth and honor cannot. Yet this sort of desire, though able to be satisfied, nonetheless occurs repeatedly and so must repeatedly be sated.[85] Hence, like wealth and honor, it is an ideal image through which to motivate, perpetually, the quest for wisdom.

---

[82] The Hebrew text is somewhat difficult. For a discussion, see Murphy, *Proverbs*, 233–235; Plöger, *Sprüche Salomos*, 354–55.

[83] Whybray, in *Proverbs*, 415, for instance, writes: "The universal view that here (both in v. 15 and v. 19) it [הון] has the meaning of 'sufficiency' is based mainly on the context." Cf. E. Kutsch, *TDOT* 3:364–68, esp. 366.

[84] Burke, *Rhetoric*, 274.

[85] Hence the often close association, not only in Proverbs and HB but in other

In Proverbs these three images—wealth, honor and sexual fulfillment—are closely related and interact with one another in important and complex ways. Each is associated with the quest for wisdom and serve as important rhetorical motivations. Each image, moreover, like one of Burke's god terms represents both what it literally points to and symbolically all that is desirable. Hence for the sages, it is not only a quest for a certain degree of material prosperity which, as a necessary component of a good life, must be ordered under the rubric of wisdom, but social status and sexual fulfillment as well. As I suggested above, for the ancient sages, the desire for these lesser goods must be subordinated to the desire for wisdom's virtues; and the book's task is largely to redirect the hearer's desires for these lesser goods toward a desire for wisdom. However of the three—riches, honor and sexual fulfillment—images of material wealth (and lack) are most prominent in the book. It is these images of riches, which represent all that a reader or hearer of the book might find desirable, that the discussions in the following chapters will highlight.

2.2.e. *The Act-Consequence Nexus*

Along with images of material riches, the book of Proverbs contains a good deal of retributive rhetoric, and the Act-Consequence nexus (or *Tun-Ergehen Zusammenhang*) is usually presented as a notion fundamental to the sages' thought. The act-consequence nexus or what I call in relation to the discourse of wealth and poverty, a wisdom prosperity axiom, is usually characterized as the belief that the wise and righteous are inevitably rewarded for their deeds and the wicked and foolish punished. Because the wisdom Proverbs offers often appears as observations of the natural and social worlds and draws on images well-known from those realms, the book's cause and effect rhetoric, its wisdom prosperity language, is generally interpreted in a literal fashion as the sages' quasi-empirical description of how the world works.

literature as well, of food imagery with sexual themes and implications (e.g., Prov 5:15–20; 9:1–6, 13–18). Like sexual desire, hunger can be sated, but it inevitably reappears and must be sated again and again. On food and sex in the Bible see Ken Stone, *Practicing Safer Texts: Food, Sex, and Bible in Queer Perspective* (London and New York: T&T Clark, 2005).

In a famous article entitled, "Gibt es ein Vergeltungsdogma im Alten Testament?" Klaus Koch suggested that in Proverbs (and elsewhere in HB) good and evil consequences automatically followed good and wicked behavior as a result of these actions rather than as the direct judgment of the deity.[86] Although Koch's views have been challenged, scholars take the idea of a *Tun-Ergehen* connection in Proverbs very seriously.[87] Whether or not a mechanistic universe or the deity is thought ultimately responsible for the retributive process, it is a kind of empirically verifiable act-consequence schema that is thought to be characteristic of the sages' thought. Matthew J. Goff's formulation of the matter in his book on the Qumran wisdom text 4QInstruction, for example, is characteristic and testifies as to how widespread and commonplace this understanding remains. For Goff, the traditional wisdom of a book like Proverbs "teaches that knowledge can be acquired through an empirical understanding of reality that fosters clear understanding of how consequences result from actions."[88]

However, as almost all commentators on Proverbs recognize in some form or another, such an act-consequence viewpoint corresponds rather poorly to the world as it is experienced by many. Bad things, all too often, do happen to good people; and one assumes this was the case in ancient Israel and Judah as well. Hence, how the ancient sages negotiated this contradiction between the world espoused in the text they produced and the empirically verifiable world needs to be explained. As I indicated above some scholars, such as Van Leeuwen, indicate that although the sages believed that this was truly how the world works, they nonetheless recognized exceptions to the general *Tun-Ergehen* rule. Others, such as Pleins, view the sages' act-consequence thinking as the blatantly self-serving ideology of an upper class elite.

---

[86] Klaus Koch, "Gibt es ein Vergeltungsdogma im Alten Testament?" *Zeitschrift für Theologie und Kirche* 52 (1955): 1–42.

[87] It seems likely to me that in Proverbs, or anywhere in HB, ancient Israelite and Judean writers and readers would consider YHWH to be the driving force behind any formulation of retribution, even if this is not explicitly stated. Von Rad's view is similar; see *Wisdom in Israel*, 92. Koch gestures in this direction, but is most concerned to demonstrate that in HB certain kinds of consequences follow certain kinds of acts inevitably.

[88] Matthew J. Goff, *The Worldly and Heavenly Wisdom of 4QInstruction* (STDJ 50; Leiden: Brill, 2003), 43. Cf. von Rad's comments regarding "experiential knowledge" and Proverbs in *Wisdom in Israel*, 1–8.

Neither of these typical approaches is entirely wrong. However, they are also not fully satisfactory precisely because they appear to understand the act-consequence rhetoric of Proverbs, which often employs wealth and poverty language, in an overly literalistic fashion as that which is presumably empirically verifiable, and assume the ancient sages did so as well. The tension between the world the text of Proverbs presents and the world of human experience remains. One should, however, recall Ricoeur's suggestion that this sort of tension may function as a cue that one ought not try too hard to understand such rhetoric literally.

It is, for instance, possible to explain Proverbs' act-consequence rhetoric largely in terms of didactic ends and pedagogical strategies, as Bergant at points seems to do.[89] The hearer or reader of the book is promised good or evil in order to encourage that person to follow the book's instruction. Such an understanding may be largely correct (Proverbs is moral instruction). For those who recognize the book's didactic intent it might also minimize the tension between the act-consequence world of the text and the real world experiences of certain readers, the former being a kind of pedagogical hyperbole. This sort of understanding, however, perhaps does not do full justice to the powerful act-consequence rhetoric that one finds in Proverbs.

In her study of the book of Job Carol A. Newsom offers a richer account of how one might understand the retributive rhetoric of Israelite and Judean wisdom literature as something more than pedagogical hyperbole.[90] Although an act-consequence rhetoric may appear as literal observations or descriptions of reality, for Newsom such rhetoric, which she discusses in relationship to the speeches of Job's friends, is nonetheless not the kind of language one ought to understand literally. She observes that most recognize such a view is too easily contradicted to pass as true if taken as empirically verifiable on a consistent basis. Rather Newsom intimates that this sort of rhetoric is not so much describing everyday reality as it is making certain claims about the deep structures of reality, despite the fact that this fundamental essence of the cosmos may *not* be

[89] Bergant, *Israel's Wisdom Literature*, 78–107.

[90] Carol A. Newsom, *The Book of Job: A Contest of Moral Imaginations* (Oxford: Oxford University Press, 2003), 115–125.

empirically verifiable. As Newsom suggests, the persuasiveness of the rhetoric of moral retribution in the 'fate of the wicked' poems in Job is not based on reasoned argument and empirical observation—precisely the kinds of procedures that are typically considered the hallmark of wisdom thinking. It depends instead on the rhetoric of tropes and images, which do not try to give evidence so much as to *make evident.*

I wish to claim that the *Tun-Ergehen* rhetoric of Proverbs also represents such an effort at "making evident the nature of the world."[91] And the world that the sages' act-consequence language strives to make evident is one in which the very structure of reality favors virtue and opposes vice. Thus for Proverbs, to act righteously and wisely is to align oneself with the structures of creation; to act foolishly and wickedly is to oppose the organization of reality. Hence the book's assured claims about the prosperity of the wise and righteous and the demise of the foolish and wicked. This unveiling of the "true" structure of the cosmos, moreover, is in essence the fundamental point of Prov 8:22–31, which claims that Wisdom was with God at creation. Regardless of the precise nature of Wisdom's relationship to the deity, creation, and humanity in this passage (all of which are the topic of much scholarly discussion), the text fundamentally is concerned to express Wisdom's intimate and intricate relationship to the created order (and the deity).

The "truth" of the sages' act-consequence rhetoric thus has to do primarily with how one *perceives* the world.[92] The retributive rhetoric of Proverbs constructs a kind of wisdom mythos, a pattern of values and beliefs that symbolically at the level of the structure of the cosmos express the characteristics attitudes of the ancient sages. In this mythos, adherence to wisdom and virtue lead to well being or human flourishing. Yet the believability of the wisdom mythos does not depend on exceptionless empirical verifiability of the claims about wisdom and prosperity inherent to Proverbs' act-consequence rhetoric. The wisdom mythos rather shapes the way people "see" things. As an ideological construct, the mythos produces subjects who in fact

---

[91] Newsom, *The Book of Job*, 118–119.

[92] As Newsom writes, "one cannot convince another of the truth" of the perceptions generated through the wisdom literature's act-consequence rhetoric "by means of argument, for the issue is fundamentally one of perception itself." *The Book of Job*, 121.

will perceive and understand their experience of reality in accordance with the ideological description presented by the mythos. Hence although a good deal of non-conforming examples might be readily noticed by those not shaped by the wisdom mythos, for those operating under the constraints of the mythos such non-conformities may not prove problematic. Rather such instances will tend to be screened out as not diagnostically significant. The mythos will tolerate a certain level of mixed experience of conformity and non-conformity to its claims, though of course there is a ultimately a limit to the amount of anomaly any such mythos might tolerate.

Drawing on the work of Alsdair MacIntyre, Newsom calls the perception of the cosmos or the kind of narrative about the world, which the wisdom mythos tells through its act-consequence schema, an "iconic story." The truth of an iconic story, moreover, "its perceived fit with reality or lack of it, has to be assessed in relation to the particular social formation in which the story is embedded and in which it functions."[93] Newsom explains further:

> Iconic narratives encode fundamental commitments, social roles, and profiles of virtue that constitute the community. These narratives make meaningful—and therefore possible—certain forms of action. That is, only within the contours of such narratives do certain kinds of action acquire meaning and so become the things one does or refrains from doing. These narratives ring true because they define the horizon of meaningful action within an already given social and moral world.[94]

The already given social and moral world, the particular social formation, which the iconic narrative of the wisdom prosperity rhetoric in Proverbs is related to, is that of the ancient Israelite and Judean scribal culture. The act-consequence iconic narrative has to do with the "foundational commitments" of the literati that produced Proverbs. It is not a naïve or simply literal account of the nature of the world they inhabited.[95] Although the actual experiences of any particular

---

[93] Newsom, *The Book of Job*, 122.

[94] Newsom, *The Book of Job*, 122.

[95] Cf. Newsom, *The Book of Job*, 123. Von Rad (*Wisdom in Israel*, 64) appears to gesture toward a similar understanding when he writes: "What the sentences teach already surpasses any objective material knowledge in so far as it is dealing with perceptions which have been acquired in connection with a truth for which one has already decided. It is, in other words, a truth to which one has already committed oneself; one could even call it a truth which has to do with character rather than with the intellect."

wise individual perishing, or wicked person prospering, might contradict the act-consequence iconic narrative, these exceptions have no explanatory value for the sages. In Newsom's words, although "such things may happen," "they are perceived as anomalies." However, "the story of the wicked overtaken by calamity, like the story of the restoration of the good person, rings true *because it is consonant with the foundational values of the society*" or social formation that tells and hears the story—in the case of Proverbs the scribes of ancient Israel and Judah (Yehud).[96] Because these scribes believe so fundamentally in the value of righteousness and in the ability of the virtues of wisdom's way to produce a good and flourishing human life, the claims of an act-consequence rhetoric about the nature of reality itself can be perceived as true, despite some empirical evidence to the contrary. This sort of understanding of the act-consequence schema as iconic story, however, also warns against caricaturing the sages' instruction and understanding of their world and the moral life in simplistic, quasi-empirical terms. Although not sketching fully the complexity of the situation, scholars such as Van Leeuwen are thus in a sense correct in insisting that the sages held strong beliefs about the *Tun-Ergehen Zusammenhang* but also recognized exceptions to the act-consequence rule. When it comes to the discourse of wealth and poverty, it is important to remember that the sages are less concerned with offering observations and primarily concerned with communicating their fundamental values. They do this within the symbolic framework of the act-consequence nexus and with literary skill.

2.3. Conclusions and Thesis

The language of wealth and poverty in Proverbs appears in significant contexts in each of the two major divisions of the book—chapters 1–9 and 10–31. In each section, moreover, the text employs this wealth and poverty rhetoric in analogous ways. Hence the discourse of wealth and poverty in the different sections of Proverbs ought to be considered together. Scholars, moreover, often detect in Proverbs a kind of act-consequence rhetoric, or wisdom prosperity axiom, where literal material wealth is construed not only as a good, but

[96] Newsom, *The Book of Job*, 124; italics added.

also as a kind of automatic reward for obedience to instruction and the attainment of wisdom, while poverty is reckoned the inevitable result of disobedience and ignorance. A certain inconsistency or "ambiguity" is said to arise not only from the fact that a number of sayings seem to relativize the act-consequence view, but because many verses also encourage particular benevolent conduct on behalf of the poor and criticize the rich.

This ambiguity is not adequately explained away by various appeals to the provenance of the book's wealth and poverty sayings. I contend, rather, that it arises in part from three related matters: the belief that Proverbs is best understood as a simple guide to success, often primarily conceived in terms of material prosperity; an overly literalistic reading of the book's wealth and poverty language; and a misperception (again an overly literalistic understanding) of Proverbs' act-consequence mode of thinking. My re-examination of the prologue suggests that it is better to regard the book more fundamentally as moral instruction rather than as a simple guide to success. I likewise contend that together with the "two ways" rhetoric of especially chapters 1–9, the prologue provides the reader of Proverbs with an important hermeneutical orientation. The text's opening lines invite the reader to explore the book's figurative structures. Likewise I contend that "wealth" imagery is not only the kind of language that can function as an especially effective rhetorical motivation, it is in fact an important symbol of the desirable in Proverbs. In addition, I argue that the book's act-consequence rhetoric is not the kind of language one ought to regard in an overly literalistic manner as reflecting the sages' quasi-empirical observations of the world. Rather it provides the symbolic framework within which the values and virtues the text wishes to articulate find meaning and make sense. My consideration of the discourse of wealth and poverty in Proverbs will take all of these sorts of findings into consideration.

In what follows I will argue that beginning already in chapter one the dominant, instructing voice in Proverbs deploys a rhetoric of wealth and poverty and in so doing positions itself at the outset of its discourse to exercise a good deal of control over the symbolic usages and associations of a cluster of terms for wealth and poverty/rich and poor that appear throughout the rest of chapters 1–9 as well as throughout the book's subsequent collections. The instructing voice exercises its control over the discourse of wealth and poverty primarily in two ways. First, it simply offers *direct, concrete instruction* regarding a broad range of economic matters—e.g., how one should conduct business or manage one's material resources or what perspectives and actions ought to be embraced or avoided in regard to wealth and poverty and the rich and poor. This economic ethic is representative of, and belongs to, the way of wisdom. But the book also employs the language of wealth and poverty as *motivational symbols* in *meshalim* that should be understood more *figuratively*. The rhetoric of wealth in these instances serves to underscore the desirability of the way of wisdom generally and the values or virtues associated with that way. The rhetoric of poverty depicts the undesirability of the vices that belong to the way of folly.[97] These sorts of sayings are not directly related to matters of literal wealth and poverty, but depend upon an implicit understanding of the value of wealth. Though sometimes employing an act-consequence rhetoric and implicitly promising well being or hardship to the hearer, neither sort of saying, moreover, ought to be reduced to a flat, literal or quasi-empirical description of the world of objects. Rather, the iconic narrative of the act-consequence rhetoric underscores the fundamental importance the values and virtues of the book held for the ancient scribes who produced and used the book, scribes whose interests and horizons of concern should likewise not be collapsed into those of the economic and political elite on the one hand, or the rural folk, on the other hand.

The language of wealth and poverty is employed in these two main ways—as direct instruction and as motivational symbol—throughout the book of Proverbs, though other strategies are taken up as well. In chapters 1–9 the rhetoric of wealth is predominant and is most often employed as a *positive* motivational symbol, though the teaching voice does offer particular economic instruction as well. In chapters 10–31, alongside the rhetoric of wealth, the text takes up the language of poverty much more fully. As in chapters 1–9 these sections also employ the rhetoric of wealth and poverty as motivational symbols. Wealth language remains a positive motivational symbol while the rhetoric of poverty functions as a *negative* symbol. These

[97] Perhaps more than any other commentator, Bergant recognizes the motivational aspects of Proverbs rhetoric. See *Israel's Wisdom Literature*, 78–105.

later chapters also offer more direct, practical instruction regarding poverty and wealth.

As I will argue in the following chapters, the book of Proverbs also employs identifiably different rhetorics depending on the purpose or focus of its instruction and the discourse of wealth and poverty/rich and poor in the book is actually made up of at least three recognizable sub-discourses. The first of these sub-discourses I call a *wisdom's virtues discourse*, since it is not so much concerned with instructing the hearer specifically on matters of wealth and poverty/rich and poor as with persuading the hearer to choose the way of wisdom and to acquire the virtues associated with that way. The second, because it is concerned with encouraging right practices in the market place and promoting kindness to specifically the poor, I call a *discourse of social justice*. This discourse is reminiscent of a larger biblical and ancient Near Eastern discourse of social maintenance and Proverbs seems largely to have adopted it for its own instructional end without much alteration. The third sub-discourse likewise possesses unique rhetorical features and is quite critical of the social effects resulting from excessive wealth or excessive lack. Because in this discourse (unlike the previous two) the sages appear primarily to be offering certain kinds of observations of the social world, I call it a *discourse of social observation*.

Because the characteristics of the wisdom's virtues discourse and the discourse of social justice emerge first in chapters 1–9, in the following discussion the wealth and poverty passages in this section of Proverbs will be treated first, in Chapter Three, as a discrete unit. Following this discussion, the *wisdom's virtues discourse* and the *discourse of social justice*, as they begin to emerge in chapters 10–31, will be explicated in Chapter Four. As is to be expected with closely related discourses, however, it will become clear that at points the preferred discourse features of one sub-discourse overlap and intersect with another and, in fact, stand in a mutually interpreting dialogue with one another. Hence I will suggest in Chapter Five that the wisdom's virtues and social justice discourses discussed in Chapter Four reveal a kind of literary and moral Gestalt to Proverbs. Through the lens of this Gestalt it will become clear that a number of other wealth and poverty sayings in Proverbs might be understood as also belonging either to the wisdom's virtues discourse or the discourse of social justice. This same Gestalt, I will argue, also provides a hermeneutical position for recognizing and understanding the third sub-discourse of wealth and poverty in Proverbs: the discourse of social observation.

By attending to the book's rhetorical and figurative imagination, this project will thus reveal that through their discourse of wealth and poverty the ancient sages of Proverbs were not terribly concerned to offer sociological observations regarding the origins of rich and poor persons. It will also reveal that they were concerned to offer much more than simple economic advice to their hearers. The study will reveal rather that the rhetoric of desirable wealth in Proverbs is much more intimately linked to the book's overall effort to construct a particular moral identity for the hearer or reader; its attempt to form a wise person. In so doing, however, the study will also demonstrate that the discourse of wealth and poverty in Proverbs, though complex and certainly not seamless, is less ambiguous and more coherent than is usually thought.

CHAPTER THREE

THE DISCOURSE OF WEALTH AND POVERTY IN PROVERBS 1–9

3.1. Wealth as Motivational Symbol in Proverbs 1 (1:10–19)

The rhetoric of wealth and poverty in the book of Proverbs is first taken up in 1:10–19, soon after the prologue comes to a close. In these lines one can detect both the birth of the figurative use of wealth and poverty language as motivational symbols and how the dominant voice in the text (here the instructing voice of the father or teacher) begins to claim this powerful rhetoric for itself and its own use.[1] The passage, which is full of language that belongs to the metaphorical complex of walking and the way (e.g., vv. 10, 11, 15, 16), introduces and discredits an opposing discourse, the voice of sinners, depicted as violent robbers, who attempt to lure the hearer onto their illicit path with the promise of wealth.[2] The text reads:

(10) בני אם־יפתוך חטאים אל־תבא׃ (11 אם־יאמרו
לכה אתנו נארבה לדם נצפנה לנקי חנם
(12) נבלעם כשאול חיים ותמימים כיורדי בור
(13) כל־הון יקר נמצא נמלא בתינו שלל
(14) גורלך תפיל בתוכנו כיס אחד יהיה לכלנו
(15) בני אל־תלך בדרך אתם מנע רגלך מנתיבתם
(16) כי רגליהם לרע ירוצו וימהרו לשפך־דם
(17) כי־חנם מזרה הרשת בעיני כל־בעל כנף
(18) והם לדמם יארבו יצפנו לנפשתם
(19) כן ארחות כל־בצע בצע את־נפש בעליו יקח

10) My son, if sinners entice you, do not go.[3]
11) If they say: "Come with us, let us set an ambush to shed blood, let us lie in wait for the innocent (without cause!);

[1] The passages in chs. 1–9 that employ a wealth and poverty rhetoric to construct a concrete economic ethic for the hearer will be treated below.

[2] An alternative, but not entirely dissimilar analysis of competing discourses in Prov 1–9, is Carol A. Newsom, "Woman and the Discourse of Patriarchal Wisdom: A Study of Proverbs 1–9," in *Gender and Difference in Ancient Israel* (ed. Peggy L. Day; Minneapolis: Fortress, 1989), 142–160.

[3] The rendering of the passage largely follows NJPS. In this line (v. 10), as many note, the MT's *tōbeʾ* might be corrected to *tōʾbeh*—a form derived from א-ב-ה ("be willing")—as is the case in multiple MSS (according to Fichtner's *BHS* annotations).

12) Like Sheol, let us swallow them alive,
whole, like those who go down to the Pit.
13) We shall obtain every precious treasure;
we shall fill our homes with loot.
14) Throw in your lot with us; we shall all have a common purse."
15) My son, do not set out with them; keep your feet from their path.
16) For their feet run to evil; they hurry to shed blood.
17) In the eyes of every winged creature the outspread net means nothing.[4]
18) So they lie in ambush for their own blood; they lie in wait for their own lives.
19) Such are the paths of all who pursue unjust gain; it takes the life of its possessors.[5]

By allowing the "sinners" to be the first to deploy a rhetoric of riches the instructing voice at the outset of the book intimates the ambivalent status of material wealth in Proverbs as a good, but not an ulti-

---

See Michael V. Fox, *Proverbs 1–9: A New Translation with Introduction and Commentary* (AB 18a; New York: Doubleday, 2000), 85. It is, however, simpler to re-point the consonants as *tābô*ʾ—the 2nd m. sg. *qal* jussive of ב-ו-א, as in a minority of MSS (sometimes *plene*, *tābô*ʾ; again, so Fichtner's *BHS* notes). This preserves the consonantal text and requires no complex explanation regarding apocopation, elision, or Aramaisms. It also fits well in the metaphorical complex of "walking" and the "way" prominent in the passage. Probably MT's אל תבא אם־יאמרו evolved from an original אל תבא בם אם־יאמרו through haplography (i.e., with the idiom בוא ב, "have dealings with"; cf. Jos 23:7, 12; Gen 49:6; and the similar phrase with את in Ps 26:4; Prov 22:24). If the *sôp pāsûq* at the end of v. 10 belongs after אם־יאמרו in v. 11 as the stanzas in L suggest, the proposed original wording also reveals a smoother poetic progression: i.e., after the introductory בני the line would chiastically begin and end with אם + impf.; moreover, by one popular means of reckoning Hebrew poetic meter, namely syllable counting, the proposed original wording (excluding the introductory בני) reveals eight syllables in each half of the line. See Wilfred G. E. Watson, *Classical Hebrew Poetry: A Guide to its Techniques* (2nd ed. reprt. with corrections; Sheffield: Sheffield Academic Press, 1995), esp. 87–113. The existence of meter in Hebrew poetry, however, has been questioned by among others, James L. Kugel, *The Idea of Biblical Poetry: Parallelism and Its History* (New Haven: Yale University Press, 1981), esp. 301.

[4] The line is a *crux*. See G. R. Driver, "Problems in the Hebrew Text of Proverbs," *Biblica* 32 (1951): 173–197, esp. 173–74. For various ways the verse has been and might be rendered, see Fox, *Proverbs 1–9*, 88–89.

[5] NJPS's rendering of ארחות as "fate" is ambiguous. It may highlight the proposed emendation of the term to אחרית ("end, outcome")—as in, e.g., Fichtner's *BHS* notes and C. H. Toy, *Proverbs: A Critical and Exegetical Commentary on the Book of Proverbs*, (rprt., Edinburgh: T&T Clark, 1988), 18; 1899 original. But cf. Fox, *Proverbs 1–9*, 90. Given the prevalence of the moral metaphor of "walking" and the "way" in this chapter, MT's ארחות ought to be preserved and the rendering "paths" to be preferred, even if the term is understood to include a sense of the "end" of one's path or conduct.

mate good. On the one hand, verse ten reveals that what the robbers have to say, the son will find appealing. Their words will be enticing to the simple youth (פתה; v. 10).[6] And what the sinners promise is "all kinds of precious wealth" (כל הון יקר)—enough to fill their houses (v. 13). However, on the other hand, the father insists that the result of the robbers' marauding and murdering is not the wealth they promise, but ironically the very fate they inflict on others (v. 18; cf. v.11). Using the same language they used (cf. vv. 16, 18), the father asserts that the sinners' way is a way of death and what they pursue is not כל הון יקר, but what he renames "unjust gain" (בצע; v. 19).[7]

The enticement with riches, which the sinners hold out, implies a recognition on the text's part that wealth is something the hearer will find desirable. It is this wealth that the passage assumes the son will find attractive, not merely the robber's violent undertakings.[8] That part of the appeal of the sinners' speech (for example, the promise of a "common purse") is an invitation to "comradeship" (Fox) or to "a successful community with egalitarian and utopian claims" (Van Leeuwen) is perhaps implicit, but in the sinners' speech itself the emphasis is on the wealth to be gained (vv. 13a, b; 14a).[9] However, the robbers' words imply that they have a skewed understanding of the role and nature (i.e., the value) of desirable material goods. They

[6] The *piel* verb and the substantive(s) "simple" (פתי, פתאים/פתים; e.g., in 1:4, 22, and frequently) are derived from the same III-weak root. The sinners' alluring words are paralleled by those the instructing voice deploys later in the passage, as well as those the strange or foreign woman speaks in Prov 7. See the following and cf. Fox, *Proverbs 1–9*, 93–94; Otto Plöger, *Sprüche Salomos (Proverbia)* (Neukrichen-Vluyn: Neukirchener, 1984), 15; Richard J. Clifford, *Proverbs: A Commentary* (OTL; Louisville: WJK, 1999), 38.

[7] On the root ב-צ-ע in HB, see P. J. Harland "בצע: Bribe, Extortion or Profit?" *VT* 50 (2000): 310–22. Cf. D. Kellerman, "בצע," *TDOT* 2: 205–08.

[8] *Pace* R. N. Whybray, *Proverbs* (NCBC; Grand Rapids: Eerdmans, 1994), 39. Fox, is closer to the mark when he suggests the text is primarily concerned with instructing the son to "shun violence" and that "evil is self-destructive." As he also notes, however, it is the sinners' *speech*, not their crime that is attractive. See Fox, *Proverbs 1–9*, 93. I would add only that the end of which the sinners *speak* is the acquisition of wealth.

[9] Newsom, for instance, argues that the son is being asked to align himself with the discourse and ideology of his peers over and against the hierarchical authority of the father, an authority which generational and social differences afford him. See "Woman and the Discourse," 142–160, esp. 145. Cf. Fox, *Proverbs 1–9*, 93; Raymond C. Van Leeuwen, "Proverbs: Introduction, Commentary, and Reflections," *NIB* 5:37.

overvalue wealth and pursue it by violence and injustice. The instructing voice, by contrast, insists that wealth, though clearly something that entices, is not so valuable as to justify its acquisition by any or unjust means.

The imagery of violence and death associated with the sinners in the passage is also significant in regard to the text's claims about the value of wealth. It indicates that the sinners' confusion regarding the role of riches in human flourishing actually sets them on a path that moves them directly against the grain of the set of social virtues the prologue values most: justice, righteousness, and equity (see Chapter Two). Instead of enhancing social ties as do the virtues articulated in the prologue, the robbers' confusion regarding wealth ends up destroying such bonds and breeding brutality, as the rhetoric describing their actions—"setting an ambush," "shedding blood," "lying in wait," "swallowing up," and "booty"—makes clear.[10] Instead of leading to a flourishing life, the sinners' passionate pursuit of wealth leads to ignoble death, for themselves and others, as the images of Sheol and the Pit in v. 12 indicate.

The wealth the sinners promise, moreover, represents the appeal of their manner of life and not simply literal riches. Several features of the text point to its symbolic nature. First, although at this point in the book it is not yet well established, the passage invokes the metaphorical complex of the "way."[11] This suggests that the story of 'the sinners who entice the son' is designed to say something about the moral life generally and in particular about the choice the hearer faces between the pattern of life offered by the robbers, on the one hand, and that offered by the instructing voice, on the other hand. The passage deploys several other types of figurative language as well. In v. 11, for instance, the robbers' stated purpose is full of irony. In their pursuit of wealth, they choose their victims randomly

[10] That the father has the sinners' themselves describe their pursuit of wealth in language that carries clear connotations of violence and marshal overtones (e.g., "booty"; שלל) is a not so subtle negative judgment on the robbers. However, in 31:11, the "Woman of Worth," who at least in part represents Wisdom, is also said not to lack שלל. This is a description at the end of the book of the locus of genuine worth (see Chapter Five). It re-accents the robbers' terminology and counters the claims they make at the book's outset.

[11] Fox also underscores the importance of the moral metaphor of the way in the passage and recognizes in the criminals' words a claim in competition with that of the father and wisdom. See below and *Proverbs 1–9*, 85, 89–90, 94.

or "without cause." In the end, however, their endeavors prove to be without cause in another sense, since they are clearly not able to enjoy the wealth they gain. The sinners also offer the hyperbolic claim in v. 13 that they will obtain "every precious treasure" and "fill" their homes with booty. Moreover, in at least two instances, this, the book's initial didactic tale, clearly makes use of metaphoric language. The robbers boast that, like the mythological Sheol, they will swallow their victims 'alive and whole' (v. 12) while the father claims that it is "unjust wealth" that will "rob" the sinners of life (v. 19). Finally, the enigmatic and textually problematic folk-like proverb of v. 17, which appears to be introduced to support the father's reckoning of matters, intimates that the telling of the entire incident is not an end in itself, but like the use of folk proverbs in general, is designed to communicate something about human life and the ways of humans in the world.

The agents and goals of the initial brief narrative in Proverbs thus ought to be read not merely as literal descriptions of real robbers seeking gain, but in a more allusive sense as well; they are tropes or figures. The sinners are not simply a youth gang, but a figure for all of the things that, for Proverbs, constitute the wrong way and lead to death. They are the persuasive voices of all the discourses, or that diffuse social script alluded to in Chapter Two, that compete with the father's words. Correspondingly, "wealth" ought not to be viewed only as literal riches, but as a symbol for all that is alluring and desirable in this social script. The wise and discerning person, who is seeking to understand Proverbs' moral instruction, will hear both levels—the story and the meaning for which it is a trope.

Importantly, by insisting that the sinners' path actually leads not to wealth but to death, the father also undermines and discredits the larger social script to which the sinners' words belong. What they say, including what they say about wealth, is simply unreliable. If what the robbers say is untrue, it then behooves the son to heed the father's words. What *the father says*, including what he says about wealth, is what becomes important.[12]

[12] Of course, the father's voice, which introduced the sinners' discourse, has controlled their words from the beginning; cf. Newsom, "Woman and the Discourse," 144. Yet despite this underlying control, the sinners' promise of wealth remains an

3.2. Wealth as Motivational Symbol in Proverbs 2–9

The instructing voice's deployment of the rhetoric of wealth as a motivational symbol, which begins in chapter one, can be traced throughout the rest of chapters 2–9. In 2:4–5; 3:14–16; 4:5–7; 8:10–11; and 8:18–21 the instructing voice, be it the father or personified Wisdom, continues to broaden and strengthen its hold on such language, creating symbolic associations of its own choosing and simultaneously undermining competing claims regarding riches and wealth.[13] In each of these instances this voice, which in chapter one ostensibly permits the sinners to attempt to persuade the son of the desirability of their way by means of the rhetoric of wealth, itself employs an expanded vocabulary of wealth as a positive motivational symbol designed to encourage the son to pursue the way of wisdom.

3.2.a. *Proverbs 2:4–5*

In 2:1 the instructing voice begins a long conditional sentence directly addressing a young man (בני).[14] The contrast between the sinners' discourse in chapter one and the father's words here in chapter two is stark. The father employs an expanded vocabulary of wealth and promises the hearer something quite different than do the robbers. The instruction in 2:1–3 claims: if "you" (m. sg.) will "take my words"

enticing and potentially dangerous competing discourse to which to expose the hearer. Hence, far from being redundant—as especially older commentators sometimes claimed—the repetition of "my son" (בני) in vv. 10 and 15 serves to reestablish and reiterate the patriarch's position of authority vis-à-vis the hearer. Toy, in *Proverbs*, 16–17, for example, notes that the בני of v. 15 might be justified, but is not translated in LXX and "is unnecessary at the beginning of the apodosis, and is rhythmically undesirable, it is better to omit it." See the similar comment of W. O. E. Oesterley, *The Book of Proverbs with Introduction and Notes* (London: Methuen & Co., 1929), 9. Cf. Fichtner's notations in the *BHS* apparatus.

[13] These passages do not represent all of the subsequent passages in chs. 1–9 that deploy wealth and poverty rhetoric, but only those that use such rhetoric as motivational symbols. As noted above, other texts will be treated below in the section regarding direct instruction. Although the father's and Woman Wisdom's voice are distinguished, most obviously in terms of gender, they represent a single, patriarchal cultural voice.

[14] On the nature of this conditional sentence see Toy, *Proverbs*, 31–32; Roland E. Murphy, *Proverbs* (WBC 22; Nashville: Thomas Nelson, 1998), 14; Clifford, *Proverbs*, 46; Arndt Meinhold, *Die Sprüche* (2 vol.; ZBK; Zürich: Theologischer Verlag Zürich, 1991), 1:79.

and "treasure up my commandments" (מצותי תצפן אתך; v. 1); and attend to wisdom, discernment, and understanding (vv. 2–3); and, in 2:4–5:

אם־תבקשנה ככסף וכמטמונים תחפשנה
אז תבין יראת יהוה ודעת אלהים תמצא

> If you seek it as you do silver and search for it as for treasures, then you will understand the fear of the Lord and attain knowledge of God.

In the sinners' speech material wealth is the goal of the actions in which they invite the hearer to participate and the kinds of actions presented as necessary to achieve the goal of attaining wealth were things like setting an ambush and "concealing" oneself (צ-פ-ן). In the father's speech, however, wealth imagery plays a slightly different role, a role that serves to underscore for the hearer the value of wisdom.

Notice first that in 2:1 the father deploys the same verb (צ-פ-ן) that the sinners did in 1:11, although with a slightly different nuance or accent. For the father, the sense of "concealing" gives way to the sense of "storing up"; and by making "my commandments" the object of צ-פ-ן, the father's speech likens instruction to some material thing that is particularly valuable.[15] The comparison of wisdom with that which is valuable is further underlined by the advice in v. 4. The son is to seek insight (תבונה) and understanding (בינה), which are the antecedents in v. 3 of the 3rd f. sg. verbal suffixes in v. 4. These terms in Proverbs are essentially synonymous with the meta-virtue of wisdom, and the father's use of simile to move the hearer, rhetorically, to acquire them reveals explicitly the line's metaphorical qualities.[16] The son should seek after such virtues "*as* for silver" (ככסף) and "*as* for treasures" (כמטמונים). Notice as well that the object

[15] For צ-פ-ן with the sense of treasuring up valuable items, see Prov 13:22, which speaks of storing up חיל ("wealth"), and Song 7:14 where agricultural products ("mandrakes," "choice fruits") are stored up. More generally, in Ps 31:20 God's "good things" (טובך) are stored up. As in Prov 2:1, in a number of passages in HB the use of צ-פ-ן reflects an extension of meaning, from storing up physical objects to storing up intangible goods such as a divine "word" (אמרתך; Ps 119:11), "skill" (תושיה; Prov 2:7), and "knowledge" (דעת; Prov 10:14). In Prov 7:1 the father likewise exhorts the son to treasure up מצותי ("my commandments").

[16] Gerhard von Rad likewise recognizes terms such as wisdom, understanding, and insight are essentially synonymous in Proverbs. See *Wisdom in Israel* (London: SCM, 1972), 53.

or goal of the father's advice in 2:4–5 is not wealth as it was in the sinners' speech, but the attainment of wisdom's virtues, namely "fear of the Lord" and "knowledge of God," as the result clause of line five (signaled by אז, "then") makes clear. These phrases hearken back to the book's motto in 1:7 and the important proverbial virtue mentioned there: "the fear of the Lord."

Hence in 2:4–5 the instructing voice in essence draws on that broad social script that overvalues wealth in order, in a Bakhtinian sense, to "color" the hearer's orientation to virtue. Wisdom, not riches, is what should be most valued. The language of wealth in Proverbs has quickly become an important textual symbol of the desirable.

One further feature of Prov 2:4–5, or more specifically a feature of the larger passage of which 2:4–5 is a part, ought to be highlighted. I suggested in Chapter Two that "fear of the Lord" (see 1:7) was a virtue on a par with the other virtues mentioned in the prologue proper. After 2:5 alludes to this quality of character, the passage continues by alluding precisely to other virtues articulated by the prologue. In 2:6 the text underscores the intellectual virtues of wisdom, knowledge and understanding (cf. 1:2), claiming that these are from the Lord:

כי־יהוה יתן חכמה מפיו דעת ותבונה

> For the Lord gives wisdom; from his mouth come knowledge and understanding.

Verse 7 subsequently has the deity, who must be the subject of the verbs in the line, essentially serve as a moral paradigm for the hearer by stating that YHWH himself "treasures up" (צ-פ-ן) the practical virtue of "resourcefulness" (תושיה).[17] As the line continues, YHWH is described as a shield for those who walk blamelessly in order, so verse 8 explains, "to guard the paths of justice" (לנצר ארחות משפט). Verse nine, which is a further result clause in chapter two's long conditional sentence, subsequently offers another explicit allusion to the social virtues highlighted by the prologue. As with v. 5, v. 9 notes, via the Hebrew term אז ("then"), the goals of the father's instruction about treasuring up commandments and wisdom while

[17] The first word of v. 7 is a Ketiv-Qere (יצפן—וצפן). With Plöger (*Sprüche Salomos*, 23) and others, the Qere is to be preferred.

underscoring for the hearer the value of the social virtues by calling these "good."

אז תבין צדק ומשפט ומישרים כל־מעגל־טוב

Then you will understand justice and righteousness and equity, every good course.

3.2.b. *Proverbs 3:14–16*

After a series of imperatives in 3:1–12 charge the son to tend to instruction (see below), v. 13 declares the one who finds wisdom and understanding to be "happy" (אשרי אדם מצא חכמה). Subsequently, in 3:14–16 the instructing voice again takes up the rhetoric of wealth as a positive motivational symbol and expands its control of this language by expanding its symbolic associations. Specifically, the text introduces three new terms ("trade value," "gold," "rubies"); and what was implicit in 2:4 is made explicit. Wisdom, now personified as a woman, is said to be *better* than silver and other treasures. The text reads:

(14) כי טוב סחרה מסחר־כסף ומחרוץ תבואתה
(15) יקרה היא מפניים וכל־חפציך לא ישוו־בה
(16) ארך ימים בימינה בשמאולה עשר וכבוד

14) Her value in trade is better than silver, her yield greater than gold.[18]
15) She is more precious than rubies, all of your goods cannot equal her.[19]
16) In her right hand is length of days, in her left, riches and honor.[20]

---

[18] The rendering of the passage follows NJPS.

[19] The rendering of פנינים (the Qere, which is to be preferred to the Ketiv פניים; cf. 8:11) as "rubies" is not certain. Alternatives include "corals" and "pearls." See Toy, *Proverbs*, 68; Fox, *Proverbs 1–9*, 157; Hans F. Fuhs, *Das Buch der Sprichwörter: Ein Kommentar* (Forschung zur Bibel 95; Würzburg: Echter Verlag, 2001), 79.

[20] Among others, Fox, in *Proverbs 1–9*, 157, has suggested "riches and honor" may be an instance of *hendiadys*, meaning something like "honorable wealth." However, each term is better considered individually as emblematic of what the hearer would consider desirable—i.e., here material wealth *and* social status. As Clifford writes, ancient Mediterranean societies "put great value on honor and reputation and on the avoidance of public shame." See *Proverbs*, 54. On this topic see further J. G. Peristiany, ed., *Honour and Shame: The Values of Mediterranean Society* (Chicago: University of Chicago Press, 1966); see especially the article by Julian Pitt-Rivers, "Honour and Social Status" in the same volume. Cf. Victor H. Matthews and Don C. Benjamin, eds. *Honor and Shame in the World of the Bible* (Semeia 68; Atlanta: SBL, 1994).

Wisdom's worth in this passage is first expressed in commercial terms. The text claims that "her [Wisdom's] value in trade" is greater than the commercial and financial gains that silver can offer (טוב סחרה מסחר־כסף).[21] Likewise that which Wisdom produces, expressed via the agricultural image of the "yield" (תבואה), surpasses the value of gold and rubies. None of the son's "goods" (חפץ), the text says, can equal her.

Some commentators contend that the association of Wisdom with wealth in these verses (and elsewhere in Prov 1–9) implies that Wisdom promises the hearer literal material advantages.[22] The instructing voice, however, does not reflect neatly a wisdom prosperity axiom as this is regularly understood, but is concerned with persuading the hearer of the incomparable value of the personified meta-virtue of Wisdom. By means of the comparative (*ṭôb-min*) construction, vv. 14–15 function to underscore the advantage wisdom holds *over* wealth, not the wealth wisdom will produce. The verses do not say that wisdom brings riches, but, in expanding the analogy of 2:4, that wisdom is *better than* riches.[23] The father adopts the language of material

[21] From the root ס-ח-ר are derived several economic terms. The *qal* act. part. in HB, for instance, is often best rendered "merchant" (e.g., Gen 23:16; 37:28; 1 Kings 10:28, etc.) while in later Hebrew texts סחרן is a "traveling merchant." Both terms are probably extensions of the root's base meaning "to pass through"—i.e., merchants would have to "pass through" various regions to do business. See Marcus Jastrow, *Dictionary of the Targumim, Talmud Babli, Yerushalmi and Midrashich Literature* (New York: Judaica Press, 1996), 972; one volume reprint of the two volume 1971 original. Here in Prov 3:14 *saḥar* ("value in trade") reverberates with these kinds of economic connotations (cf. Is 23:3, 18; Prov 3:14; 31:18).

[22] For example, although Toy recognizes that in this passage the "excellence of wisdom is *figurative*," he nonetheless adds: "Here we have an explicit statement of the material rewards that attend her [Wisdom]. . . . The riches and honor, here mentioned in addition to long life, are to be taken *literally*." The conception of wisdom found here includes "qualities that usually secure both wealth and the esteem of men." The "qualities" Toy has in mind are "prudence" and "sagacity," but it is not entirely clear how or why he thinks these normally lead to riches and honor. See *Proverbs*, 68–69; italics added. Whybray, in *Proverbs*, 66, likewise avers: "It is *material* advantages that the author has in mind. In other words, it is more advantageous to put the acquisition of wisdom first as an immediate goal rather than **silver** or **gold**, because in the end it will bring even greater and more durable material rewards" (bold-type in original). Christine Roy Yoder in *Wisdom as a Woman of Substance: A Socio-Economic Reading of Proverbs 1–9 and 31:10–31* (BZAW 304; Berlin: W. de Gruyter, 2001), 97 writes similarly: "The son should strive to acquire her [Wisdom] because, in the end, she will bring him even more wealth, property, and good fortune (3:16–17)." Cf. Clifford, *Proverbs*, 54.

[23] Meinhold similarly recognizes that for this passage "precious metals . . . despite

wealth and economic comparison (סחר) to convince the son to choose Wisdom's way. Indeed not only does she "hold" the enticements of riches and other valuable items, as v. 16 reveals, she herself is more valuable than these inducements. Even if measured against valuable silver, gold, and rubies, Wisdom must be said to be most valuable.

The final stich of 3:15 ("all of your goods [חפץ] cannot equal her") likewise intimates that Wisdom's wealth here ought to be reckoned less as something she literally can pass on to humans and more as a symbol of her worth. Although חפץ can carry the meaning "goods," and the economic terminology in the passage, suggests that such a rendering is appropriate here, in BH the word more generally means "desire," "delight," "pleasure."[24] Wisdom thus can be said to be not only better than wealth, but also better than anything the son might "desire."[25] The multivalency of חפץ, which points toward both "material goods" and the broader notion of "desire," anticipates, and is a reflex of, the text's use of other images to speak of wisdom's desirability (e.g., "honor" in 3:16). It also colors the other wealth imagery in the line. All of it functions together as a symbol of what is alluring in order to communicate to the son Wisdom's desirability and to persuade him to pursue her as he might any desirable good, whether wealth or, as the passage's personification of Wisdom as a woman also hints, sexual satisfaction.[26]

The rhetoric of 3:16, however, may in fact seem to suggest that Wisdom will bring the son real material rewards, since this line states that she is not merely *like* or *better than* riches, but that, along with "length of days" and "honor," she actually possesses wealth. It would not be unreasonable to assume, then, that the one who finds Wisdom would subsequently find these other things as well.

their great material worth do not in the slightest come close to the worth of wisdom" (*Edelmetallen . . . trotz ihres hohen materiellen Wertes nicht im entferntesten an den Wert der Weisheit heranreichen*). However, he nonetheless continues by stating that this does not exclude the fact that, "wisdom for her part helps one acquire wealth" (*Weisheit ihrerseits zu Reichtum verhilft*). See *Die Sprüche*, 1:80–81. Similarly, Fox, *Proverbs 1–9*, 156; Leo G. Perdue, *Proverbs* (Interpretation; Louisville: WJK, 2000), 101–104.

[24] In later texts composed in classical Hebrew חפץ can also come to mean something like "business activities." This, for instance, is in my view sometimes the case in the Qumran wisdom text 4QInstruction. The translation above, which renders the term "goods," is adopted from NJPS.

[25] Cf. Van Leeuwen, "Proverbs," *NIB* 5:53; Fox, *Proverbs 1–9*, 156–157.

[26] Though the erotic dimensions of Woman Wisdom are not in this instance highlighted as they are elsewhere (e.g., 4:5–8; see below).

However, two observations speak against the view that the text ought to be regarded primarily as literally promising the one who finds wisdom material wealth. First, the passage again reveals a certain tension regarding the value of wealth. On the one hand, verses 14–15 have just emphasized Wisdom's value over material goods—a fact that calls into question the ultimate worth of riches. Verse 16, on the other hand, claims that Wisdom possesses wealth. As in chapter one this tension invites the reader to consider the possibility that this *mashal* is employing the rhetoric of material riches (and other desirable images) in a non-literal fashion.

Second, Wisdom in 3:16 is personified.[27] Personification is a literary device by which an abstract notion or inanimate object is said to possess personal qualities or characteristics.[28] With the very introduction of this figure we are thus already in the realm of the figurative. Hence, although any good and flourishing life that wisdom will produce must include a degree of real material prosperity, in this line it is best to say that personified Wisdom is depicted as holding riches

[27] The image of personified Wisdom has been much discussed. It may find its background in Egyptian mythology surrounding Isis or *Maʿat*. In Egyptian iconography the goddess *Maʿat* can be represented holding what many biblical scholars, following Kayatz, identify as the symbols of life and wealth; see especially Christa Kayatz, *Studien zu Proverbien 1–9* (WMANT 22; Neukirchen-Vluyn: Neukirchener, 1966), 102–117. The Hebrew text perhaps is drawing on this mythic imagery, but see Fox's critique in "World Order and *Maʿat*: A Crooked Parallel," *JANES* 23 (1995): 37–48 and in *Proverbs 1–9*, 157. Yoder reviews a number of scholarly positions regarding Woman Wisdom in *Woman of Substance*, 4–13 and argues that real, though somewhat exceptional, women of the Persian period Levant are best regarded as forming the background to the woman of substance in Prov 31:10–31 *and* that Woman Wisdom in chapters 1–9 is depicted as just such a woman. Cf. Claudia V. Camp's more extensive survey of the scholarly landscape in *Wisdom and the Feminine in the Book of Proverbs* (Sheffield: Almond, 1985), 21–68. Other studies concerned with the figure of Woman Wisdom include Silvia Schroer, *Die Weisheit hat Ihr Haus Gebaut: Studien zur Gestalt Sophia in den Biblischen Schriften* (Mainz: Grünewald, 1996) and Bernhard Lang, *Wisdom and the Book of Proverbs: An Israelite Goddess Redefined* (New York: Pilgrim, 1986). On the title page, the subtitle of the latter book, however, is given as "A *Hebrew* Goddess Redefined." The work is a revision of Lang's 1975 Tübingen dissertation, which appeared as, "Frau Weisheit: Deutung einer biblischen Gestalt."

[28] The *Oxford English Dictionary* states that personification "is the attribution of personal form, nature, or characteristics; the representation of a thing or abstraction as a person: esp. as a rhetorical figure or species of metaphor." *Oxford English Dictionary* (prep. by J. A. Simpson and E. S. C. Weiner; 2nd ed.; Oxford: Clarendon, 1989), 11:604. Yoder, in *Woman of Substance*, 1, who cites this same definition, notes a number of instances of personification in the Hebrew Bible (e.g., Zion in Jer 4:31; Lam 1–2, 4; etc.).

primarily because the text recognizes its addressee would find such wealth valuable and desirable. The rhetoric of honor and long life in the line function similarly.

Hence in 3:14–16 Proverbs deploys images from several easily recognized spheres of human life—namely, the social (honor) and physical (long life) realms along with, of course, the economic sphere (riches). These familiar images of what humans often find valuable and desirable provide a conceptual bridge by which the hearer can come to comprehend the value that wisdom possesses in the moral sphere. As a symbol, the wealth imagery in the passage points not merely to literal wealth, but also beyond itself, to all that is desirable.

By valuing Wisdom in terms of the lesser goods of wealth, status, and long life, the text in 3:14–16 also makes it difficult for the hearer to confuse these goods, mere components of a flourishing life, with the good life or the way of wisdom itself. Earlier the father acknowledged the sinners' competing discourse in order to discredit it. Here the instructing voice in a sense attempts to screen out the message of the same broad social script that the sinners' words represent—a script which promotes beliefs and ideologies other than those of the father (i.e., beliefs, perhaps, which suggest the accumulation of riches, honor, etc. is the best means to human flourishing). The text again wants to be certain that the voice of the father is the one to which the son attends.

3.2.c. *Proverbs 4:5–9*

At the beginning of chapter four the instructing voice addresses an audience cast in the plural. Having recalled the guidance he received from his own father (vv. 3–4), the father or teacher in 4:5–9 switches to a m. sg. form of address and deploys the rhetoric of wealth. The passage reads:

(5) קנה חכמה קנה בינה אל־תשכח ואל־תט מאמרי־פי
(6) אל־תעזבה ותשמרך אהבה ותצרך
(7) ראשית חכמה קנה חכמה ובכל־קנינך קנה בינה
(8) סלסלה ותרוממך תכבדך כי תחבקנה
(9) תתן לראשך לוית־חן עטרת תפארת תמגנך

5) Buy Wisdom, buy understanding; do not forget and do not turn from the words of my mouth.
6) Do not abandon her and she will guard you. Love her and she will protect you.

7) The beginning of wisdom is "buy Wisdom!" and with all your possessions "buy understanding!"[29]
8) Cherish her and she will exalt you; she will honor you if you cling to her.[30]
9) She will set on your head a graceful garland, a beautiful crown she will bestow on you.

The passage is complex and rich with two further distinct discourses of desire—erotic, marriage language and the language of social status—interacting with the rhetoric of wealth.[31] The fact that the lines, especially v. 9, depict Wisdom engaging in acts that normally would be the provenance of humans indicates that she is again personified,

---

[29] The line is not present in the Greek. Although the syntax is difficult, the verse is understandable. For a discussion see Fox, *Proverbs 1–9*, 175.

[30] סלסלה is a *hapax* and is translated in a variety of ways: "hug her" (NJPS); "prize her highly" (NRSV). Plöger, *Sprüche Salomos*, 44–45 renders "value her highly" (*Schätz sie hoch ein*). Fox notes that the word's "root-meaning is apparently 'be/make high.'" Hence he suggests translating the term as "exalt," "cherish." See *Proverbs 1–9*, 175; cf. 171. "Cherish" is perhaps the best rendering. It preserves the notion of elevation, albeit social elevation, which the following two terms underscore: ותרוממך and תכבדך. It also gestures toward the erotic element that the final term in the verse, תחבקנה, suggests.

[31] In verses five and seven the text deploys what at least initially appears to be an economic rhetoric. Verse five exhorts the hearer to "acquire" or "buy" (קנה) Wisdom and understanding. Verse seven, in a play on the root ק-נ-ה, similarly commands one to "acquire" (קנה) Wisdom and understanding with all of one's "acquisitions" (קנינך). Verses six, eight, and nine, by contrast, make use of erotic, marriage imagery, as many have noted. See especially Meinhold, *Die Sprüche*, 1:91–93; Yoder, *Woman of Substance*, 95–96; Clifford, *Proverbs*, 61–62; Murphy *Proverbs*, 27; Perdue, *Proverbs*, 114. Fuhs (*Das Buch der Sprichwörter*, 93), however, believes it is "very questionable" (*sehr fraglich*) if the passage deploys wedding imagery. Fox (*Proverbs 1–9*, 173–174) also claims: "Nothing in the present passage alludes to marriage." He and others (e.g., McKane) consider the image of Wisdom here in 4:5–9 to be one of a "patroness." See Fox, *Proverbs 1–9*, 178; William McKane, *Proverbs: A New Approach* (Philadelphia: Westminster, 1970), 306; cf. Whybray, *Proverbs*, 78. Verse six, however, also admonishes the hearer not to "abandon" (אל־תעזבה) Wisdom, but to "love" her (אהבה). The root ע-ז-ב, which normally means "to abandon," can also carry the sense of divorce, as in Prov 2:17 where the adulterous woman abandons or "divorces" her husband, "the companion of her youth." Cf. Isa 54:7 and see Yoder's similar comments in *Woman of Substance*, 95–96. The Hebrew אהב ("to love"; v. 6) largely carries the same range of meanings as the English "love"—including its erotic possibilities. The first word of v. 8, סלסל, is a *hapax*. Its meaning is disputed, but the parallel verb חבק ("to embrace," "hug") is deployed in Song 2:6 and 8:3 in what are plainly erotic contexts. For a discussion of the term see Toy, *Proverbs*, 88–89; Fox, *Proverbs 1–9*, 175. Verse eight likewise takes up the rhetoric of social status where it is claimed a heightened passion for Wisdom results in an increase of one's honor. Returning to the erotic, verse nine speaks of garlands and crowns, terms which elsewhere in HB appear in the contexts of weddings (e.g., Song 3:11). Cf. Whybray, *Proverbs*, 78; Clifford, *Proverbs*, 61–62.

and that the reader is once more in the realm of the figurative. Moreover, although it is perhaps possible to purchase certain kinds of knowledge, it is impossible to buy wisdom, as especially vv. 5 and 7 command. Indeed even if the figure of Wisdom here is based on real Persian period women as Yoder has argued, Wisdom herself is not a real woman that one might acquire or marry. The literal interpretation of the lines thus produces, in Ricoeur's idiom, an absurdity that forces the reader to search for an alternative, metaphorical understanding.

Despite the commands to "buy" wisdom, the instructing voice in Prov 4:5–9, which exhorts the son to recognize the woman's attractive features and embrace her to himself, is attempting to persuade the son of Wisdom's desirability primarily in terms of erotic imagery. Such a rhetorical move is not surprising since elsewhere in Prov 1–9 the text deploys a good deal of erotic language to speak of, especially, the desirability of the strange or foreign woman (e.g., 6:24–35) and Woman Folly (9:13–18). Proverbs, however, speaks of the desirability of these women via a rhetoric of illicit sexuality—e.g., adultery (ch. 6), and figuratively, "stolen water" and bread eaten in secret (ch. 9). Like the robbers' riches in Prov 1, together these two women represent all that is alluring on the wrong way.[32] By contrast, the desirability of the woman in 4:5–9—i.e., Woman Wisdom—is presented in terms of what the instructing voice deems legitimate erotic terms associated with marriage imagery (as probably is the woman of chapter 31:10–31).[33] Just as in chapter one the instructing voice values wisdom's way by employing a positive economic rhetoric,

[32] As many have noted, where the image of one of the women is invoked the other is simultaneously evoked. Murphy (*Proverbs*, 282), for instance, writes: "Folly resembles the Woman Stranger and her machinations" and "chap. 9 suggests a symbolic identification of Woman Stranger with Woman Folly." Cf. Perdue, *Proverbs*, 89; Whybray, *Proverbs*, 54–56. On the figure of the strange woman, see further, Claudia V. Camp, "What's So Strange about the Strange Woman?" in *The Bible and the Politics of Exegesis* (ed. David Jobling et al.; Cleveland: Pilgrim, 1991); Fox, *Proverbs 1–9*, 252–262; Christl Maier, *Die "Fremde Frau" in Proverbien 1–9: Eine exegetische und sozialgeschichtliche Studie* (OBO 144; Freiburg: Universitätsverlag; Göttingen: Vandenhoeck & Ruprecht, 1995); Joseph Blenkinsopp, "The Social Context of the 'Outsider Woman' in Proverbs 1–9," *Biblica* 72 (1991): 457–73; Harold C. Washington, "The Strange Woman (אשה זרה/נכריה) of Proverbs 1–9 and Post Exilic Judaean Society," in *Second Temple Studies 2. Temple Community in the Persian Period* (ed. Tamara C. Eskenazi and Kent H. Richards; JSOTSup 175; Sheffield: JSOT, 1994), 217–242.

[33] Yoder's thesis in *Woman of Substance* that Woman Wisdom is presented as a Persian period "woman of substance," presupposes a similar notion.

which is distinguished from the invitation to thievery that the sinners employ, here too in contrast to the illicit descriptions of the strange woman and Woman Folly elsewhere in chapters 1–9, the father chooses to emphasize Wisdom's desirability to the son by means of a related, but distinct and legitimate, rhetoric of desire. Woman Wisdom is to be acquired as the young male addressee would obtain a good wife, as Yoder has pointed out. Wisdom, moreover, is not to be divorced (v. 6) and is an appropriate object of the hearer's desire, as the imperatives "love" (v. 6), "cherish," and "cling" (v. 8) indicate. For her part Wisdom will play the part of a good bride offering the son a (marriage) garland and crown (v. 9); and the one who pursues Wisdom passionately as a lover/bride, she will reward with honor (v. 8).

However, again, this erotic imagery points to the text's metaphorical qualities since, as I stated above, Wisdom is not a real woman. The instructing voice of Proverbs knows that the attainment of honor and erotic fulfillment, like wealth, are things the imagined hearer will likely crave, and for this reason deploys the rhetoric of sex and social status to demonstrate the desirability of the way of wisdom.[34] Whereas the patriarchal imagination envisions shame and death for the one who chooses the illegitimate path of adultery (cf. 6:23–35) or the adulterous way of folly (cf. 9:13–18), the claim that union with this woman brings "honor" and exaltation belongs, by contrast, to the patriarchal imagination regarding marriage (cf. 31:23).

It is however, with the use of terms derived from ק-נ-ה in 4:5 and 7 that both the erotic, marriage language of the passage and its rhetoric of social status intermingle as well with an economic discourse. The economic resonances of קָנָה are especially evident in 4:7. The words וּבְכׇל־קִנְיָנְךָ קְנֵה בִינָה, however, are somewhat ambiguous. The phrase might mean "acquire understanding *along with* all your possessions"—where wisdom (i.e., understanding) is understood to be as valuable as any other possessions one might acquire. That is, 'whatever you get, be sure to get wisdom too!' However, the verb קָנָה is often deployed in economic contexts where it carries the mean-

[34] Recall that, as with wealth imagery, the rhetoric of sex and honor are ideal rhetorical motivations. Each possesses what Burke would call a built-in mechanism of "interference" that allows it perpetually to motivate. See Chapter Two above.

ing "to buy."[35] On a number of occasions in HB, the root appears as well with the preposition *bet* functioning as the *bet preti* or "*bet* of exchange." This is the case in Gen 47:19, 2 Sam 24:24, Is 43:24, Amos 8:6, and 1 Chr 21:24, for example. Given the rather frequent use of economic language in Proverbs, it is likely that the *bet* of בכול is functioning in this economic sense here as well. The lines are thus best rendered, "in exchange for all your possessions buy understanding;" or, "with all your possessions, buy understanding."[36] The imperatives of verse five (קנה) should thus be rendered as "buy" as well.

Hence, whereas Prov 3:14–16 uses the economic language of economic exchange (סחר) to suggest that Wisdom's value exceeds that of material wealth, the teacher in 4:5–9 insists one should not only seek Wisdom as one might seek wealth, but also that one should spare no expense to acquire this valuable commodity. Together with the fact that wisdom is not something that can ordinarily be purchased, this ironic and hyperbolic exhortation points to the figurative nature of the passage. In the symbolism of the instruction "all your possessions" is a further trope for all those things (e.g., wealth, status, sex) besides wisdom, which might be the focus of the hearer's desire and his overly zealous pursuits.

Notice, too, that the father's economic rhetoric in 4:5–9 once more stands in sharp contrast with that of the sinners' in 1:13. The robbers

---

[35] The same consonants carry other connotations that are significant for the study of Proverbs (e.g., "create," "bear a child"; see esp. Gen 4:1 and cf. Prov 8:22 and Wisdom's relationship to the deity described there). In these instances, however, the term is sometimes reckoned as a distinct root, II, related to a third weak root attested in other West Semitic languages such as Ugaritic.

[36] Verse seven, however, remains difficult. It is not present in LXX and some commentators, such as Clifford (*Proverbs*, 60), believe it should be omitted. Nevertheless, his rendering of the line ("The beginning of wisdom; acquire wisdom; at the cost of all your other acquisitions, acquire insight") suggests he too understands the *bet* of *bkwl* as the *bet preti*. Whybray (*Proverbs*, 77) similarly renders the phrase in question in a manner consonant with my analysis: "at the price (even) of all your possessions." Like Clifford, Toy also believes v. 7 should probably be omitted. However, one of the translations of the verse that he offers is in line with what I am suggesting. He writes: "the Heb. reads: . . ., or *buy wisdom, and, with all that thou hast gotten, buy*, etc., that is, buy wisdom at the price of all thy property." See Toy, *Proverbs*, 88; italics original. Van der Weiden, by contrast, understands the *bet* in the phrase בכל־קנינך as the *beth-comparativum*: "*plus que tout ce que tu possèdes*" ("more than all you possess"). See W. A. van der Weiden, *Le Livre des Proverbes: Notes Philologiques* (BEO 23; Rome: Biblical Institute Press, 1970), 45.

in chapter one make the attainment of wealth the end of life. They consider riches to constitute an ultimate good to be acquired at any cost, including that of injustice and violence. The father, by contrast, exhorts the hearer to "acquire" (קנה) wisdom and discernment "in exchange for all your possessions" (בכל קנינך). He casts riches only as a means to a flourishing life. The implicit logic of the passage is that by giving up something of value (one's possessions) one will acquire something that is, or will prove to be, of greater worth (wisdom). Although the sinners' wealth in chapter one is ostensibly precious and ultimately something that requires one's life, it is initially presented to the hearer as easily attainable. Acquiring wisdom, by contrast, is, according to the instructing voice, costly business. It requires that one give up all of the possessions one might normally desire.

If, however, it is clear that ק-נ-ה belongs primarily to the realm of economic discourse in 4:5–9, it can also be said to belong to the realm of erotic, marriage discourse, which I already suggested plays and important role in the passage. Although a variety of usages are attested, in at least one instance in HB the root קנה is used in the context of acquiring a wife. In Ruth 4:10 (cf. 4:8 and the more obscure 4:5) Boaz says: "Ruth the Moabite, the wife of Mahlon, I will acquire as my wife" (קניתי לי לאשה). The precise meaning of Boaz's words in relation to his acquisition of Elimelech's and Naomi's field and to Ruth herself is obscure, as is the ritual subsequently enacted by Boaz and his countrymen. However, unlike the *levir* (cf. Deut 25), a kinsman redeemer (גואל) in ancient Israel, which is what Boaz is said to be in Ruth, would only be obliged to purchase or acquire land that was in danger of being sold, or rescue kin from debt slavery. He would not be obligated to generate offspring for a deceased kinsman through marriage of the kinsman's widow. Hence it appears in Ruth 4 that Boaz is announcing that will take Ruth as a bride, regardless of whether the closer redeemer in the story is to "acquire" Elimelech's and Naomi's field.[37]

[37] Such an understanding of the scene makes sense of the consonantal Hebrew text of Ruth 4 and explains why the nearer redeemer relents in his intention to redeem Elimelech's field upon hearing of Boaz's intention to "marry/acquire" Ruth. If Boaz and Ruth produce a child, that child might be in the position to claim ownership of the land through a reckoning of lineage through Ruth's first husband (presumably Chilion; cf. Ruth 1:5), the son of Elimelech and Naomi. See Tod Linafelt, *Ruth* (Berit Olam; Collegeville, MN: The Liturgical Press), 63–76. Linafelt's commentary is published as a single volume with Timothy K. Beal's commentary on Esther.

Elsewhere in Proverbs the son is also instructed to call Wisdom his "sister" (אחת; 7:4), a term that in the Song of Songs (4:9, 10, 12; 5:1) is paralleled with "bride" (כלה) and "spoken by a man to his beloved."[38] This broader context, along with the fact that in Mishnaic Hebrew the root ק-נ-ה can also be used of acquiring a wife, intimates that קנה in Prov 4:5 and 4:7 might carry traces of its uses in the kinds of marriage contexts alluded to in Ruth.[39]

The instructing voice in 4:5–9 thus makes use of distinct rhetorics of desire drawn from the economic, erotic, and social spheres in order to emphasize wisdom's appeal. Although these different sorts of rhetoric merge in the passage so that one might say, as Yoder has argued, the son in v. 4 is being exhorted to acquire Wisdom as he might acquire or purchase a wife who would socially and economically profit him, the meta-virtue of wisdom is not something for which one could literally exchange one's possessions. She, moreover, is not herself a real woman who can be purchased as a bride. The language of the verse thus must be regarded as figurative. The verses highlight the value and desirability of wisdom.

3.2.d. *Proverbs 8:10–11*

It is not until 8:10–11 that Proverbs again employs the rhetoric of wealth as a positive motivational symbol. In this passage, after personified Wisdom proclaims she offers shrewdness, instruction, noble things, truth, and knowledge, she uses the language of wealth in a direct appeal to a young man. Her claim that she is better than rubies and that no "goods" can equal wisdom reads:

קחו־מוסרי ואל־כסף ודעת מחרוץ נבחר
כי־טובה חכמה מפנינים וכל־חפצים לא ישוו־בה

Take my instruction rather than silver, knowledge rather than choice gold.
For wisdom is better than rubies; no goods can equal it. (Prov 8:10–11)

[38] Yoder, *Woman of Substance*, 95. Yoder also notes that, "some of the women addressed as sister (אחת) in letters from Elephantine were probably wives" and that "in Egyptian, husband and wife were often designated" as "brother" (*sn*) and "sister" (*snt*). The designation of Wisdom as a sister likewise evokes Abram's/Abraham's insistence that his wife Sarai/Sarah be represented as his sister in Genesis 12:13 and 20:2 (cf. Isaac's representation of Rebekah in Gen 26:7 as well).

[39] Jastrow, *Dictionary*, 1391. See as well Fox, *Proverbs 1–9*, 174, who writes: "To be sure the verb *qanah* 'acquire' is used of taking a wife in MH." He adds, however, that "it is not so used in the Bible." Fox, at this point in his commentary, does not address Ruth 4:5 or 4:10. Cf. Fuhs, *Das Buch der Sprichwörter*, 93.

The vocabulary in these lines is reminiscent of 2:4 and 3:14–15, but here personified Wisdom herself rather than the father addresses the hearer with the rhetoric of wealth.[40] She also uses the imperative as did the teaching voice in chapter four. Taken together these features contribute to a forcefulness of language most evident in the first stich of verse ten. It literally reads: "Take my instruction and not silver!"[41] This kind of formulation leaves nearly nothing to inference. Though the second half of verse ten and verse eleven employ the language of comparison as earlier passages do, in the first half of verse ten Wisdom does not state that she is *as* valuable, or even *more* valuable, than wealth; nor is the addressee admonished to use material possessions to acquire her. Rather she states clearly and simply that the hearer, the one who would be wise, should *not* acquire "silver," but only her instruction and knowledge.

This is strong rhetoric and Proverbs 8:10–11 is another instance where any suggestion that an "act-consequence" notion is at work in Proverbs needs nuance. A position like Whybray's, for instance, is inadequate. He suggests the text in 8:10 can insist on the value of wisdom over riches because ultimately wisdom will provide the son with practical skills that will allow him not only "to make money but to keep it and increase it."[42] However, as we have seen, the rhetorical force of 8:10a suggests not merely that wisdom is more valuable than riches, but that the son should not bother to accumulate wealth at all. The text at this juncture (as was the case in the prologue) employs no cause and effect rhetoric and says nothing about any ultimate attainment of wealth as a goal of wisdom.

McKane is closer to the mark when he writes:

---

[40] Verse 11 slips back into the third person, which might imply that Wisdom's direct address has ended, at least temporarily. But it is simpler to understand *personified* Wisdom to be speaking of the value of the comprehensive (or meta) *virtue* of wisdom so that verse 11 remains a part of her direct speech.

[41] For the syntax see *Gesenius' Hebrew Grammar* edited by A. E. Cowley and E. Kautzsch (*GKC*) paragraph *152g*.

[42] Whybray, *Proverbs*, 104. Yoder describes the rhetoric of chs. 1–9 as a whole in a similar fashion, though it is unclear precisely how she understands it to be functioning. She writes: "The sage assures the young men that if they seek her [Wisdom] diligently, they will find her and reap socio-economic rewards. In this act-consequence worldview those who call Wisdom their 'sister' are guaranteed to get ahead while conversely, the foolish live in poverty, the just fruits of their laziness and immorality." If the son "chooses wisely, he will live richly." See Yoder, *Woman of Substance*, 103–104; cf. 97.

> The intention vv.10f. is not to speak disparagingly of the value of coral, silver, gold and delights or pleasures. On the contrary, in order that the comparison should have point, the great value of these other commodities has to be assumed. These are indeed great prizes and they are in no way incompatible with wisdom or righteousness or knowledge (cf. v. 18), provided they exist within a framework of values in which the priority of wisdom, with its derivatives, discipline and knowledge, is assumed. Otherwise wealth may be vulgarity and a man may have it without *kābōd*—without *gravitas*—in which case it will detract from, rather than add to, his status. The man of weight in the community has a material prosperity which befits his status, but the man who has gold and silver is not necessarily a man of weight.[43]

McKane is correct in that the passage is not so much relativizing the value of material wealth as it is simply insisting that wisdom is remarkably valuable; and far from deprecating the value of riches, the instructing voice is exploiting the image of riches in order to demonstrate Wisdom's worth. As in 3:15, the multivalent חפץ in 8:11 likewise points to the more abstract notion of "desire." None of the son's desires (in whatever form—erotic, economic, social status) are as "desirable" as wisdom. This, however, once more suggests that any understanding of the wealth rhetoric as primarily literal language must give way to a symbolic understanding, something that McKane's analysis does not make clear.

McKane is also close to the mark in suggesting that riches are not "incompatible with wisdom . . . provided they exist within a framework of values in which the priority of wisdom . . . is assumed." However, he introduces the notion of honor and social status here in a manner that is somewhat curious and misleading. There is, in fact, no explicit mention of "honor" (כבוד) in the passage and McKane seems to imply a parity or equality between wisdom and high social status. Although honor or high social status, along with wealth and erotic fulfillment, is an aspect of human flourishing, and in the sages' wisdom mythos ought to be what the wise person receives, it too is merely an aspect of Proverbs' vision of the good life. Like wealth, it too is a lesser good that needs to be properly ordered under wisdom. Though absent in this passage, when the rhetoric of honor is present in Proverbs it functions, as has been noted, in a way analogous to wealth imagery (cf. 3:14–16; 4:5–9). It demonstrates the

[43] McKane, *Proverbs*, 346.

desirability of the virtuous life of wisdom; and its deployment in this manner functions in part precisely to prevent the hearer from mistaking the attainment of this lesser good with what it considers the true key to human flourishing—the virtues of wisdom's way.

Finally it is important to recognize that in 8:10–11 matters concerning wisdom are framed for the hearer as a choice. The instructing voice recognizes that its addressee will encounter other voices or competing discourses—i.e., the general and diffuse social script already spoken of—that will tell him to choose wealth and that the acquisition of riches (or other lesser goods such as honor), and not wisdom's virtues, is the key to human flourishing. In this sense the "great prizes" (McKane) of vv. 10–11 are "incompatible with wisdom" for, as has been suggested, the inordinate pursuit of lesser goods, especially if it leads to the kinds of deeds in which the sinners in chapter one engage, will undermine the realization of the flourishing life characterized by the social equity and harmony that Proverbs, from the book's outset, envisions.

3.2.e. *Proverbs 8:18–21*

A few verses later in 8:18 personified Wisdom again employs the rhetoric of riches. After claiming in vv. 12–16 that she possesses a litany of virtues (knowledge, foresight, counsel, resourcefulness, courage, and the ability to rule justly), Wisdom turns finally to the language of wealth in addressing a young man. In v. 17 she promises to be found by those who love and seek her, with vv. 18–19 adding:

עשר־וכבוד אתי הון עתק וצדקה
טוב פריי מחרוץ ומפז ותבואתי מכסף נבחר

> Riches and honor belong to me, enduring wealth and success.
> My fruit is better than gold, fine gold, and my produce is better than choice silver.[44]

In this final, explicit, mention of wealth in chapters 1–9 the instructing voice continues, as Bakhtin might suggest, to color wealth and poverty rhetoric with its own hues. The text introduces in verse 19, for instance, the term פז, which is paralleled with חרוץ, a word which itself up to this point has only been employed twice (3:14; 8:10).

[44] The translation follows NJPS.

The passage is also reminiscent of 3:14–16 where Wisdom likewise is said to be better than precious metals (cf. 8:10–11) and to hold riches and honor. As in that chapter, it is sometimes thought that Wisdom here (v. 18 in particular) is literally promising the hearer literal material rewards.[45] The not unreasonable assumption is that if Wisdom possesses wealth, then the one who finds wisdom will naturally attain wealth too. However, the tension noted earlier between the claim that wisdom is "better than" wealth, but also "possesses" wealth (8:10–11, 18 vs. 8:19) once more emerges in these *meshalim*. As in chapters three and four, the personification of Wisdom also suggests the text ought to be regarded as operating in a metaphorical manner. The point is not merely that the one who possesses the intellectual, practical, and social virtues that comprise the comprehensive (or meta) virtue of wisdom will necessarily attain to wealth. Nor is the point simply that the wise person will strive after wealth only in legitimate and righteous ways.[46] Rather the verse describes the accoutrements that adorn Wisdom in order to demonstrate the desirability and value of the virtue for which she is a personification. As in 3:14–16, not only does she possess desirable things, an enticement in themselves, she herself is again said to be more valuable than these enticements. By explicitly taking up the rhetoric of valuable

[45] For instance, Plöger (*Sprüche Salomos*, 90) claims the things that wisdom promises "are surely 'material goods,' such as riches . . ." (*sind sicherlich >>materielle<< Werte, wie Reichtum* . . .). Garrett recognizes that not all of Wisdom's "benefits are material in nature," but nonetheless writes that Wisdom's claim to bestow wealth "should be taken in a literal rather than a metaphorical sense; through wise behavior one can attain material prosperity." See Duane A. Garrett, *Proverbs, Ecclesiastes, Song of Songs* (NAC 14; Nashville: Broadman Press, 1993), 108. Others likewise seem to assume that Wisdom's gifts, including wealth, should be understood in a straightforward literal manner. Cf. Toy, *Proverbs*, 169–170; Clifford, *Proverbs* 95; Perdue, *Proverbs*, 142; Murphy, *Proverbs*, 51. McKane, too, believes wisdom will bestow literal wealth, but distinguishes this from "vulgar opulence." He insists that Wisdom offers both wealth and property, but again that this is not "meretricious or speculative wealth." Rather it is "located in a framework of values and is an ingredient of a way of life which bestows *gravitas* and social wholeness." See McKane, *Proverbs* 350. This is close to my position, but see my comments on 8:10 above. Whybray offers a less sophisticated account. He writes: "'The wealth offered by Wisdom is not to be understood in a figurative sense but is quite literally material wealth which, because it is gained through Wisdom rather than directly as an end in itself, is more worthwhile than gold and silver obtained in the usual way without regard to her." See *Proverbs*, 126. See also Yoder, *Woman of Substance*, 97, 103–104.

[46] See, for instance, Fox, *Proverbs 1–9*, 278. Even if the latter is the case, it is not necessarily the whole point.

material wealth and associating it with Wisdom, the instructing voice first and foremost is employing wealth language as a textual symbol of the positive, desirable, and valuable in order to convince its addressee of the value of the virtuous life.[47] One should not deny that the rhetoric includes a general promise of good things (including material well-being). However, to make the acquisition of actual riches the point of the teaching is to overstate that element and distort the nature of the rhetoric.[48]

The most significant aspect of 8:18, however, is the particularly forceful way the line ties together much of what comes before. The Hebrew, recall, reads:

עשר־וכבוד אתי הון עתק וצדקה

The first two words here—riches and honor—are identical to the last two words of 3:16 and the thrust of the rhetoric in both texts is to a large extent the same (see above). The second half of 8:18, however, is more intriguing.

Recall that in chapter one, the abstract and general term הון was on the lips of the sinners, who were promising the son "all precious wealth" (כל הון יקר). The instructing voice, however, discredited this claim, and since that point has responded to the sinners' offer by itself employing the rhetoric of "all kinds of wealth" in order to persuade the son to choose the right way, even while largely avoiding the wealth language the sinners employ. Instead of speaking of הון ("wealth") the instructing voice of chapters 1–9 makes use of more concrete images of gold, silver, coral, etc., as well as the rhetoric of economic exchange.[49]

---

[47] Yoder in *Woman of Substance*, 103, too, recognizes that wealth or "money" is one of the "primary means by which the sage *motivates* the young men to choose Wisdom," but apparently accepts that this motivation is to be understood as a literal promise, i.e., resulting in real material rewards for the one who chooses wisdom. I.e., she suggests that "money . . . becomes an objective means to evaluate *human* worth" (italics added). However, it is not that "economic success is the mark of superior moral character whereas poverty signifies moral deficiency," but rather simply that material wealth is the means by which the text values the ways of wisdom and folly. Wealth and poverty language does not "evaluate *human* worth" but rather the worth or relative desirability of virtue and vice.

[48] The act-consequence nexus, recall, is not a mechanistic order through which one can infallibly predict outcomes. Rather it is a symbolic construction of the world within which the values and virtues of the sages make sense.

[49] Besides the sinners' use of the term in 1:13 and Wisdom's words here in 8:18,

In fact one can trace a progression in Proverbs' use of the rhetoric of wealth thus far. After the sinners are done speaking, the instructing voice in chapter two admonishes the son to seek wisdom *as* he would silver and treasures. In chapter three the father is clear that Wisdom, who holds "riches" (3:16), possesses a value that is *greater than* that of gold, rubies, as well as various kinds of "goods" or "desires" (something only implicit in chapter two). In chapter four the father, in appealing to the authority of his father, next employs the *imperative* (vs. the indicative in the preceding) to admonish the son to *use* whatever material possessions he has *in order to acquire* Wisdom—so much more valuable is she than wealth. In 8:10–11, it is *personified Wisdom herself* who admonishes the son in the imperative. She cries: "Take my teaching and not silver!"—reiterating how much better she is than gold, corals, or any good or desirable thing. Now in 8:18, the text takes up the sinners' own terminology (הון), but utters it with what in a Bakhtinian sense might be called a unique accent. Wisdom possesses something slightly, but significantly, different than the wealth the sinners promise. She holds not "precious wealth" (הון יקר), but "lasting wealth" (הון עתק).

The *hapax* עתק (*ʿātēq*) is a difficult and obscure word. The root ע-ת-ק, however, is attested 20 times in MT, including three times in Aramaic, and its basic sense seems to be something like "move forward."[50] In Proverbs another form of the root appears only in 25:1, which introduces the collection of sayings that Hezekiah's men העתיקו ("copied," "transmitted"). Yet forms of the root are translated variously in different contexts throughout the Bible. Here in Prov 8:18 Plöger, for instance, believes the thrust of the root suggests the "increase of wealth" (*Vermehrung des Vermögens*) and renders הון עתק as "*Vermehrtes Vermögen*" or "increased wealth."[51] In Job 21:7 the root ע-ת-ק is again deployed in connection with wealth language. In this verse the protagonist asks:

מדוע רשעים יחיו עתקו גם־גברו חיל

Why do the wicked live on, prosper and grow wealthy?[52]

הון only appears in the direct instruction of 3:9 (see below) and in 6:31 where the adulterer, it is claimed, will loose all the wealth of his house. Besides 8:18, the general and abstract עשר ("riches") likewise appears in chs. 1–9 only in 3:16.

[50] H. Schmoldt, "עתק," *TDOT* 11:456–58.

[51] Plöger, *Sprüche Salomos*, 90.

[52] The translation follows NJPS.

Job is lamenting the fact that in contrast to his own situation, it often appears that the unjust, and all that is theirs (cf. Job 21:8–13), flourish over the years—i.e., they and their wealth "endure." Although various translations have been proposed for the adjective *ʿātēq* in Prov 8:18, it should be understood in the context of the kinds of issues with which Job is wrestling and is best rendered something like "enduring."[53] As does Job in Job 21:7, the instructing voice in Prov 8:18 is at least in part making a claim about who and what perseveres. Job (at this point in his discourse) perceives matters one way: the wicked and their wealth endure. Proverbs, however, insists that it is Wisdom who holds "wealth" that endures.

From at least Ptahhotep, ancient Near Eastern wisdom literature (especially the Egyptian instructions) has often been concerned with communicating to its audience the unpredictable nature of wealth.[54] The wisdom tradition also demonstrates a concern that its audiences distinguish, or be able to discern, what is valuable (including material wealth) in terms of what is "enduring" or "long lasting" and not easily lost. What exactly the various wisdom books have in mind by deploying such rhetoric of course requires close consideration of each text. In Proverbs, however, Wisdom's riches, the valuable and desirable thing she possesses, are the virtues of wisdom's way. And for this book, it is this symbolic "wealth" that endures in contrast to the wealth of the sinners, which they clearly do not live to enjoy (1:18–19).[55]

---

[53] Toy uniquely translates הון עתק as "lordly wealth" in *Proverbs*, 168–69. But this is not a good rendering; cf. the discussion in Fox, *Proverbs 1–9*, 277–278.

[54] Consider, for example, maxim 30 in Ptahhotep, which resonates with Qohelet's sense that enjoyment of life's goods is a gift of God. It reads: "If you are great after having been humble, have gained wealth after having been poor in the past, in a town which you know, knowing your former condition, do not put your trust in wealth which came to you as a gift of god; so that you will not fall behind one like you, to whom the same happened." The Instruction of Any says more concisely: "As to him who was rich last year; He is a vagabond this year." Similarly Ankhsheshonq 18:17 reminds its hearer that, "Wealth comes to an end," and in 26:7–8 (in a manner similar to Prov 11:24) that, "There is he who saves and does not profit. All are in the hand of the fate and the god." The examples could be multiplied. The translations are all from Miriam Lichtheim, *Ancient Egyptian Literature: A Book of Readings* (3 vols.; Berkeley: University of California Press, 1973).

[55] Cf. maxims 5, 6, and 19 in Ptahhotep, which resonate with a perspective found in Proverbs. For example, maxim 5 reads in part: "Baseness may seize riches, yet crime never lands its wares; In the end it is justice that lasts." Maxim 6: "If a man says: 'I shall be rich' . . . 'I shall rob someone,' he will end being given to a stranger. People's schemes do not prevail, God's command is what prevails." After the warning, "Guard against the vice of greed," maxim 19 states: "That man endures whose rule is rightness." All translations are from Lichtheim, *Ancient Egyptian Literature.*

Proverbs knows that material riches (and other lesser goods) are important and desirable aspects of a flourishing life. But Proverbs also recognizes that these by their nature must remain external to the one who possesses them. They are thus subject to changes in a person's fortune and inherently unreliable and ephemeral (something Job knows all too well). As a component of a person's character, however, wisdom's virtues by contrast are internal to the one who possesses them and so not subject to changes in circumstance and fortune. Thus they are enduring and so imminently more reliable, valuable, and desirable than any external good. In the idiom of the wisdom mythos I spoke of in Chapter Two, they are part of the genuine structure of the cosmos. Wisdom's "wealth" is hence "true" or "real" wealth. It is "wealth" that is genuinely valuable and the key to human flourishing. It is "enduring" and leads to "life."

However, Wisdom possesses not simply enduring wealth, but "lasting wealth *and righteousness*" (*הון עתק וצדקה*). The NJPS translation renders צדקה in 8:18 as "success" and the NRSV as "prosperity." Likewise Clifford translates "rich rewards;" Yoder adopts the rendering "prosperity" without comment.[56] As with decisions to render השכל in 1:3 along the lines of "success" (see Chapter Two) such translations of צדקה appear based on a notion that the point of Proverbs is to serve as a guide to successful living, including especially the attainment of material prosperity. The close proximity of the rhetoric of material wealth to צדקה in 8:18 may also lead translators to seek out parallel economic meanings for this term, especially if one understands the כבוד in the verse as pointing to material wealth (or the entire phrase עשר וכבוד as *hendiadys*).[57]

These sorts of interpretations and renderings of 8:18 are not impossible. Moreover, up to this point I have been highlighting the figurative use of economic language as a means of ascribing worth to wisdom and its virtues so that it might seem appropriate to regard the rhetoric of righteousness in 8:18 to be functioning in an expanded sense as well. However, nowhere else in Proverbs does צדקה carry the sense of "prosperity." Although texts such as Joel 2:23 are sometimes

[56] Clifford, *Proverbs*, 91. Yoder, *Woman of Substance*, 98–99. Oesterley (*Proverbs*, 60) writes: "in the present context it [צדקה] has the sense of 'prosperity.'" Plöger (*Sprüche Salomos*, 90) writes similarly; cf. Toy, *Proverbs*, 168–170.

[57] As suggested above, however, it is better not to treat the phrase as an instance of *hendiadys*. For כבוד with the meaning "wealth," see M. Weinfeld, "כבוד," *TDOT* 7:22–38, esp. 25–26.

marshaled as evidence for such a usage elsewhere in HB, the meaning of the word in such passages is ambiguous.[58] As I just noted Prov 8:18–21 also marks the pinnacle of a progression in the discourse of wealth and poverty in the first major section of the book—chapters 1–9. Together with the fact that verse 8:18 deploys language that hearkens back to key phrases in earlier chapters—i.e., the prologue's underscoring of "justice and righteousness and equity" (צדק ומשפט ומישרים) and the robbers' claim to be seeking "all precious wealth" (כל הון יקר)—these observations suggests that one should strive to discern how the passage fits more precisely within this larger discourse.

As I just intimated, "righteousness," is one of the key notions the text uses to express the virtue of social justice, which the prologue indicates is of primary importance to Proverbs. To be precise, in 1:3 the term employed was צדק rather than צדקה. Yet the two words are cognate forms and each evokes ancient Near Eastern notions of social justice.[59] This is especially so when they are deployed in close connection with other social justice terms, as in the prologue where משפט and מישרים follow צדק immediately. Such is also the case here in chapter eight, for verse 20 has personified Wisdom declare:

בארח־צדקה אהלך בתוך נתיבות משפט

I walk on a way of righteousness, in the midst of a path of justice.

The rhetoric of the second half of v. 18 thus is not so much valuing the virtues of wisdom (as previous wealth language in chapters 1–9 has done) as 1) *explaining why what she possesses is so much more valuable than literal wealth.* Wisdom and the virtues of wisdom's way not only belong to the structure of the cosmos as the wisdom mythos suggests, they are enduring, long lasting, and not subject to changes in circumstance and fortune. The stich, however, also 2) *reminds* the

[58] See Oesterley, *Proverbs*, 60 and especially Toy, *Proverbs*, 169–170 who offers a fuller explanation and further potential parallels. See, too, the discussion in Fox, *Proverbs 1–9*, 278; Plöger, *Sprüche Salomos*, 90; and below. In later Hebrew, of course, צדקה can carry an economic connotation and mean something like "almsgiving"; see Jastrow, *Dictionary*, 1263–64. However, this reflects a development from its usual meaning of "righteousness" in biblical Hebrew.

[59] For a discussion of ancient Near Eastern terminology and ideas of social justice see Moshe Weinfeld, *Social Justice in Ancient Israel and in the Ancient Near East* (Jerusalem: Magnes, 1995).

reader of *what Proverbs understands one of the most important virtues of wisdom's way to be*—social justice and harmony. Thus one ought to say the *waw* in v. 18's וצדקה functions as an epexegetical or "explanatory *waw*" and the term (צדקה) should be translated in its usual way, and as it is universally rendered in verse 20, i.e., as "righteousness."[60]

Finally, as with the rhetoric of 3:16 and 8:18, some commentators will understand Wisdom's concluding words in this section of Proverbs, namely 8:21, as a straightforward promise of literal material rewards for the one who attains wisdom—though often with the caveat that the wise person will gain wealth by honest means and that material prosperity is subordinated to Wisdom's morality.[61] After speaking of her "fruit" and "produce" in v. 19 and the nature of her way in v. 20, Wisdom states in v. 21:

להנחיל אהבי יש ואצרתיהם אמלא

I will bequeath to those who love me wealth; I will fill their treasuries.[62]

Wisdom here promises יש to the ones who love her and will fill the storehouses of the same. The word יש (regularly the particle of existence, "there is") in this instance is usually rendered something like "inheritance" or "wealth." This is perhaps appropriate.[63] If so, by

[60] For the epexegetical *waw* see *GKC*, paragraph *154a* n. 1. With this emphasis on justice Proverbs also resonates with other ancient Near Eastern wisdom instructions like Ptahhotep. See again the sayings from Ptahhotep cited in n. 53 above—especially maxims 5 and 19. Many commentators likewise indicate that צדקה in 8:18 ought to be translated in its usual way. See, for example, McKane, *Proverbs*, 350; Perdue, *Proverbs*, 142. These, however, either do not discuss the term in much detail or do not understand the meaning of צדקה in quite the manner I do; and none relate it to the virtues articulated in the prologue. McKane, for instance, notes only (though correctly) that to translate צקדה as "'success' or 'prosperity' is to oversimplify the relation of 'rightness' to 'wealth.'" Perdue suggests that "righteousness" in 8:18 should be understood as "the just order that pervades the cosmos, regulates and sustains human society, and enables its kings and governors to rule wisely." Again though there is certainly an aspect of this in the "social justice" connotations I am arguing for, this heavily cosmic slant obscures the concrete particulars of the biblical vision of social justice and seems a more appropriate description of (Woman) Wisdom than the nature of the righteousness she is said to possess. See further Fox, *Proverbs 1–9*, 278, who writes that "there is no need to ascribe a special sense" to צדקה in 8:18. He, however, suggests the term here "refers to wealth gained righteously and honestly" (see below). Cf. Plöger, *Sprüche Salomos*, 90.

[61] See Van Leeuwen, "Proverbs," *NIB* 5:92; Garrett, *Proverbs*, 108. Cf. Meinhold, *Die Sprüche*, 1:143; Fox, *Proverbs 1–9*, 278.

[62] The translation follows NRSV's rendering of יש.

[63] Such a rendering, however, is by no means certain. In classical Hebrew יש is thought to function as a substantive meaning "possessions," or something similar,

this point in Proverbs 1–9, a wise and discerning reader however knows how to hear and understand this wealth trope, occurring as it does in a clearly symbolic context where personified wisdom acts. The term יש here not only points to wisdom's promise to deliver material security, it is a symbol that points to the value and desirability of virtue and all the well-being that comes from attaining it. Personified Wisdom is primarily promising to bequeath to the one who finds her an ultimate good and the particle is probably bettered rendered something like "being," "existence" or "life"—an understanding which also accords well with the book's larger rhetorical strategy of the two ways.[64] Having made the turn from the concrete language of precious metals and treasures to general and abstract "wealth" terminology by employing הון in 8:18, the instructing voice has simply continued on this course by substantivizing the particle of existence in v. 21.

Similarly, when Wisdom in 8:21 promises to fill her lovers' storehouses, it is necessary to ask with what she is promising to fill them. Perhaps it is some kind of material good, the inheritance or "wealth" mentioned earlier in the passage, for instance. The nature of the metaphor in the immediate context, however, suggests that what is most likely to be set in these storehouses is Wisdom's harvest of v. 19—i.e., "her fruit" and "her produce." Yoder argues that "the emphasis in the immediate context on wealth and riches (esp. 8:18, 21) suggests that the 'fruit' and 'yield' of which she speaks are her monetary earnings." This may be true to the extent that Wisdom is metaphorically presented as a potential, profitable bride. However, it is again important to remember that Wisdom is not a real Persian period woman of worth, whether or not Proverbs describes her in such terms or not. If the text is not literally promising the hearer baskets of figs and olives or barns full of grains (i.e., real fruit and produce), it is also not only or primarily promising monetary earnings.[65]

only here and in Sirach 42:3 (less likely in Prov 13:23 and 20:15). In the Ben Sira passage, however, the marginal reading of MS B, וישר, suggests that ויש may be an error; or at least it may not be the best reading. Jastrow, *Dictionary*, 598, also lists "wealth" as one of the appropriate renderings of the term in rabbinic literature, but "being" and "substance" as well, which, I will suggest, are better translations of the term in 18:21. Cf. Fox, *Proverbs 1–9*, 278.

[64] See the previous note and esp. Jastrow, *Dictionary*, 598.

[65] Yoder, *Woman of Substance*, 99.

The agricultural images in 18:21 rather are symbols that point not merely to themselves but to the value or desirability of Wisdom and her virtues—i.e., that which the instructing voice has been highlighting from the beginning of its instruction (from the prologue on). As with 4:5–8, and other passages throughout chapters 1–9, the text in 8:21 employs images from familiar realms to express something about the intangible and less familiar sphere of moral life. In this case, the economic rhetoric of agricultural bounty combines with traces of a discourse of erotic desire (note the language of "love" in v. 19) to express the desirability of the virtuous life of wisdom.

It is, of course, not inevitable that every reader will regard the *meshalim* of 8:18–21, or others in Proverbs, in the figurative manner for which I have been arguing. However, for the one who takes seriously the prologue's invitation to pursue Proverbs' wisdom through a consideration of the book's tropes and figures, the text points in this direction, inviting the reader or hearer not to neglect the text's literal meaning, but to move beyond it.

3.3. Direct Instruction in Proverbs 1–9

I suggested above that Proverbs employs the rhetoric of wealth and poverty primarily in two ways: as a symbol to value virtue and in direct instruction concerning economic matters. Chapters 1–9 are most concerned to present the value and desirability of wisdom's way. They do not offer as much direct economic instruction or observation as subsequent chapters. Nonetheless, the instructing voice in these initial chapters occasionally employs the rhetoric of wealth and poverty to begin constructing a concrete economic ethic for its addressee. Personified Wisdom and the father instruct the son how he should act in a variety of circumstances where matters of wealth and poverty/rich and poor (and other economic issues) are at stake. Although such direct wealth and poverty instruction is distinct from the symbolic and motivational use of such language, it emerges from the same moral horizon; namely, a concern that wisdom's vision of a good and flourishing life, with its emphasis on virtue, and especially the virtue of social justice and harmony, find expression.

3.3.a. *Proverbs 3:9–10*

In chapter three, via a series of imperatives in verses 1, 3, 5, and 7, which are coupled with a motivational clause of some sort, the father exhorts the hearer to tend to instruction and his commandments, to hold fast to truth and faithfulness, to trust in the Lord, not to be wise in one's own eyes, and to fear the Lord. The instructing voice then in 3:9–10 admonishes the son:

כבד את־יהוה מהונך ומראשית כל־תבואתך
וימלאו אסמיך שבע ותירוש יקביך יפרצו

> Honor the Lord with your wealth and with the first fruits of all your produce.
> And your barns will be filled with grain, your vats will burst with new wine.[66]

There is little about 3:9 to suggest that the rhetoric of riches is being used figuratively as a positive motivational symbol.[67] In this verse, however, the father employs the same term as the sinners do in chapter one, הון ("wealth"). But as is the case in that chapter, the father clearly distinguishes his discourse of wealth from that of the robbers'. Whereas the sinners were attempting to lure the son onto their path by the promise of הון יקר, here the father instructs the son specifically as to what he should do with his הון. The deployment of the imperative, moreover, reinforces the patriarch's claim to authority over the hearer. What *the father* has to say about wealth is once more what matters, not any other discourse or social script; and in this instance he insists the son fulfill his cultic duties, as the language of the second verse half intimates.[68]

---

[66] "Grain" is *śābāʿ* ("abundance, satiety"). Older interpreters (e.g., Toy, *Proverbs*, 62; Oesterley, *Proverbs*, 21; cf. Fichtner's notes in the *BHS* apparatus) noting the LXX rendering (πλεσμονῆς σίτου) suggest emending (to *šeber*). However, the Phoenician Karatepe inscription (A III 7–9) provides a Semitic parallel for the usage (שבע ותרש). See Herbert Dönner and Wolfgang Röllig, *Kanaanische und Aramaische Inschriften* (3 vols.; Wiesbaden: Harrasowitz, 1962), 1:69 (text # 26). See further Mitchell Dahood, *Proverbs and Northwest Semitic Philology* (SPIB 113; Rome: Pontifical Biblical Institute, 1963), 9. Cf. McKane, *Proverbs*, 294; Fox, *Proverbs 1–9*, 151–52.

[67] As I argued above, however, the instructing voice can also take up this same wealth vocabulary (הון) in more figurative terms (e.g., 8:18).

[68] The phrase ומראשית כל תבואתך resonates with the cultic language associated with the presentation of the first fruits and most commentators understand the verse as one of the few allusions in the book to the Israelite cult. Particularly Deut 26:2, but also sometimes Exod 23:19 and Num 28:26 are adduced as parallels. However,

In 3:10, although the father does not employ explicit wealth and poverty vocabulary, the line's agricultural imagery nevertheless creates a vision of prosperity so that this verse, too, should be said to belong to the discourse of wealth and poverty. The point of verse ten is to motivate the hearer to obey what is said in verse nine. Taken together the two lines suggest a cause and effect relationship between honoring YHWH with one's wealth and material blessing; hence the lines are a good example of Proverbs' wisdom prosperity, or act-consequence, frame of reference. Interpreters generally recognize this rhetoric of promise and usually understand such language in simple literal fashion as a straightforward assurance of material prosperity.[69] However, as I suggested in Chapter Two, expressions of the act-consequence nexus are not the kind of talk one ought to understand in simple literal fashion. The wisdom mythos predisposes the sages to "see" an act-consequence mechanism at work in the world and to screen out non-conforming examples. Such rhetoric thus should not be thought to be presenting a vision of the world

since the imperatives of earlier verses urge the son to take some action regarding some intangible (e.g., v. 1 instruction and commands; v. 3 "faithfulness" and "truth"; v. 4 "favor"; v. 5 YHWH himself), one is tempted to render 3:9 with Cohen as: "Honor the Lord more than your wealth and more than your choicest income." See Haim Cohen, "Two Misunderstood Verses in the Book of Proverbs," *Shnaton* 11 (1997): 139–152. (Cohen's article is in Hebrew, but an English summary is provided on pp. XVI–XVII.) So too Fuhs, *Das Buch der Sprichwörter*, 74. Such a sentiment would not be out of place in Proverbs 1–9. The weight of scholarly opinion, however, is against Cohen and Fuhs. See, for example, Plöger, *Sprüche Salomos*, 32, 34–35; McKane, *Proverbs*, 293; Murphy, *Proverbs*, 21; Clifford, *Proverbs*, 52; Whybray, *Proverbs*, 63. Toy (*Proverbs*, 62), however, is skeptical that 3:9 alludes to the cult; cf. Fuhs, *Das Buch der Sprichwörter*, 74. For a further, brief critique of Cohen's suggestion, see Fox, *Proverbs 1–9*, 151. Other possible cultic allusions in the book include: 14:9; 15:8; 20:25; 21:3, 8, 27 and perhaps 20:9 and 30:12. On the question of wisdom's relationship to the cult more generally see, for example, Leo G. Perdue, *Wisdom and Cult: A Critical Analysis of the Views of Cult in the Wisdom Literature of Israel and the Ancient Near East* (Nashville, 1975); cf. von Rad, *Wisdom in Israel*, 186–89.

[69] Without hinting that the gifts of 3:10 ought to be considered in anything other than a literal manner, Toy, for instance, writes that, "the reward for honoring Yahweh is here physical." See *Proverbs*, 63. Similarly, Whybray notes: "This is the most blatant expression in the Old Testament of the principle of *do ut des*—the offering of gifts to God solely in order to elicit material rewards from him." See *Proverbs*, 63. Van Leeuwen speaks of a "practical 'payoff'" and a "natural outcome" and "natural symmetry" between that which one gives to God and the "blessings . . . which ensue." See "Proverbs," *NIB* 5:49. Fox too states that, "God will reward gifts to him (v. 9) by enhancing the giver's own prosperity." See *Proverbs 1–9*, 151.

that is verifiable in some empirical fashion. It rather has to do with a certain perception of the nature of creation and a subsequent effort at ordering one's life by wisdom's virtues so that it is in sync with the generative forces of the cosmos.

In regard to 3:10 in particular, notice that the language of "blessing," with its images of overflowing barns and bursting vats, is paradisiacal or utopian. The text's rhetoric is one of extravagance. It is this extravagance that signals v. 10's formulation of the act-consequence nexus is an idealized one. Although 3:9 offers direct instruction regarding wealth and so can be said to be constructing a kind of concrete economic ethic for the hearer, 3:10 motivates this concrete instruction in a manner analogous to the way the text so often elsewhere motivates the quest for wisdom. Proverbs 3:10, that is, taps into the wisdom mythos and certainly constructs for the reader a general promise of well being, which surely includes a degree of material prosperity. However, to focus too fully and literally on the images of material prosperity is again to overstate that element of the promise and to distort the thrust of the rhetoric. Those who strive to understand the sage's "tropes" and "figures" will recognize that these agricultural symbols represent not merely a promise of material well being, but reveal as well that the father's demand in v. 9, as an aspect of the way of wisdom, is not taxing but pleasant and appealing—i.e., valuable and desirable.[70]

3.3.b. *Proverbs 3:27–28*

After the first twelve verses of chapter three implore the addressee to hold to the father's teaching and vv. 13–26 extol the benefits of wisdom, v. 27 begins a series of negative commands (vv. 27–31) that

[70] So too the medical image of 3:8 motivates the instruction of 3:7. Few, however, would argue that in these verses the sages' words suggest they believed that "fearing YHWH" and "turning from evil" would produce a literal "potion for the bones" (שקוי לעצמות). Clifford, for instance, intimates that vv. 7–8 promise "health, renewed physical energy." See *Proverbs*, 52. Similarly, Garrett writes that, "health naturally proceeds from the peaceful and well-ordered life that is submitted to God." See *Proverbs*, 81. Clearly for these writers "potion for the bones" is a trope for health. Though accepting the figurative nature of the image, the line's act-consequence rhetoric, however, is still often understood in a overly literalist manner. Health, a powerful symbol of well-being, should be viewed less as an automatic reward for the wise than a further image deployed to speak of the well being wisdom offers.

offer direct instruction regarding how the wise person will (or will not) live. The entire sub-section of vv. 27–31, which is followed by a number of motivations in vv. 32–35, might best be read together. However, only verses 27–28 reveal a concern with economic matters, albeit implicitly; an explicit wealth and poverty rhetoric is absent. Given the important figurative uses of wealth and poverty language elsewhere in Proverbs 1–9, the absence of explicit wealth and poverty terminology in a proverb that is likely concerned with economic issues is a first indication that these lines are of a different order than many of the passages discussed above. The lines read:

אל־תמנע־טוב מבעליו בהיות לאל ידיך לעשות
אל־תאמר לרעיך לך ושוב ומחר אתן ויש אתך

> Do not withhold good from the one who deserves it when you have the power to do it [for him] [71]
> Do not say to your fellow, "Come back again, I'll give it to you tomorrow," when you have it with you.

There is some uncertainty as to whether the father is offering instruction regarding almsgiving or borrowing, or presenting a general call to benevolence. If the concern is almsgiving, the son is to give what he is able and not attempt to remove himself from the obligation that the instructing voice places upon him to be kind to one in need. If, however, the phrase (word) "one who deserves it" (בעליו; lit. "its owner") does not mean 'one who deserves it because that person is in want,' but 'one who deserves it because that person is a creditor,' the father is admonishing the son to pay back debts in a timely and proper manner.

It is best to consider the lines to be concerned with giving to one who is impoverished. Injunctions to show kindness to the poor are common in Proverbs, as a consideration of the discourse of social justice will make clear (see Chapter Four). The LXX likewise understands an economic context of almsgiving, speaking in 3:27 of one who is "poor" (ἐνδεῖ). This view was adopted by subsequent Jewish interpreters as well.[72] Moreover, although elsewhere in Proverbs (par-

[71] The phrase "from the one who deserves it" renders מבעליו, which properly speaking is a plural form. The translation understands ידיך with the Qere as the sg. ידך. For the idiom לאל יד, see Gen 31:29; Deut 28:32; Mic 2:1; and cf. Oesterley, *Proverbs*, 26; Murphy, *Proverbs*, 20.

[72] On the interpretation of the line in subsequent Jewish tradition see Clifford,

ticularly the sentence sayings of chs. 10–29) טוב carries broader connotations of well being, verse 27's suggestion that the hearer might actually have in his possession that which he ought to give indicates as well that this term, and the lines generally, have to do with some kind of real transfer of material wealth.

The patriarchal voice in 3:27–28 thus is not employing economic rhetoric to a larger didactic end as do many other wealth and poverty verses in Prov 1–9. It is rather offering the hearer concrete instruction regarding the way in which he should handle his wealth in relation to a needy person in particular. The lines presuppose that the son may be disinclined to act in the prescribed manner. This is likely due to the fact that the text recognizes its hearer is susceptible to a wrong understanding regarding the role of wealth in human well being. He is likely not only to overvalue it and pursue it passionately, but to hold on to it at all costs, even the cost of the well being of another.

3.3.c. *Proverbs 6:1–5*

The father begins chapter six by presenting three potential roles he hopes the hearer will reject, but knows him susceptible to playing: the person involved in surety matters (vv. 1–5); the lazy person (vv. 6–11); and the deceptive scoundrel (12–15).[73] In the description of the first of these roles (vv. 1–5), the instructing voice employs an explicit economic rhetoric. The father imagines a situation where the son is (already) mixed up in a troubling affair: "My son, if you have provided surety to your neighbor" (v. 1). The father proceeds to instruct his pupil how such a state of affairs should be handled: "So do this, my child" (v. 3). He likens a person found in such a

Proverbs, 58. Fox names Rashi, Ramaq, Radaq, "and many others" in this regard. See *Proverbs 1–9*, 165. Alonso Schöckel and Vilchez appear to adopt a view similar to the traditional one, citing Deut 15:9. See L. Alonso Schöckel and J. Vilchez, *Proverbios* (Nueva Biblia Española, Sapienciales I.; Madrid: Ediciones Cristiandad, 1984), 189. See too Perdue, *Proverbs*, 108. Fox, however, argues that the passage does not have to do with "charity or kindness" but with a general obligation to assist others. See *Proverbs 1–9*, 164–65. Similarly, McKane understands the injunction broadly as a general call to benevolence and helpfulness. See *Proverbs*, 299; cf. Toy, *Proverbs*, 77–78.

[73] The essential features of 6:6–11 are taken up in the nearly identical 24:30–34, treated in Chapter Four.

situation to an animal ensnared and taken by a hunter or fowler (vv. 2, 5). The one who goes surety is similarly "trapped" by his words and, the text claims, his very life is endangered. Hence the addressee in 6:3 is commanded to "grovel" and "badger" his neighbor in order to free himself from his economic obligation. The passage reads in its entirety:

(1) בני אם־ערבת לרעך תקעת לזר כפיך
(2) נוקשת באמרי־פיך נלכדת באמרי־פיך
(3) עשה זאת אפוא בני והנצל כי באת בכף־רעך
לך התרפס ורהב רעיך
(4) אל־תתן שנה לעיניך ותנומה לעפעפיך
(5) הנצל כצבי מיד וכצפור מיד יקוש

1) My son, if you provide surety to your neighbor, if you clap hands for a stranger;
2) If you have ensnared yourself by the words of your mouth, if you are captured by the words of your mouth;
3) Do this, then, my son and save yourself, for you have come into the hand of your neighbor. Go grovel and badger your neighbor.
4) Do not give sleep to your eyes nor slumber to your eyelids.
5) Escape like a gazelle from a hunter, like a bird from the hand of the fowler.[74]

The Hebrew of verse one is somewhat ambiguous. Particularly problematic is the rendering of the verb ערב, which can mean to "provide surety, act as guarantor" or "seek surety." Although the neighbor (רע) in the verse might be the borrower, this is not likely. As Fox notes, verse three warns of "falling into the power of 'your neighbor'" and that "a guarantor does not become dependent on the borrower's good will but on the creditor's." It thus makes the best sense to "identify the 'neighbor' as the lender and the 'stranger' (זר) as the borrower" and so the addressee as guarantor.[75] Hence, in the translation above, the hearer is imagined as providing surety "to" his neighbor and "for" a stranger.

Because advice regarding surety is not uncommon in biblical and ancient Near Eastern wisdom literature, and because other verses in Proverbs that speak of the practice are similar in sentiment to 6:1–5,

[74] Reading מציד ("from a hunter") instead of MT's מיד ("from a hand"). The translation follows Fox, *Proverbs 1–9*, 210.

[75] Fox, *Proverbs 1–9*, 211.

a small excurses of sorts on the topic is appropriate here.[76] This small detour will also shed more light on the symbolic relationship of Prov 6:1–5 to the remainder of the instruction as well.

The practice of surety is designed to protect a lender from incurring financial loss by permitting a third party to act as a guarantor to a loan arrangement.[77] One might stand surety out of compassion or obligation, as Sirach 29:14 implies. Or, one might stand surety for profit. As Fox suggests, "the likely motive for vouching for a stranger would be to receive a fee for the service," a practice to which Sirach 29:19 alludes.[78] In either case there is the sense in the wisdom literature that standing surety is risky business. Wisdom writers may also express some discomfort with a 'profit motive' when it comes to standing surety. This sort of view, in any case, would be consistent with Proverbs' sense that wealth ought not to be overvalued and passionately pursued. Though not speaking of surety specifically, the Egyptian Ankhsheshonq 16:12, likewise offers some economic instruction that focuses on a profit motive:

> Do not borrow money at interest in order to live well on it.[79]

However, the economic riskiness of standing surety seems to be a more important reason for the sages' discouragement of the practice. In a few lines subsequent to the one just cited (21–22), Ankhsheshonq explicitly recognizes the risky nature, not of surety, but of lending, including lending that might be motivated in part by compassion:

> Do not lend money at interest without obtaining a security.
> Do not be too trusting lest you become poor.

Ankhsheshonq's sentiment seems consistent with Prov 22:26–27 where the riskiness of standing surety is highlighted:

> אל־תהי בתקעי־כף בערבים משאות
> אם־אין־לך לשלם למה יקח משכבך מתחתיך

---

[76] In Proverbs itself see 11:15; 17:18; 20:16; 22:26–27; 27:13. See further Sir 8:13; 29:14–20. Several passages from Egyptian instructions resonate with Prov 6 as well (see below).

[77] Alternatively, a lender might be protected by receiving from the borrower a deposit of some valuable item or the borrower's pledge of property or children. See Fox, *Proverbs 1–9*, 215.

[78] Fox, *Proverbs 1–9*, 215.

[79] The translation of this and the following lines from Ankhsheshonq and Any are from Lichtheim, *Ancient Egyptian Literature*.

> Do not be one of those who give their hand, who stand surety for debts, lest your bed be taken from under you when you have no money to pay.[80]

Beyond this common evaluation of the dangers of surety, wisdom voices also seem to understand financial dealings to be particularly risky when they involve strangers or foreigners; and the sages are especially concerned with this state of affairs. The final lines of Any 5, for instance, say:

> Let your hand preserve what is in your house; Wealth accrues to him who guards it; Let your hand not scatter it to strangers, lest it turn to loss for you. If wealth is placed where it bears interest, it comes back to you redoubled; Make a storehouse for your own wealth, your people will find it on your way. . . . Protect what is yours and you find it. Keep an eye on what you own, lest you end as a beggar. He who is slack amounts to nothing. Honored is the man who's active.

Any 6 continues:

> Do not rely on another's goods; Guard what you acquire yourself; Do not depend on another's wealth, lest he become master in your house.

Ankhsheshonq 9 similarly instructs:

> Do not dwell in a house in which you get no income. Do not entrust your wealth to a house of profit. Do not put your wealth into a house only. Do not put your wealth in a town to which you must send.

Neither Ankhsheshonq nor Any is talking about surety in particular, but broader economic activities. In any case, Any does not appear to censure a profit motive. There is, however, a sense that securing one's wealth is hard work, not the project of slackers; it is also a task that doesn't work well when strangers or outsiders are involved. Both of these themes resonate with Prov 6, which after speaking of surety on behalf of the זר ("stranger"), continues with instruction to the lazy person (vv. 6–11). Proverbs 6:1–5 together with at least 11:15, the nearly identical 20:16, and 27:13 are also explicitly concerned with economic dealings with outsiders and specifically with standing surety on behalf of the זר and/or the נכריה/ם, the stranger or foreigner.

---

[80] The translation follows NJPS. The verse's similarities with Egyptian instruction are intriguing as the line comes from the so-called Amenemope section of Proverbs.

The other verse concerning surety in Proverbs that has not yet been mentioned is 17:18:

אדם חסר־לב תוקע כף ערב ערבה לפני רעהו

A person lacking sense claps the hand to stand surety to his neighbor.

This line speaks of standing surety לפני רעהו, "in the presence of his neighbor." Although the translation of these two words is simple, exactly what they mean is not so clear. However, as with the preposition in 6:1's ערבת לרעך, the לפני of 17:18 likely indicates that the neighbor is again the creditor, not the borrower. The stranger or outsider, of course, is not explicitly mentioned in 17:18. Yet, given the anxiety other surety proverbs express about such a situation, it is likely 17:18 shares this concern and the third party is a stranger. Although skeptical of this possibility, McKane is nonetheless correct when he writes in regard to 17:18 that "the neighbor may be the one to whom the guarantor will be liable, should a third party for whom he has assumed financial responsibility be in default of his obligations."[81]

One of the themes that lends some unity to chapters five and six in Proverbs, and hence is significant for understanding Prov 6:1–5, is a general concern with what brings on ruin. This concern is essentially a particularizing of the general act-consequence principle of the wisdom mythos that intimates that wisdom brings good things and folly bad. However, chapter five and the first verses of chapter six are also concerned with the *stranger* who ensnares (cf. 5:22 and 6:2 and the shared language of capture; לכד) and who brings destruction. In chapter five it is the זרה with whom one is tempted to commit adultery. She is, on the literal level, most likely the wife of another man. But she is also a symbol of the way of folly.[82] In the first five verses of chapter six, the text is concerned with the stranger זר for whom one is tempted to stand surety. As I suggested (following Fox), it makes the most sense to assume that Prov 6:1 is concerned with remunerative surety—standing surety for profit, to gain valuable wealth. If so, the two sections in Prov 5–6, the one concerned with the strange woman and the other concerned with the strange borrower, share a logical, symbolic structure: that which is

[81] McKane, *Proverbs*, 503.
[82] As I suggested above in the discussion of Prov 4:5–9.

strange/foreign appears desirable (sexually or economically), but ultimately is not so and ends in destruction.

It thus seems that the problem with standing surety for strangers in 6:1–5 is not so much the profit motive, or attaining profit not by one's own labor (though as I intimated there may be some dis-ease with this). Rather it is the fact that standing surety is *especially* risky. This is likely due to the fact that strangers are prone to disappear more readily than neighbors. Standing surety for a זר creates a situation where one is at the mercy not only of the creditor/neighbor, but of the more ephemeral stranger/borrower as well. It places the guarantor in a particularly precarious social and economic position.

This understanding of Prov 6 also helps to explain Sirach's relative openness to surety practices. Proverbs is most often, as in 6:1–5, concerned with surety on behalf of a stranger. Sirach, however, is regularly concerned with standing surety not for strangers, but for a neighbor (Sirach 29:14). This is still risky business but, he seems to imply, somewhat laudable (cf. 29:14, 20). Sirach, it appears, sees some potential social benefit from standing surety for a neighbor—perhaps an increase, or maintenance, of social cohesion. However, he is skeptical where surety practices are socially detrimental (cf. 29:15–16, 19). Indeed when Ben Sira is critical of surety measures he is critical of a) the debtor who does not sufficiently respect the guarantor's economic risks (29:15–16); and b) the one who strives to profit unduly from surety practices (Sirach 29:19). Both Sirach and Proverbs thus likely recognize that the profit motive is a significant reason why someone might choose to stand surety for another. Moreover, both can be somewhat critical of this, either implicitly (Proverbs) or more explicitly (Sirach). Nevertheless, for Sirach, the risks associated with standing surety for a neighbor are tolerable because of the potential social benefit. For Proverbs, however, where the borrower is not envisioned as a neighbor, the risk is too high. There is not the possibility for the same kind of communal benefit Sirach imagines.

Finally, to return to the larger context of Prov 5–6: The instruction in 6:1–5 regarding standing surety for a stranger/outsider is, on one level, good, old fashion ancient Near Eastern wisdom advice. The text's disapproval is motivated by the risky character of the practice. Yet because of the parallel structure of the two chapters in general and the particular fact that the strange woman in chapter five is both literally the wife of another man *and* a symbol for the way of folly, the conventional advice about surety in 6:1–5 is also woven into the larger symbolic system of Proverbs. The verbal and thematic links of the "stranger" or "foreigner" and the danger associated with these constitute the key links. For Proverbs, to stand surety for a stranger, quite simply, but also symbolically, is to travel the 'adulterous' path of folly.

3.4. Conclusions

Already in chapter one the figurative aspects of Proverbs' wealth and poverty language is discernable. The sinners deploy the rhetoric of riches in an effort to lure the hearer to their way. The wealth they offer, however, functions largely as a symbol of all that is desirable on the path of folly. In the following chapters the instructing voice similarly employs the rhetoric of wealth to convince the addressee of the desirability of wisdom's path and to motivate him to choose that path. Although the instructing voice largely avoids the abstract language of wealth that the sinners employed in Prov 1, one can trace a progression in the father's and Wisdom's use of wealth and poverty language. Their discourse culminates in Wisdom's claim in 8:18 that she possesses not הון יקר, as the robbers did, but הון עתק, precious or enduring wealth—symbolic "wealth"—which is defined as the kind of virtue that the prologue highlights in 1:3, justice (צדקה).

The teaching voice in the book's first collection, however, also uses the language of wealth and poverty in non-figurative ways to construct for the hearer a concrete economic ethic. In both types of instances, and throughout Proverbs more generally, the sages' can employ a cause and effect rhetoric. This cause and effect language, however, is not one that ought to be understood in simple literalistic fashion. Rather the text's act-consequence rhetoric projects a symbolic sapiential narrative in which the wise and righteous are rewarded while the wicked and foolish come to naught. The truth of such a view is not based solely, or even primarily, on empirical evidence, in the sense that any objective observer would be able to confirm or disconfirm the claim. Rather it emerges from, and depends upon, a particular perception of the cosmos, a wisdom mythos. It is through this perception that the virtues and values that Proverbs promotes—often through its discourse of wealth and poverty—make sense and become meaningful. It is through the ideological lens of this wisdom mythos that the sages construe and view their world. Hence they are predisposed to order a variety of experiences and to promote a variety of values as consonant with the mythos that claims the cosmos favors a life of virtue.

Finally, though I have not yet made the designation explicit, the material in the book's initial chapters that makes use of wealth language as a motivational symbol belongs to Proverbs' wisdom's virtues discourse and that which offers direct instruction to the hearer belongs to the discourse of social justice. The nature and contours of these sub-discourses of wealth and poverty, along with the discourse of social observation, however, become especially evident in chapters 10–31.

CHAPTER FOUR

THE WISDOM'S VIRTUES DISCOURSE AND THE DISCOURSE OF SOCIAL JUSTICE IN PROVERBS 10–31

The material that makes up Proverbs 10–31 is formally distinct from what is found in chapters 1–9. Unlike the instructional poems of the book's initial chapters, which have a father/teacher or personified Wisdom instructing a son or pupil directly, chapters 10–31 are primarily collections of short, anonymous sentence sayings.[1] Yet despite the shift in predominant forms, the instruction of 10–31 shares the same underlying organizing assumption as chapters 1–9—the rhetorical strategy of the two ways. On the one hand "wisdom" and its functional synonyms (understanding, insight, etc.) together with the "wise" and "righteous" persons continue to serve as the text's primary positive rubrics. On the other hand, the "fool" and the "wicked" person along with "folly" and "wickedness" continue to function as the composition's primary negative rubrics. Like the material in chapters 1–9, what the various *meshalim* of later chapters recommend can be characterized as belonging to the way of wisdom and righteousness, and what they disavow to the way of folly and wickedness. Although the text is often explicit in naming what belongs to each path (as especially in chs. 10–15, through antithetical parallelism), elsewhere this distinction is more implicit and the text continues to expect the hearer to possess a certain literary competence and to discern what belongs to each way. As a collection, the purpose of the material in chapters 10–31, as with that of the first nine chapters, is to teach a person about the right way of virtue.

The wealth and poverty sayings in the later chapters of Proverbs also underscore the continuity between chapters 1–9 and 10–31. The

[1] Though, of course, Prov 22:17–24:22, the so-called Amenemope section of the book, along with ch. 30 (a disparate collection of the sayings of Agur and other sayings) and ch. 31 (the instruction of Lemuel's mother and the poem to the woman of worth) should be distinguished from the larger sentence collections of 10:1–22:16, the "Further Sayings of the Wise" in 24:23–34, and chs. 25–29. Occasionally in the non-sentence collections different textual voices are credited with the teachings in a superscription (e.g., Agur in 30:1; Lemuel's mother in 31:1).

vocabulary of wealth and poverty in the sentence sayings, for instance, is quite similar to that of chapters 1–9. However, whereas the early chapters have comparatively little to say about poverty and the poor, the later chapters take up such language much more fully. The text employs poverty rhetoric both as a negative trope to impel the addressee to pursue virtue and shun vice, and in order to construct for the hearer a specific economic ethic. As with the other material in the later chapters, the hearer or reader of the wealth and poverty sayings of chapters 10–31 also often must discern precisely what virtue the text wants to inculcate in its addressee (or what vice it hopes will be avoided).

In the final form of the book, the first collection in Proverbs (chs. 1–9) serves as a hermeneutic framework for the proverbs in subsequent collections, encouraging the hearer or reader to view the later instruction as consonant with what the more personalized instructing voice of chapters 1–9 offers.[2] Furthermore, even if in its *Ur*-form Proverbs 1:2–6 (7) was intended only as an introduction to some *Ur*-form of chapters 1–9, the purpose (i.e., to learn intellectual, practical, and social virtues) and the invitation (i.e., to understand the text's tropes and figures) that this prologue articulates are appropriate for the subsequent sections of the book as well. To understand fully how the wealth and poverty sayings in the sentence collections are functioning it is thus necessary to inquire about the didactic end of each proverb, to ask what place the saying holds in the text's larger moral discourse, and to consider how wealth and poverty language functions to help any particular saying reach that end. In this regard it is important to remember not only the prologue's invitation to read wisely, but to recall as well that the form of the sentence proverbs is reminiscent of folk proverbs and hence evokes the communicative and metaphorical strategies common to folk proverbs.

[2] See Raymond C. Van Leeuwen ("Proverbs: Introduction, Commentary, and Reflections," *NIB* 5:24), who states that chapters 1–9, together with chapters 30–31, form "an interpretive 'frame' through which to view the small wisdom utterances they enclose." Fox, too, speaks of chapters 1–9 as an "introduction" to the rest of the book. See Michael V. Fox, *Proverbs 1–9: A New Translation with Introduction and Commentary* (AB 18a; New York: Doubleday, 2000), 25. Carole R. Fontaine states similarly that chs. 1–9 "act as a theological and literary prologue to the proverb collections that follow." See her "Proverbs" in the *Women's Bible Commentary* (ed. Carol A. Newsom and Sharon H. Ringe; expanded edition; Louisville: WJK, 1998), 154. Cf. Chapter Two, n. 75.

Recognizing the figurative aspects of the wealth and poverty proverbs of chapters 10–31 is vital if one is to avoid a misleadingly literalistic interpretation of the book's wealth and poverty sayings as well as an overly simplistic understanding of its act-consequence rhetoric.

Finally, in the second half of Proverbs it is also possible, more than in the initial collection, to distinguish when the book employs wealth and poverty language in distinct ways—e.g., as a motivational symbol or as direct and concrete economic instruction. In the latter chapters one is especially able to discern the book's three closely related, but distinct (sub)-discourses of wealth and poverty, which I call a "wisdom's virtues discourse," a "discourse of social justice," and a "discourse of social observation." This chapter is concerned with the wisdom's virtues discourse and the discourse of social justice. The following chapter will first consider more fully the book's moral and literary Gestalt—its ethical vision and its rhetorical and figurative patterns of language use—that both the poems of chapters 1–9 and the sayings considered in this chapter establish. Subsequently, other proverbs in chapters 10–31 will be analyzed in light of this Gestalt and shown to belong either to the wisdom's virtues or the social justice discourse, or to the book's third sub-discourse of wealth and poverty, the discourse of social observation.

4.1. The Wisdom's Virtues Discourse in Proverbs 10–31

4.1.a. *Characteristics*

The wisdom's virtues discourse is by far the largest of Proverbs' three sub-discourses of wealth and poverty. The sayings that belong to it can be distinguished by several characteristic linguistic and rhetorical features.

First, although proverbs comprising the wisdom's virtues discourse can use a broad range of terms and images, this discourse prefers a particular abstract, or better, "impersonal" vocabulary for wealth and poverty derived from particular roots (e.g., ע ש ר, ה-ו-ן, ר-י-ש, ח-ס-ר). Occasionally the wisdom's virtues discourse employs a comparative construction. In such instances the personal language of "rich" and "poor" (i.e., rich or poor "person"), expressed by means of the substantivized adjective or participle, is used. In these comparative constructions the poor (usually a form derived from ר-י-ש) are also always grammatical subjects. They are, along with the rich, doers or actors. By contrast, in most other instances in Proverbs where this sort of personal language is employed (e.g., in the discourse of social justice), the poor are always objects, grammatically speaking.

As in chapters 1–9, the *meshalim* in the later chapters of Proverbs that belong to the wisdom's virtues discourse also generally function figuratively and features internal to the individual proverbs regularly signal a saying's metaphorical qualities. As I suggested above, however, the book's prologue also directs the hearer or reader to attend to the book's tropes wisely. It will thus be important to recall that the form of these short sayings is also reminiscent of folk proverbs that both regularly employ metaphor, and are habitually employed metaphorically to say something about human life and activity.

Recognizing the figurative aspects of the wisdom's virtues discourse is important, for sayings belonging to this sub-discourse are not usually concerned to say something about wealth and poverty. Rather, they promote a larger didactic end. They employ the rhetoric of wealth and poverty primarily as tropes to mark the relative value of virtue and vice and are designed to encourage the hearer or reader to adopt the way of wisdom and to reject folly. As with much of the wealth and poverty language in chapters 1–9, the wealth and poverty rhetoric in chapters 10–31 often represents that which the hearer or reader will find desirable and valuable; or in the case of poverty images that which is undesirable. Material wealth in these later chapters remains a good and valuable thing. But as in chapters 1–9, in the moral vision of the wisdom's virtues discourse, riches belong to a set of lesser goods, the attainment of which should never be confused with the acquisition of a more fundamental good, wisdom and its virtues.

As is also the case in earlier chapters, the wisdom's virtues discourse in the second half of Proverbs attempts to persuade the hearer of the desirability of wisdom and its virtues over and against an implicit social script (a kind of competing discourse), which contends wealth and other lesser goods are, in fact, ultimate goods. Subsequently the text employs images of precisely those lesser goods that the hearer values but may tend to overvalue. If in chapters 1–9, however, Proverbs uses the rhetoric of wealth and poverty as motivational symbols to get the hearer to recognize generally the *value* of wisdom's way over that of folly's, in chapters 10–31 it also uses such rhetoric as motivational symbols to persuade him to accept the particular *values* (i.e., the virtues) of that way and to shun all that belongs to folly's path. The virtues promoted by the wisdom's virtues discourse in chapters 10–31, moreover, are consonant with those broad virtues and values the prologue stresses, especially that of social equity and harmony.

4.1.b. *Figurative Wealth and Poverty Sayings*

Several sayings in Proverbs 10–31 employ a wisdom vocabulary and an economic rhetoric that is very similar to certain *meshalim* of chapters 1–9. As with the proverbs of the initial chapters, these sayings likewise reveal that the text employs wealth and poverty language in figurative ways. Consider, for instance, the following proverbs:

קנה־חכמה מה־טוב מחרוץ וקנות בינה נבחר מכסף

> Buy wisdom! So much better is it than gold. The acquisition of understanding is preferable to silver. (Prov 16:16)[3]

למה־זה מחיר ביד־כסיל לקנות חכמה ולב־אין

> What good is money in the hand of a fool to purchase wisdom, when he has no mind? (Prov 17:16)[4]

אמת קנה ואל־תמכר חכמה ומוסר ובינה

> Buy truth; and do not sell wisdom or instruction or understanding. (Prov 23:23)[5]

---

[3] The MT's *qĕnōh* is peculiar. The vowels are appropriate to a m. sg. imperative or infinitive construct of the strong root. However, the expected form of the III-*heh* infinitive would be *qĕnôt*, as at the beginning of the second stich. Rather than emend the consonantal text it is better to re-point the first word as the m. sg. imperative of a III-weak root, *qĕnēh*. The interrogative מה ("what") may be a dittography of the final two letters of the previous word חכמה ("wisdom"); cf. Arndt Meinhold, *Die Sprüche* (2 vol.; ZBK; Zürich: Theologischer Verlag, 1991), 2:272. However, there is no reason to delete it; cf. Roland E. Murphy, *Proverbs* (WBC; Nashville: Thomas Nelson, 1998), 118. As Otto Plöger suggests, the saying may be the end product of what were originally two riddles: "What is better than gold? Wisdom! What is more precious than silver? Understanding!" (*Was ist besser als Gold? Weisheit! Was ist kostbarer als Silber? Einsicht!*). See *Sprüche Salomos (Proverbia)* (Neukrichen-Vluyn: Neukirchener Verlag, 1984), 193; cf. Murphy, *Proverbs*, 122.

[4] The translation follows NJPS.

[5] The verse is not in the Greek and seems out of place in the larger passage's concern with parents. This state of affairs has given rise to a number of theories regarding the passage's composition and development. On these matters see Plöger, *Sprüche Salomos*, 275; Murphy, *Proverbs*, 176; Richard J. Clifford, *Proverbs: A Commentary*, (OTL; Louisville: WJK, 1999), 213.

Like several of the *meshalim* in chapters 1–9, the sayings just cited deploy a metaphor of commercial transaction and a rhetoric of relative value.[6] It is unlikely that these proverbs mean to suggest that in ancient Israel or Judah (Yehud) one might go out and hire a wisdom teacher.[7] Indeed, in filling out the metaphorical complex—WISDOM IS A COMMODITY—23:23 warns the hearer against "selling" wisdom as well! It is precisely the difficulty, or in Ricoeur's idiom, the absurdity, that arises when proverbs such as 23:23 are regarded literally that suggests a metaphorical quality to them. As I intimated in Chapter Three in regard to Prov 4:7, although one might conceivably purchase knowledge or some form of instruction, it is impossible to buy wisdom. The verses more fundamentally employ economic language primarily as a means of describing the worth and desirability of wisdom's virtuous way. Wisdom is like a precious good that one should seek to acquire, not peddle away.

Interpreters, however, generally overlook the metaphor that it is at work in the proverbs and often appear merely to reiterate the literal sense of the lines. Murphy, for instance, writes in regard to 17:16 that, "the fool is dumb enough to think that the acquisition of wisdom is merely a matter of a monetary transaction."[8] Similarly Plöger states that whoever thinks, "one can get anything with money" is a fool.[9] Clifford and Meinhold offer similar comments.[10] It is not, however, simply the case that the fool is a dullard who wrongly thinks he can go out and buy wisdom like a pomegranate in the market place. Rather, the wise and discerning hearer of 16:16 and 23:23, as well as 17:16, will follow the logic of the metaphor of commercial exchange and understand the proverbs to mean not only

[6] Proverbs 16:16's hearkening back to chapters 1–9 is particularly appropriate since it stands just before 16:17, the middle point of the book according to the masoretic tradition. See Meinhold, *Die Sprüche*, 2:272; Murphy, *Proverbs*, 122.

[7] Toy likewise writes: "It is doubtful that fees were taken by Jewish teachers." See C. H. Toy, *Proverbs: A Critical and Exegetical Commentary on the Book of Proverbs*, (rprt., Edinburgh: T&T Clark, 1988), 346. Cf. Meinhold, *Die Sprüche*, 2:291; Murphy, *Proverbs*, 130; R. N. Whybray, *Proverbs*, (NCBC; Grand Rapids: Eerdmans, 1994), 259.

[8] Murphy, *Proverbs*, 130.

[9] Plöger, *Sprüche Salomos*, 204; (*Für Geld ist alles zu haben*). Plöger also believes the image works best if one imagines a school situation. At least this is implicit when he writes that, "the verse can be understood outside of a school situation as well" (*Der Vers lässt sich auch ausserhalb einer Schul situation verstehen*).

[10] Clifford, *Proverbs*, 166; Meinhold, *Die Sprüche*, 2:291.

that wisdom is remarkably valuable, but that one ought to acquire that which is more valuable (wisdom) by means of that which is less valuable (wealth). The fool in 17:16, by contrast, does not know how to deploy what is less valuable (money) in order to "trade up" and acquire that which is more valuable (wisdom); hence, in the logic of the metaphor, whatever "assets" he may possess, whether economic or moral, are wasted. Because they are not integrated into a framework of values controlled by the meta-virtue of wisdom, they are only of minimal worth.

A number of other proverbs in the wisdom's virtues discourse can likewise only be understood figuratively and their wealth and poverty rhetoric understood as positively marking, i.e., "valuing," wisdom and its virtues. This is so in 10:20; 20:15; and 25:11–12. These read:

כסף נבחר לשון צדיק לב רשעים כמעט

The tongue of the righteous person is choice silver, but the mind of the wicked is like something of little worth.[11]

יש זהב ורב־פנינים וכלי יקר שפתי־דעת

There is gold, and abundance of costly stones, but lips of knowledge are a precious vessel.[12]

תפוחי זהב במשכיות כסף דבר דבר על־אפניו
נזם זהב וחלי־כתם מוכיח חכם על־אזן שמעת

Golden apples in silver showpieces is a phrase well turned; a ring of gold, a golden ornament, is a wise person's reproof in a receptive ear.[13]

---

[11] Though the expression כמעט often means something like "almost," Whybray (who refers to *GKC* paragraph *118x*) suggests that it is "probably an emphatic form of *meʿat*, 'little.'" See his *Proverbs*, 168; cf. W. A. van der Weiden, *Le Livre de Proverbes: Notes philologiques*, (BEO 23; Rome: Biblical Institute Press, 1970), 94. The proverb contrasts the "tongue," the organ of speech, with the "heart" or "mind" of a person, which is the source of that which is spoken.

[12] According to Whybray, in *Proverbs*, 295, the term יש here is sometimes reckoned as a noun ("property, possessions"), as it often is in 8:21 (see Chapter Three). There is little to commend this view since the usual meaning of the particle "there is" creates no difficulties. Whybray is correct in rejecting it. "Costly stones" sometimes rendered "jewels"—translates פנינים; cf. NJPS; Clifford, *Proverbs*, 184. The term may refer more specifically to "coral." See Whybray, *Proverbs*, 295; cf. Toy, *Proverbs*, 389.

[13] The translation follows NJPS. Although the sense of the line is clear, "the precise meaning of several words" in the verse "is doubtful." See Whybray, *Proverbs*, 363. In particular, "apples of" (תפוחי), "showpieces" (משכיות), "a well turned phrase" (דבר דבר על־אפניו), and "ornament" (חלי) have been the subject of some discussion. See Whybray, *Proverbs*, 364; Clifford, *Proverbs*, 224; Murphy, *Proverbs*, 189, 192.

These indicative statements are from three different collections of the second half of the book. They also make clear that the later chapters of Proverbs are able to use wealth and poverty imagery as tropes in sayings that must be understood figuratively. Each proverb is concerned with some notion of "right speech" ("the tongue of the righteous person" in 10:20; "lips of knowledge" in 20:15; "a well turned phrase" and "reproof" in 25:11–12). In each, however, a literal understanding of the line produces an absurdity, one that is so obvious that most readers likely unconsciously move to understanding the lines in a metaphorical sense.

The rhetorical strategy of the lines is to value virtue—i.e., what the text considers to be of worth in the moral realm—by images of material goods whose worth in the economic realm is clear, namely precious metals, coral (or jewels), and ornaments. Put otherwise, the logic of the lines is to pair a moral positive with an economic positive (10:20a; 20:15; 25:11–12) and a moral negative with an economic negative (10:20b). In 10:20, by associating the "tongue of a righteous person" with the image of precious silver, the text creates a positive valuation for this "right speech." The second half of the verse, which compares a "heart" or "mind of wickedness" with that which is "worthless," produces the opposite rhetorical effect. Importantly, however, the absurdity produced by 10:20a's copula—the tongue of the righteous person "is" choice silver—immediately gives way, as Ricoeur would suggest, to the metaphorical "is like." The simile of the second half of the verse (note the preposition *kap* in כמעט) unambiguously signals the metaphoricity of that stich. Clearly that which, on the one hand, is associated both with the צדיק (a person who embodies one of the book's primary virtues, "righteousness") and with that which is of great material worth ("choice silver") is valued and advocated by the verse. On the other hand, that which is linked with what is of no economic value and with "wickedness" (one of the book's meta-vices) is disavowed.[14]

In 20:15 the images of gold, jewels, as well as כלי יקר ("precious vessels")—which hearkens back to the robber's quest for הון יקר ("precious wealth") in chapter one—work in the same way as the rhetoric of choice silver in 10:20. They lead to an absurdity when the line

[14] Toy, in *Proverbs*, 212, makes a similar observation.

is interpreted literally and positively mark a certain kind of speech that the text views as virtuous. The "golden apples," "silver show-pieces," and golden rings and ornaments in 25:11–12, associated with a well-turned phrase and a reproach, function similarly.[15]

The sayings just cited make simple use of images from the economic realm to value a virtue—right speech—that belongs to the way of wisdom.[16] However, what particular aspects of "right speech" each saying is alluding to is not necessarily obvious on first glance. Proverbs 10:20 and 20:15 suggest that one's words reveal one's character or one's relationship to wisdom's way, i.e., to righteousness or knowledge, respectively. Proverbs 10:20 may also be concerned with the honest speech that good character produces, as two of the terms it uses, צדיק ("righteous person") and רשעים ("wicked persons"), are perhaps borrowed from the legal realm where a premium is placed on truth telling.[17] As Bakhtin would suggest, the words 'taste' of their life in that social realm (see Chapter One). Proverbs 20:15's allusion to "lips of knowledge" may likewise be underscoring the worth of the same kind of integrity in speech to which Prov 10:20 points. Indeed Prov 29:7, which more clearly alludes to a legal context than 10:20, claims that the righteous person "*knows* the rights of the poor,"

[15] The allusion to a נזם זהב ("ring of gold") in the first half of 25:11, moreover, recalls 11:22 where the patriarchal book of Proverbs is not so much concerned that its male hearers attend to "right speech," but to the "good sense" of their women, for נזם זהב באף חזיר אשה יפה וסרת טעם ("a gold ring in the snout of a pig is a beautiful woman bereft of sense," following NJPS).

[16] Nearly all commentators recognize this process of valuation. In relation to 10:20, Meinhold is representative and perhaps the most thorough in his description. See Meinhold, *Die Sprüche*, 1:178. But Whybray too writes: "In any case the sense of the line is that the speech of the righteous is of great value." See *Proverbs*, 168. Cf. Plöger's evaluation that, "This proverb . . . wishes to highlight the worth and significance of the righteous, who are recognizable through their speech" (*Dieser Spruch . . ., möchte den Wert und die Bedeutung des Gerechten hervorheben, die an seinem Reden erkennbar sind*). See *Sprüche Salomos*, 128. On the valuation at 20.15, cf. Murphy, *Proverbs*, 152; Meinhold, *Die Sprüche*, 2:338; Plöger, *Sprüche Salomos*, 235. For the syntax of the line see especially Toy, *Proverbs*, 388–89. On 25:11–12, see Murphy, *Proverbs*, 192; Meinhold, *Die Sprüche*, 2:424–25; Plöger, *Sprüche Salomos*, 300–01; Toy, *Proverbs*, 462–62; Clifford, *Proverbs*, 221.

[17] In commenting on 10:20 Murphy, in *Proverbs*, 75, likewise alludes to the trustworthy nature of the righteous person's words. Commentators, however, usually speak only generally of "righteous speech" or "*rechte Reden*;" and, in relation to lines such as 20:15 and 25:11–12, of "wise words," etc. Meinhold, in *Die Sprüche*, 2:338, in relation to 20:15, for instance, speaks of "*verständiger Rede*"—i.e., sensible, judicious, speech.

and presumably will not subvert those rights in any way, including through articulating less than truthful speech.[18] The "right speech" that is the concern of 25:11–12, however, seems to have more to do with the speech of the wise in an instructional context, where reproof offered in an effective manner would be highly valued. Yet even the "right speech" of this verse carries traces of a life of use in broader legal and moral contexts and need not be confined to the world of formal instruction, as the appearance of מוכיח in Amos 5:10; Job 9:33; 32:12; and 40:2 suggests.

The virtues of right speech that each of the sayings under consideration value via economic rhetoric can thus be seen as virtues vital to the achievement of what the prologue identifies as an essential feature of the book's purpose—the realization of social justice and harmony. For justice, righteousness, and equity (cf. 1:3) to characterize a community or society, integrity and honesty in speech and conduct (precisely the concern of 10:20 and indirectly 20:15 and 25:11–12), are indispensable.[19]

4.1.c. *Further Figurative Sayings*

A variety of other sayings in Proverbs motivate adherence to wisdom's way by deploying wealth and poverty language in a manner that must primarily be regarded as figurative. Consider first 21:20:

אוצר נחמד ושמן בנוה חכם וכסיל אדם יבלענו

> Precious treasure and oil are in the dwelling of a wise person; but a fool of a person swallows it up.[20]

The claim of 21:20, that treasure and oil, both valuable economic commodities, are to be found in the wise person's house, is some-

[18] Proverbs 29:7 belongs properly to the discourse of social justice and will be considered more fully below.

[19] Other sayings in Proverbs concerned with truthful speech and testimony include: 12:17, 22(?); 14:5, 25; 19:5, 9, 28; 21:28; 24:26, 28; 25:9, 18. Cf. 17:15; 18:5; 24:24; 28:21.

[20] Some commentators find the mention of "oil" in this verse strange. It is not present in the Greek, though the LXX itself does not reflect the MT of the verse in a straightforward manner; cf. Whybray, *Proverbs*, 313. See further Meinhold, *Die Sprüche*, 2:356; Toy, *Proverbs*, 406; Murphy, *Proverbs*, 161; Hans F. Fuhs, *Das Buch der Sprichwörter: Ein Kommentar* (Forschung zur Bibel 95; Würzburg: Echter Verlag, 2001), 295.

times regarded as reflecting a wisdom prosperity axiom.[21] However, the line does not employ a plain cause and effect rhetoric that would more clearly suggest an underlying act-consequence nexus to be at work. The proverb can be easily understood otherwise. Plöger and Clifford, for example, regard the saying as a reflection on the different manner wise and foolish people handle wealth. The wise do not squander their wealth and so their 'house'—literally speaking—will be full of valuables.[22]

Either of these lines of interpretation of 21:20—the act-consequence line or the 'squandering' line—is possible. Neither, however, exhausts the text's meaning. Although the book's prologue and the saying's form encourages a reader of Proverbs to seek out the metaphorical dimension of the *mashal*, at least one further feature internal to the proverb itself points to its figurative aspects.

The issue in 21:20 is not merely that the fool "runs through" (NJPS) or "squanders" his wealth, but that he "swallows up" (בלע) good things. As Whybray notes, the *piel* of ב-ל-ע probably nowhere in HB carries the sense of "squander."[23] It is, however, a term with a well established pattern of metaphorical usage. The robbers in Prov 1:12, recall, "swallow up" the innocent; and this same line alludes as well to the common mythological and metaphorical trope of Sheol swallowing up living beings.[24] Elsewhere in HB the term appears in various contexts where destruction is thematized.[25] As a verb of consumption בלע, moreover, invites elaboration in terms of

[21] See, for instance, Murphy, *Proverbs*, 161, who writes: "The teaching of the sages provides for prosperity as the lot of the wise person." Similarly Meinhold, in *Die Sprüche*, 2:356, avers: "That the wise person, because of his good life and the virtues he exhibits also will acquire material profit, is evident from a number of proverbs" (*Dass der Weise auf Grund seines guten Lebens und der dabei gezeigten Tugenden auch zu materiellen Gewinn gelangen würde, geht aus manchen Sprüchen hervor*). Elsewhere Meinhold's evaluation of similar proverbs is more nuanced (see below). In regard to this verse (21:20) he, like others (see the immediately following), is also open to the notion that the proverb is most concerned with the frittering away of one's wealth

[22] Plöger, *Sprüche Salomos*, 248; Clifford, *Proverbs*, 192; cf. Jutta Hausmann, *Studien zum Menschenbild der alteren Weisheit* (Forschungen zum Alten Testament 7; Tübingen: J. C. B. Mohr, 1995), 20 who sees 21:20 also as a proverb that "relativizes" wealth (cf. p. 338).

[23] Whybray, *Proverbs*, 189.

[24] Cf. Plöger, *Sprüche Salomos*, 248; Clifford, *Proverbs*, 192; Meinhold, *Die Sprüche*, 2:356; Toy, *Proverbs*, 406; Van Leeuwen, "Proverbs," *NIB* 5:194.

[25] See, for instance, Ps 124:3; Is 28:4; Hos 8:7.

food and other "consumables." In 21:20, this is metaphorically developed by means of the images of consumable oil and treasure. The wise person stores up these goods inside his house for preservation. The fool metaphorically brings them into his body in a way that exhausts them.

The particular virtue 21:20 is concerned with promoting is thus prudence, the careful husbandry of all things good and valuable. The line is a good example of the book's common use of a particular rhetorical strategy, namely, a kind of synecdoche, where 'a part stands for the whole' or 'a specific or particular stands for a general': here stewardship of treasure and oil for the virtue of prudence. The vice the line means to censure is a greed characterized by a carelessness that has an edge of destructive and insatiable desire to it. The *mashal* may also offer a kind of oblique analogy: just as riches are said to be found inside the wise person's abode, so the valuable wisdom that the wise person possesses belongs to his interior character.

To the extent that the verb בלע is a "dead metaphor" with the sense of "to consume voraciously," Prov 21:20 "works" on a literal level and can be said to carry an implicit promise of well being for the wise person. But it is also a trope for much more. It more broadly values the wise person's way of life and censures the path of the fool who "squanders" all kinds of goods, both material and moral. The underlying problem with which the verse is dealing, as the nuances of the verb בלע intimate, is that the foolish person *overvalues* lesser material goods to the point that he pursues them frenetically. In contrast to that perennial and broad social script alluded to above, which suggests material wealth or some other lesser good is the key to human flourishing and so should be pursued passionately, this text hints that it is a person's interior qualities, his wise character, which is truly valuable.

Proverbs 24:3–4 uses language and imagery that is similar to 21:20. It reads:

בחכמה יבנה בית ובתבונה יתכונן
ובדעת חדרים ימלאו כל־הון יקר ונעים

> By wisdom a house is built; and by understanding it is established; and by knowledge [its] rooms are filled [with] all precious wealth and pleasantries.

Whybray believes the imagery of a good number of sentence sayings in Prov 10–29 indicates that they are the product of the lives and experiences of small farmers in ancient Israel and thus are best read against this background in essentially literal fashion. Hence, though recognizing the language reverberates somewhat more broadly, he writes in regard to 24:3–4 that:

> The statements in these verses are in the first place to be understood literally. It is a general principle of the teaching of the book that **wisdom** will confer material prosperity on those who follow her (see, for example, 8:18, 21; 21:21), or that such prosperity will be given to the righteous (see especially 15:6) or to those who fear and honor Yahweh (so 3:9–10; 22:4).

He continues: "So what is stated here is that the followers of wisdom will so prosper materially that they will be able to build their house and furnish it with every luxury."[26]

Whybray's understanding of 24:3–4 is not uncommon.[27] However, it is not fully adequate for understanding the wealth and poverty imagery of these lines. Notice first that the picture of 24:3–4—of a house full of "all precious treasures" (כל הון יקר)—is reminiscent of the words of the robbers in chapter one, where the text invites a figurative understanding. That the following lines, 24:5–6, speak of the wise person's intellectual abilities in terms of martial images, i.e., metaphorically, likewise hints that a figurative understanding of vv. 3–4 is warranted.[28] It may also be that the language of 24:3–4 is designed to evoke an image of personified Wisdom building a house as she does in 9:1, something that likewise moves the reader into the realm of the figurative, if not the mythological.[29] Or, perhaps

---

[26] Whybray, *Proverbs*, 343–344; emphasis original.

[27] See Clifford, *Proverbs*, 214, who alludes to 3:13–20 and writes of 24:3–4 that: "Such lines assured those courting wisdom that they would have wealth." Plöger rightly opts for a more figurative understanding of the verses suggesting that it is wisdom that fills life with what is of lasting worth, but he also leaves open another position: "*doch dürfte das reale Verständnis primär sein*" ("but on the contrary it may be that the literal understanding is primary"; *Sprüche Salomos*, 279). Cf. Helmer Ringgren and Walther Zimmerli, *Sprüche/Prediger* (Göttingen: Vandenhoeck & Ruprecht, 1962), 98.

[28] Cf. Plöger, *Sprüche Salomos*, 279. Proverbs 24:5–6 reads in the NJPS translation: "A wise man is strength; a knowledgeable man exerts power; for by stratagems you wage war, and victory comes with much planning."

[29] Or the language may evoke an image of YHWH creating the cosmos by wisdom as in 3:19–20. In these lines the same three terms that 24:3–4 uses ("wisdom," "understanding," and "knowledge") likewise appear. See too the description of wisdom at 8:30; cf. further Plöger, *Sprüche Salomos*, 279. Hausmann rejects the possibility that 24:3–4 alludes to Wisdom's house building. See *Menschenbild*, 284; cf. Meinhold, *Die Sprüche*, 2:401.

one is to understand 24:3–4 to be claiming that a "household," a family unit, is only built up through the virtues the lines highlight. If so, this picture of furnishing a house(hold) demands that the wealth language of v. 4 be understood in figurative terms, perhaps even allegorically, symbolizing, for example the members of the household.

The imagery of 24:3–4 is, of course, allusive and none of the possible understandings just sketched is necessarily exclusive of the others. The lines are multivalent and permit a variety of readings, including a more literal one. However, in light not only of features internal to the line—such as (perhaps) the personification of Wisdom—but also: a) the prologue's invitation to discern the tropes and figures of the book's moral instruction; b) the form of the saying, which evokes the metaphorical functions of folk proverbs; and c) the pattern of usage of wealth and poverty language both in the similar 21:20 and elsewhere in Proverbs' wisdom's virtues discourse, a literal reading could not exhaust the line's meaning. The wise and discerning reader of Prov 24:3–4 will recognize the text to be doing more than promising material goods. By associating Wisdom's or the wise person's "house" with images of material wealth, the text can be said to be primarily expressing the conviction that wisdom's way is overflowing with value in order to persuade the hearer to pursue that way.[30] Although motivating its claims through a promise of material goods, the promise of riches is not merely a literal promise. It also symbolically undergirds the larger claim of the wisdom mythos that virtue is that which is most valuable.

4.1.d. *The Comparative Valuing*

The association of wealth images with wisdom and virtue in constructions that intimate wealth to be a reward of wisdom is one of the prominent ways the sentence material in Proverbs speaks of the value of wisdom's virtues over and against the way of folly. Indeed a number of other wealth and poverty sayings in Proverbs that employ an explicit act-consequence rhetoric will be considered in Chapter Five. However, a different set of sentence sayings in Proverbs need to be considered next, for they make no use of a cause and

[30] Cf. Murphy, *Proverbs*, 180, who also recognizes the saying's concern with "motivation."

effect rhetoric that might imply they reflect, or are the product of, a simple mechanistic wisdom prosperity view of the cosmos. Instead they simply ascribe worth to virtue and vice by means of wealth and poverty language in a comparative construction.[31] Of course, all of the texts considered thus far have been employing a conceptual comparison, at least implicitly. In fact, one could argue that all claims to value deploy comparative modes of thinking—i.e., they involve judgments of some sort of what is of more worth than something else in regard to a specific purpose or end.[32] For the moral instruction of Proverbs, the nature of this judgment has to do with the ability of wisdom, versus other goods, including wealth, to bring about a good and flourishing life.

The wealth and poverty proverbs that employ the comparative are thus significant for two reasons. They are important first because such sayings make explicit the relational aspect of the value of wisdom to which I just alluded. The comparative sayings, however, are also important because they unambiguously speak of the value wisdom's way holds *over* material wealth. Furthermore, it is largely due to the absence of an act-consequence rhetoric in this kind of proverb that ambiguity arises in the discourse of wealth and poverty for those readers who understand the sages' words elsewhere in the book to reflect a wisdom prosperity axiom in the overly literalistic manner I described above. For many, as Murphy suggests in regard to 15:16 but alluding also to 16:8 (both treated below), such comparative wealth and poverty sayings are thought to "*modify* conventional wisdom by pointing up a *paradox*," namely, that "fear of the Lord"—and here one could substitute wisdom, righteousness or any virtue the book promotes—"is *no guarantee* of prosperity and riches, even if these are the benefits promised to the wise."[33] Similarly, Hausmann, who speaks of the relative value of wealth in proverbs like 15:16; 16:8; and 28:6 (likewise discussed below) concludes that these sayings

---

[31] Comparative constructions in chs. 10–31 that do not properly belong to the wisdom's virtues sub-discourse of wealth and poverty are: 16:32; 17:12; 21:9, 19; 27:5. The comparatives of 16:8 and 21:3 on the one hand, and 27:10 on the other hand, belong to the sub-discourses of social justice and social observation respectively. These proverbs will be treated below.

[32] See C. David Grant, *God the Center of Value: Value Theory in the Theology of H. Richard Niebuhr* (Fort Worth: Texas Christian University Press, 1984), esp. 25–69.

[33] Murphy, *Proverbs*, 113 (cf. 121); italics added.

demonstrate in part that the *Tun-Ergehen-Zusammenhang* is not something that is to be found at work everywhere in Proverbs. For her, no group of sayings is so "conflicting" (*zwiespältig*) or reveals such an ambivalence in perspective as the wealth and poverty sayings.[34] Likewise Clifford, who generally regards the use of antithetical pairs in Proverbs as an effort to "describe behavior and its consequences," believes (following Hausmann) that the rich and poor sayings are an exception in this regard.[35] Similarly Plöger's comment in connection with 28:6 that "uprightness is surely no infallible prescription to gain wealth" reveals that for him elsewhere the rhetoric of Proverbs in fact more or less straightforwardly points to such a moral rule.[36]

Though not necessarily wrong, the common understanding of the comparative wealth and poverty sayings as somehow "modifying" or "relativizing" the value of wealth needs nuance. Such a view is bound up with an overly literalistic understanding of the wisdom prosperity axiom. However, as I suggested above, the act-consequence nexus has less to do with empirical verifiability and more to do with a particular perception of the world; it is an integral piece of a wisdom mythos that makes sense within, and of, a particular social formation and set of values. In other words, it is not designed to offer reliable predictions of the success (e.g., enrichment) or failure (e.g., impoverishment) of particular individual lives.

With this understanding of the act-consequence nexus in mind, it becomes clear that the wealth and poverty images in the comparative sayings function in a manner analogous to the other sayings in the wisdom's virtues discourse: they ascribe worth to virtue and vice in a straightforward and fairly simple way. Because of the explicit use of a comparative construction, these sayings offer a clear judgment about what Proverbs deems *most* valuable for attaining a good life—wisdom. For these comparative wealth and poverty sayings to work rhetorically, however, the full value and desirability of material wealth needs to be in view. Certain of these proverbs intimate as well that when the desirable lesser good of wealth is overvalued

[34] Hausmann, *Menschenbild*, 335–338; 342–44. For an account of how various scholars (e.g., Whybray, Washington, Crenshaw) attempt to resolve this tension by an appeal to the provenance of different proverbs, see Chapter Two.

[35] Clifford, *Proverbs*, 22; cf. Hausmann (*Menschenbild*, 342).

[36] Plöger, *Sprüche Salomos*, 333–34; (*Redlichkeit ist sicher kein unfehlbares Rezept, um zu Reichtum zu gelangen*).

it produces effects which run counter to what the book envisions as key to a good and flourishing life.

Consider first Prov 15:16 and 16:8.

טוב־מעט ביראת יהוה מאוצר רב ומהומה בו

Better a little with the fear of the Lord, than abundant treasure with confusion.

טוב־מעט בצדקה מרב תבואות בלא משפט

Better a little with righteousness than abundant produce without justice.

Each saying employs economic language to speak of the worth of both righteousness and fear of the Lord. The texts claim that even if one possessed these proverbial virtues and nothing much of economic value, such a condition is of more value than (lit. "more 'good' than") if one possessed an abundance of what is of clear economic value without the virtues. There is here no promise of reward, material or otherwise, but simply an ascription of worth. The logical structure of the verses insists that an economic negative (little) plus a moral positive (fear of the Lord/righteousness) is of more value than an economic positive (abundant treasure/produce) and a moral negative (confusion/injustice).

The logic of 19:1 and 28:6 is similar:

טוב־רש הולך בתמו מעקש שפתיו והוא כסיל

Better a poor person walking in his uprightness than a person of perverse lips who is a fool.[37]

טוב־רש הולך בתמו מעקש דרכים והוא עשיר

Better a poor person walking in his uprightness than a person of perverse ways who is rich.[38]

---

[37] This verse and 19:2 are not found in LXX; cf. Murphy, *Proverbs*, 141.

[38] Some manuscripts erase the differences between 19:1 and 28:6 and it is in fact tempting to call 19:1 a corruption of the proverb attested in 28:6. For instance, according to the *BHS* apparatus prepared by Fichtner, some MSS have 19:1 read, instead of שפתיו ("his [two] lips"), דרכיו ("his ways"; though possibly, if only the consonants are read, "his two ways"). This is similar to 28:6's דרכים (dual; "two ways"). In any case, 28:6's un-suffixed dual form, though perhaps an allusion to the book's two-ways doctrine (so too Whybray, *Proverbs*, 390–91), seems odd. It may be better to read דרכיו ("his ways"; less likely, "his two ways") with the Syriac and Targum (and the similar 10:9). Moreover the Syriac of 19:1 reads the final word of this line as '*tjr*' (i.e., implying a correction to, or a *Vorlage* reading of, עשיר as in 28:6). Proverbs 19:1, however, should not be emended. The term כסיל is *lectio*

The two verses are nearly identical. The language of the first half of 19:1 is the same as what is found in the first half of 28:6. The second stich of 19:1 likewise begins with the same term with which the second half of 28:6 begins, "crookedness" (מעקש; rendered above as "perverse"). The lines also both end with a colophon introduced with the pronoun הוא. The antithesis of the poor person of whom the colophon of 19:1 speaks, however, is not the rich person as it is in 28:6, but the fool. Besides this shift, the difference between the two sayings lies in the fact that 19:1 points not so much to the general way of folly, but to a particular vice that belongs to that way—improper speech. That is, whereas 28:6 contrasts the poor (economic negative) but upright (moral positive) person with the rich (economic positive) person whose "ways" are crooked (moral negative), 19:1 contrasts the poor (economic negative), but upright (moral positive) person with the fool (moral negative) whose "lips" are crooked (a further moral negative).

Several other comparative proverbs ought to be considered as well. These are:

טוב ארחת ירק ואהבה־שם משור אבוס ושנאה־בו

> Better a meal of vegetables where there is love than a fattened ox where there is hate. (Prov 15:17)[39]

טוב שפל־רוח את־עניים מחלק שלל את־גאים

> Better to be humble and among the poor than to divide the spoil with the proud. (Prov 16:19)[40]

טוב פת חרבה ושלוה־בה מבית מלא זבחי־ריב

> Better a dry crust with peace than a house full of feasting with strife. (Prov 17:1)[41]

---

dificilor and there is nothing to explain adequately why this reading might have emerged to replace an original עשיר. Cf. Hausmann, *Menschenbild*, 89; Whybray, *Proverbs*, 275–76.

[39] The translation follows NJPS.

[40] The first half of the verse ends with a Ketiv-Qere (Ketiv עניים ["poor"]; Qere ענוים ["lowly"]). The Ketiv is to be preferred. Following the logic of 15:17 and 17:1, the first stich of 16:19 ought to include a virtue followed by an image which functions to value that virtue. In 16:9, the virtue of humility is already articulated by the phrase שפל־רוח ("humble"). What is expected is an image whose value or worth is easily recognizable and "poor" fits this situation best and corresponds to the broadly economic image of dividing spoils in the second verse half. The Greek (ταπεινώσεως) appears to follow the Qere, as do several scholars. See, for example, Plöger, *Sprüche Salomos*, 194; cf. Murphy, *Proverbs*, 118.

[41] The translation follows NJPS.

נבחר שם מעשר רב מכסף ומזהב חן טוב

Repute is preferable to great wealth, grace is better than silver and gold. (Prov 22:1)[42]

Without offering a promise of reward, each proverb deploys an image of material prosperity or lack to speak of the worth of different virtues and vices.[43] Similar to other comparative sayings, the logic of the lines insists that an economic negative plus a moral positive is of more worth than an economic positive with a moral negative. The text claims the virtues of love, humility, peace, etc., even if accompanied by meager material conditions, are more desirable and valuable than what is of clear material worth where certain vices (hate, pride, strife) are prominent. Moreover, the virtues which are being positively valued (love, humility, peace) are precisely the sort that would promote the social equity and harmony Proverbs so highly values while the vices (hate, pride, strife) are those which would hinder the establishment and maintenance of this social justice.[44]

Yet also important in several of these comparative sayings (e.g., 15:17; 16:19; 17:1) is the nature of the images with which the various undesirable vices are associated. They are certainly images of prosperity and material thriving. Yet they are specifically images that emerge from the world of an economic elite. This is particularly clear in 15:17 and 17:1 where the fattened ox and the "sacrifices" mentioned in the two lines point to the consumption of meat, which in the ancient world was, except for special occasions, largely the prerogative of the wealthy. The suggestion in 17:1 that a house might be "full" of feasting or sacrifice may also intimate that sayings like

---

[42] The translation follows NJPS.

[43] Again, the sayings cited here are sometimes said to be modifying a wisdom prosperity axiom, even if not disparaging wealth. In regard to 15.17, see Murphy, *Proverbs*, 113, who speaks of both this verse and the preceding v. 16 as proverbs which "modify conventional wisdom;" see, too, Toy, *Proverbs*, 310. In regard to 16:19 see again Murphy, *Proverbs*, 122, who writes: "It is not according to the expectations of the sages, who consistently rate prosperity as a blessing that comes to the wise." For Murphy, in this saying, "the usual scale of values is turned upside down." Cf. further Clifford, *Proverbs*, 160.

[44] Although שלוה ("peace") in 17:1 does not carry the same breadth of positive connotations as שלום, the images of well being and the parallelism of the term with שלום in Ps 122:7 indicates that it can connote a kind of social well being that is more than a tranquil or "quite life" to which Toy, for example, alludes in *Proverbs*, 335.

this are, in fact, depicting the practices of an economic elite.[45] The lines may thus contain an implicit critique of a certain kind of rich person.

Proverbs 16:19, however, is somewhat more complex. In this verse the term for "spoils"—שלל—and the image of sharing it, hearkens back to the robbers' discourse in chapter one (1:13). The terminology conjures images of wealth, if not unjustly acquired, taken violently at the expense of others.[46] However, those who divide booty here are not called sinners, but the proud. Although the language primarily points to the arrogance of those who divide spoils, it also is evocative of a discourse of social status. The "proud" in this verse may perhaps be those who seek not only to enrich themselves materially (probably by violent means), but those who believe that in so doing they insure for themselves a certain social prominence. What might be perceived by some (e.g., those who abide by that broad social script already alluded to) as the attainment of two good ends, wealth and the enhancement of social status, is problematic for the sages of Proverbs. For 16:19, it is better to tread humbly wisdom's way among the "poor" (i.e., the ענוים of the K) than proudly to play "the divider of spoils."

4.1.e. *The Value of Diligence*

One of the most common virtues that chapters 10–31 speaks of is diligence. A number of sayings underscore the worth of this virtue

[45] For a similar view, see Toy's remarks in regard to 15:17 in *Proverbs*, 310, that "*fatted ox* stands for luxury in general" (italics original). On 17:1 see Van Leeuwen's comment in "Proverbs," *NIB* 5:166, that: "Only the wealthy could afford abundant ('a house full,' see 1:13) sacrifices of meat."

[46] The rhetoric of "dividing spoils" is most at home in a military context (cf. Fuhs, *Das Buch der Sprichwörter*, 259) and here carries traces of its usage in that sphere, as Bakhtin would suggest (see Chapter One). Plöger, in *Sprüche Salomos*, 194, intimates, probably correctly, that here the sense is of wealth gained unjustly. Whybray, in *Proverbs*, 247, suggests the words "to divide spoils," though originally probably a military phrase, have come to mean simply, "to be wealthy." If Whybray is correct, this may be an instance where Proverbs implicitly critiques a certain kind of zealous quest for gain as problematic. Clifford believes that the issue at stake in the verse is vainly thinking that victory has been gained by one's own prowess. See *Proverbs*, 160. Clifford's understanding of both 15:17 and 17:1 is likewise somewhat different than mine. He believes that both are in essence comments regarding what makes a true or genuine feast. See *Proverbs*, 153, 164.

and disparage its corresponding vice—laziness—by means of a wealth and poverty (or related) rhetoric. Consider the following proverbs:

ראש עשה כף־רמיה ויד חרוצים תעשיר

> A slack hand makes a poor person, but the hand of the diligent enriches. (Prov 10:4)[47]

עבד אדמתו ישבע־לחם ומרדף ריקים חסר־לב

> The one who works his land will be sated with bread, but the one who pursues vanities has no sense. (Prov 12:11)[48]

בכל־עצב יהיה מותר ודבר־שפתים אך־למחסור

> In all toil is profit, but mere talk makes only for lack. (Prov 14:23)

אל־תאהב שנה פן־תורש פקח עיניך שבע־לחם

> Do not love sleep lest you be impoverished; open your eyes, have plenty of bread. (Prov 20:13)

על־שדה איש־עצל עברתי ועל־כרם אדם חסר־לב . . .
מעט שנות מעט תנומות מעט חבק ידים לשכב
ובא־מתהלך רישך ומחסריך כאיש מגן

> By the field of a lazy person I passed, by the vineyard of one who lacks sense . . .
> A little sleep, a little slumber, a little folding of the hands to lie down
> And your poverty will come marching, and your lack like a man with a shield. (Prov 24:30, 33–34)[49]

[47] The translation understands MT's *ʿōśeh* as the f. sg. participle *ʿōśāh*. Clifford, citing an oral communication with Choon-Leong Seow, notes that the second stich forces a re-reading of the first so that the poor person (ראש) "turns out to be the object rather than the subject of the verb. 'A slack hand' makes something—a pauper!" This is correct, especially if one were reading an un-pointed text. A pointed text, however, requires a re-pointing of עשה to the f. sg. Fichtner's *BHS* notes suggest emending *rāš* ("poor person") to *rēʾš* ("poverty") as well. Murphy, in *Proverbs*, 71, re-points both ראש and עשה though the former is not necessary; cf. Whybray, *Proverbs*, 158. The various readings in the versions testify to the difficulties in understanding the verse. See Toy, *Proverbs*, 200.

[48] Except for the final two words the saying is identical to 28:19.

[49] The passage has a close parallel in 6:10–11; cf. Murphy, *Proverbs*, 186. Although not affecting the sense, inexplicably "lack" here is cast in the plural (ומחסריך). According to Fichtner's *BHS* notes the manuscripts and versions mostly read the singular. For other peculiarities of the larger passage (vv. 30–34)—e.g., the three (vs. two) stichs of v. 31—see Whybray, *Proverbs*, 356 and 96–98.

עבד אדמתו ישבע־לחם ומרדף רקים ישבע־ריש

> The one who works his land will be sated with bread, but the one who purses vanities will be sated with poverty. (Prov 28:19)[50]

Each of these lazy/diligent sayings might be said to be based on the sages' observation of the social world.[51] In fact, the poem in chapter 24 itself claims as much (24:32).[52] In contrast to the comparative sayings, each proverb also employs a cause and effect rhetoric and reflects a wisdom prosperity axiom. Such sayings, moreover, are often considered some of the most troubling words in the entirety of Proverbs, for in speaking of the consequences of sloth they appear to, in Washington's words, "blame the poor" for their poverty.[53] The ethical implications of such sentiments, however, are generally recognized and commentators are quick to note that the verses, along with the judgment they appear to espouse, are not the only word Proverbs has to speak about wealth and poverty.[54] Indeed elsewhere the book can encourage kindness to the poor and even suggest that the impoverished possess the traits of the wise.

It is precisely this sort of situation that contributes to the common evaluation that Proverbs' wealth and poverty talk is ambiguous. Of course, the communicative context that one imagines for the different sayings affects how one understands them. Some scholars explain the force of the lazy/diligent proverbs for contemporary readers by underscoring the fact that such sayings emerged from a

---

[50] Except for the final two words the saying is identical to 12:11.

[51] See, for instance, Gerhard von Rad, *Wisdom in Israel* (London: SCM, 1972), 125; German original 1970. Cf. Claus Westermann, *Roots of Wisdom: The Oldest Proverbs of Israel and Other Peoples* (Louisville: WJK, 1995), 19; German original, 1990. Proverbs 13:11 might also be added to this set. It speaks of wealth hastily gotten as dwindling (cf. 28:20, 22), while underscoring the worth of the diligent person who gathers "little by little" (על יד).

[52] "I observed (ואחזה) and took it to heart; I saw it (ראיתי) and learned a lesson." (NJPS)

[53] Harold C. Washington, *Wealth and Poverty in the Instruction of Amenemope and the Hebrew Proverbs* (SBLDS 142; Atlanta: Scholars Press, 1996), 2.

[54] See, for example, Meinhold (*Die Sprüche* 1:168), who in commenting on 10:4 reminds us that the sages never say "the poor are always the lazy (but compare 13:8) and the rich person is always the industrious worker." Rather the wise "know full well that there exists also other, for example socially caused, [forms of] poverty." The full sentence in the original reads: *Die Weisen kehren die Aussage aber nicht um, dass sie sagen würden, der Arme sei immer auch der Faule (vgl. aber zu 13, 8) und der Reiche der bienenfleissige Arbeiter, wohl wissend, dass es auch andere, z. B. gesellschaftlich bedingte Armut gibt.*

particular historical milieu. They postulate that such sayings are most likely the ideological product of an upper class (or at least middle class) milieu, with the scholars themselves rejecting such a view of the complex sociological phenomenon of poverty.[55] Others locate such sayings in the world of subsistence agriculture where it is claimed laziness was a serious matter and in fact resulted in poverty.[56]

Each of these positions is defensible. Yet such readings understand the act-consequence rhetoric of the lines in an overly literalistic fashion. A quite different understanding emerges when one considers the sayings, on the one hand, in the broader context of the book's production in a scribal milieu and, on the other hand, in relation to the text's patterns of language usage and concerns that have already been described, especially its concern with valuing and motivating virtue.

If it is correct, as I argued above, that the context for the production of the book of Proverbs is among a scribal elite, then one must ask what kind of speech act the sayings constitute within this context. Furthermore, if the book of Proverbs is a text primarily concerned with moral instruction, as the prologue suggests and the sayings considered thus far intimate, then the lazy/diligent sayings are likely not in the first place concerned with offering quasi-sociological observations about how social groups (or "classes") come to be constituted. They are not designed to answer the question of why the poor are poor or the rich are rich, or to suggest, in some literal or empirical sense, that the reward and punishment for diligence and laziness is, respectively, wealth or poverty.

[55] See J. David Pleins, "Poverty in the Social World of the Wise," *JSOT* 37 (1987): 61–78, esp. 61; Bruce V. Malchow, "Social Justice in the Wisdom Literature," *BTB* 12 (1982): 120–124, esp. 121. Both represent the tendency of locating Israelite wisdom literature in a royal or upper class setting, a view based primarily on analogies with other ancient Near Eastern wisdom material that seems to find its provenance in or near the royal court. For an oft cited version of this view of the setting of Proverbs, see H.-J. Hermisson, *Studien zur israelitischen Spruchweisheit* (WMANT 28, Neukirchen-Vluyn: Neukirchener, 1968). Cf. von Rad, *Wisdom in Israel*, 11–12; Michael V. Fox, "The Social Location of the Book of Proverbs," in *Texts, Temples, and Traditions: A Tribute to Menahem Haran* (ed. Michael V. Fox et al.; Winona Lake, Ind.: Eisenbrauns, 1996), 227–239, esp. 236.

[56] See Washington, *Wealth and Poverty*, 184–85; cf. Westermann, *Roots*, 18–20; R. N. Whybray, *Wealth and Poverty in the Book of Proverbs* (JSOTSup 99; Sheffield: JSOT, 1990), 30–31; and Friedemann W. Golka, *The Leopard's Spots: Biblical and African Wisdom in Proverbs* (Edinburgh: T&T Clark, 1993).

The logic of the lines—the pairing of a moral negative with an economic negative—is analogous to the logic of many sayings belonging to the wisdom's virtues discourse that have already been considered. Much of the wealth and poverty vocabulary in the lines—terms such as מחסור (12:27; 24:34), and especially forms derived from ע-ש-ר and ר-י-ש (10:4; 24:34)—is likewise typical of sayings belonging to the wisdom's virtues discourse. By contrast, sayings that are primarily concerned with articulating something about the condition of the poor belong to the social justice discourse (see below) and normally deploy a different kind of rhetoric (e.g., דל, אביון, עני), as do proverbs belonging to the discourse of social observation (see Chapter Five).

Although the lazy/diligent proverbs offer a promise of well being through images of material wealth and lack, as with 24:3–4, the book's prologue, the folk-like form of the sayings, and the patterns of metaphorical usage already established by the wisdom's virtues discourse suggests that these promises ought not to be understood only as literal promises of literal wealth. That is, the emerging moral and literary Gestalt of the book indicates the promise of wealth in the sayings serves a broader symbolic purpose. As is typical of the wisdom's virtues discourse, the lazy/diligent proverbs cited above employ an economic discourse as a clear and easily recognizable measure of the value of the virtues and vices of which they speak. They function to persuade the hearer of the value and desirability of a variety of virtues (working the land, toiling, remaining active), and the undesirability of certain vices (pursuing vanity, idle talk, love of sleep, slackness, lack of sense). As with other wisdom's virtues proverbs, the specific, individual virtues and vices in the different sayings also function as a kind of synecdoche (the particular for the universal) for a more general virtue or vice, in this case diligence and laziness, usually represented in Hebrew by the term חרוץ on the one hand, and רמיה (or a form of the root ע-צ-ל) on the other.[57]

That the lazy/diligent sayings are first and foremost concerned with saying something about virtue and vice and are not primarily offering literal promises or comments on the origins of rich and poor

[57] A form of ע-צ-ל appears in Proverbs at 6:6, 9; 10:26; 13:4; 15:19; 19:15, 24; 20:4; 21:25–26; 22:13; 24:30; 26:13, 14, 15, 16; 31:27. The term רמיה appears at Prov 10:4; 12:24, 27; 19:15. The term חרוץ is attested at Prov 10:4; 12:24, 27; 13:4; 21:5; cf. Hausmann, *Menschenbild*, 138.

people is clear as well from one further observation: they belong to a larger group of lazy/diligent proverbs that do not always employ an economic rhetoric. Proverbs 10:26 is a good example:

כחמץ לשנים וכעשן לעינים כן העצל לשלחיו

> Like vinegar to the teeth and like smoke to the eyes, thus is the lazy person to the one sending him.

Proverbs 15:19 is significant as well, for this proverb contrasts the lazy person not with the diligent person, but with upright persons—the ישרים—a term that belongs fundamentally to moral discourse.[58]

דרך עצל כמשכת חדק וארח ישרים סללה

> The way of a lazy person is like a hedge of thorns, but the path of the upright is paved.[59]

Both 10:26 and 15:19 follow a logic analogous to the lazy/diligent proverbs discussed above. However, instead of pairing a moral negative with an economic negative, 10:26 pairs a moral negative (a lazy person) with an image of negative physical sensation (vinegar to the teeth and smoke to the eyes). Proverbs 15:19 builds, especially, on the moral metaphor of the way. On the one hand, it associates a moral negative (a lazy person's way) with a navigational negative (a hedge of thorns); on the other hand, it associates a moral positive (the upright person's path) with a navigational positive (pavement).

Proverbs 12:27 likewise is clearly more concerned to say something about virtue than with offering an observation about the rich and poor. It reads:

לא־יחרך רמיה צידו והון־אדם יקר חרוץ

> A lazy person does not roast his game, but the precious wealth of a person is diligence.[60]

---

[58] Other sayings in Proverbs that have to do with diligence and laziness, but which do not draw on explicit wealth and poverty language include: 12:24; 13:4; 18:9; 19:24; 22:13; 26:13–16. Proverbs 21:25–26, more explicitly, has to do with the economic virtue of generosity. In these lines the lazy person refuses to labor, but the righteous person gives freely.

[59] The translation follows NJPS.

[60] The verse is problematic. The sense of the first stich is either that the slothful person has no game to roast or is too lazy to bother. The meaning of the verb חרך, however, is uncertain. It is a *hapax* in HB and, according to Whybray, the rendering "roast" is a conjecture based on the verb's sense in post-biblical Hebrew and Aramaic where the meaning "singe" or "char" is attested. Whybray reports as

The line is a *crux*, which, however, when read in the context of the book's effort to value virtue and vice, begins to make some sense. Although the second half of the verse employs wealth terminology, the first verse half is not an economic saying and indicates that the line's principle focus is on the virtue of diligence. Moreover, though the second stich is difficult, Rashi's suggestion that it means something like "but the precious wealth of a person is (to be) diligent" is on target. Such a rendering, unlike certain proposals for emendation, preserves the intertextual echo with the sinners' rhetoric of chapter one.[61] This echo evokes a contrast between the robbers' quest for הון יקר—"valuable wealth," which leads to violence and death rather than well being—and the truly valuable virtue of diligence, figuratively called הון אדם יקר ("a person's precious wealth"). The line also plays on the word חרוץ, which besides "diligent" can also mean "gold."[62] According to this proverb, the precious wealth of a person is not "gold," as one might suspect, but the attainment of virtue, diligence.

The lazy/diligent sayings that use economic imagery thus are a subset of a larger group that deploy a variety of images and belong to the ancient sages' efforts at moral instruction. The sort of speech act these lazy/diligent sayings constitute is thus clarified: their purpose is not to explain disparities in the distribution of wealth, but like the other sayings belonging to the wisdom's virtues discourse, to recommend a virtue and to discourage a vice. The hearer of the

---

well that modern Hebrew attests the meaning "roast" for this root and that medieval Jewish commentators understood the word in Proverbs similarly. See *Proverbs*, 198; cf. Murphy, *Proverbs*, 88. In regard to the second half of the verse, Driver understands יקר to have been transposed with חרוץ and "to mean not so much 'precious' as 'heavy', which is the literal force of the root." He confidently states: "surely the true reading is simply והון אדם חרוץ יקר 'but the wealth of the diligent man is much.'" See G. R. Driver, "Problems in the Hebrew Text of Proverbs," *Biblica* 32 (1951): 173–197, esp. 180. This is an attractive option and appears to be how Clifford (*Proverbs*, 128) understands the line. Nonetheless it should be rejected. It obscures an important intertextual allusion to the "precious wealth" promised by the robbers in ch. 1. Although חרוץ is properly the adjective "diligent" rather than the noun "diligence," Rashi understands the sense correctly: "the wealth of a person is (to be) diligent"—cited by Toy, *Proverbs*, 258 and Murphy, *Proverbs*, 88; cf. below. Murphy also appears to accept the re-ordering of the terms suggested by Driver, but preserves the meaning of "precious" for יקר: "but the wealth of a diligent person is precious." For other possible understandings of the second stich, see Toy, *Proverbs*, 258–59 and cf. Fuhs, *Das Buch der Sprichwörter*, 209, 214–15.

[61] For these proposed emendations, see n. 60.

[62] Cf. Prov 3:14; 8:10, 19; 16:16.

lazy/diligent wealth and poverty sayings is being rhetorically prodded into a life of industrious activities with the threatening rod of poverty or dispossession behind him and the carrot of financial security or abundance dangled in front of him.

4.1.f. *Conclusions*

The primary concern of the wealth and poverty proverbs considered in this section is to insist on the incomparable value of wisdom's virtues and to communicate the undesirability of folly's vices. The majority of the sayings considered contain features internal to the proverbs themselves that highlight their figurative qualities. However, a figurative understanding of the different wealth and poverty proverbs is further supported by the prologue's invitation to discern the book's tropes. It is supported as well by the very form of the sayings, which is reminiscent of folk proverbs that regularly function metaphorically to say something about human life. As *meshalim*, all of the wealth and poverty proverbs considered thus far ought to be understood as containing and constituting genuine tropes that the hearer or reader is invited to discern. A good number of the wealth and poverty sayings considered thus far, moreover, do not employ any sort of act-consequence rhetoric. Certain sayings, however, do employ images of material well being in a manner that intimates a wisdom prosperity axiom or an act-consequence nexus is, in some sense, to be discerned in Proverbs. Yet, as I have shown, aspects of even these sayings point to their figurative qualities, or otherwise indicate that their wealth and poverty language and act-consequence rhetoric should not be read in an overly literal fashion.

The patterns of usage of wealth and poverty language established by this initial analysis of the wisdom's virtues discourse in Prov 10–31 (and in chapters 1–9) should encourage one to view similar images elsewhere in the collections—e.g., in sayings that employ a more explicit cause and effect rhetoric—less as literal promises than as analogous rhetorical motivations. As I will suggest in Chapter Five, the wealth and poverty sayings in Proverbs that deploy a more explicit act-consequence rhetoric do not merely offer simple promises of prosperity. They also serve a broader symbolic purpose. Though promising material reward, in so doing they sure up the wisdom mythos that insists on the incomparable value of a life of virtue, a manner of being which the cosmos itself favors.

4.2. The Discourse of Social Justice in Proverbs 10–31

4.2.a. *Characteristics*

The wisdom's virtues discourse in Proverbs employs the rhetoric of wealth and poverty in order to persuade the hearer or reader of the value of wisdom's way and particular virtues associated with that way. Although assuming the value and desirability of riches, it has little concrete instruction to offer concerning economic matters, except cautions against overvaluing wealth. The various sayings of chapters 10–31 considered thus far propose little that might imply a particular concrete economic ethic or suggest how a reader or hearer of the book should regard wealth and poverty or act toward the poor or rich.

Yet Proverbs is far from silent on such matters. The text in fact is quite explicit in its insistence that one engage in fair economic practices, particularly as regards the use of weights and measures. It also recommends to the hearer a general stance of kindness to the poor and at points is very specific in stating that this kindness should be embodied in just dealings with the poor, especially in the legal sphere. Several sayings in Proverbs also underscore the role of a royal figure or political elites in maintaining minimum standards of justice for the economically marginalized, and this aspect of Proverbs' instruction is reminiscent of a larger biblical and ancient Near Eastern royal ideology of social maintenance. The book appears simply to have adopted features of that paternalistic discourse into its own ethical vision and one can say, in Bakhtinian terms, the proverbial rhetoric carries traces of its life of use in that broader sphere.[63]

Although the text's insistence that justice and kindness be shown the poor is clearly a virtue and value that belongs to the way of wisdom, the sayings that commend such a stance employ a wealth and poverty rhetoric that is distinct from the wisdom's virtues discourse. In contrast to that discourse, these sayings prefer the personal language of the "poor person," especially the substantivized

[63] On this larger ideology of social justice in the ancient Near East, see F. Charles Fensham, "Widow, Orphan, and the Poor in Ancient Near Eastern Legal and Wisdom Literature," *JNES* 21 (1962): 129–139; Moshe Weinfeld, *Social Justice in Ancient Israel and in the Ancient Near East* (Jerusalem: Magnes, 1995).

adjectives דל, אביון, עני, and appear either as indicative statements or admonitions. The poor in these sentences are also, grammatically speaking, always objects acted upon, not subjects who act. The rhetoric of wealth and poverty in this group of proverbs, moreover, unlike those comprising the wisdom's virtues discourse, does not regularly function figuratively in the service of a larger didactic end. Although several of the Proverbs employ metaphors, there is nothing in the sayings that suggests the sayings are concerned to offer the hearer anything other than instruction about wealth and poverty. The particular modes of conduct and general dispositions that this discourse of wealth and poverty recommends to the hearer or reader have to do specifically with the hearer's character and real economic practices. Taken together, sayings in Proverbs that exhibit these features make up, within the larger moral discourse of the instruction, a second discernable sub-discourse of wealth and poverty, which I call a discourse of social justice.

4.2.b. *Justice in Economic Practices*

The most obvious manner by which Proverbs attempts to construct a particular economic ethic for its hearers is in its insistence that the hearer who would be wise act rightly and fairly in the economic sphere by using accurate weights and measures. Several proverbs make these kinds of concerns explicit.

מאזני מרמה תועבת יהוה ואבן שלמה רצונו

> False scales are an abomination to the Lord; an honest weight pleases him. (Prov 11:1)

פלס ומאזני משפט ליהוה מעשהו כל־אבני־כיס

> Just scales and balances are the Lord's; all the weights in the bag are his work. (Prov 16:11)

אבן ואבן איפה ואיפה תועבת יהוה גם־שניהם

> False weights and false measures; both are an abomination to the Lord. (Prov 20:10)[64]

[64] In the Hebrew the phrases "false weights" and "false measures" are literally "stone and stone" and "*ephah* and *ephah*" respectively. The repetition (as in 20:23a) probably is an allusion to the practice of deceptively employing two sets of measures and weights. Cf. Murphy, *Proverbs*, 151.

תועבת יהוה אבן ואבן ומאזני מרמה לא־טוב

> False weights are an abomination to the Lord; dishonest scales are not good. (Prov 20:23)

Each of these proverbs evaluates the importance of the use of fair or dishonest weights and measures (particular economic practices) by reference to YHWH rather than some lesser locus of value, say wealth (cf. 14:31 below). Here the deity is the touchstone for determining the worth of virtue and the one who motivates adherence to the ethic the sayings promote. Proverbs 11:1; 20:10; and 20:23 negatively evaluate, and hence discourage, the use of false weights and measures by calling these תועבת יהוה, an "abomination to the Lord." Although nothing in the lines creates and absurdity that would force a re-reading of the saying in metaphorical terms, the language of abomination that the lines employ has a rich and varied range of usage. The term תועבה itself appears at least ten times in Proverbs.[65] The basic meaning of the root appears to be "to abhor, loathe" and the rhetoric is perhaps most familiar from the realm of the cult where it can, among other things, evaluate negatively the use of unclean animals for food (Deut 14:3) and certain sexual practices (Lev 18:22). However foreign gods (Deut 32:16) and the customs of foreign nations (1 Kgs 14:24) can also be described as תועבה. Amos (5:10; cf. 6:8) and Micah (3:9), moreover, deploy this rhetoric not only to speak of cultic shortcomings, but to evaluate the relationship of these shortcomings to violations in the moral, especially economic realm. In an ethical sense, all that is "irreconcilable with YHWH's nature and rejected by him," is תועבה.[66] In short, that which is an abomination to YHWH is something offensive, detestable, or abhorrent to this deity. Such, for Proverbs, is the use of dishonest weights and measures.

The second half of Prov 20:23 also more broadly calls the use of false weights "not good." Though this may be a simple evaluation of the practice, it resonates with those sayings to be considered below where the language of the "good" is more intimately related to virtue—i.e., associated with what is "good" or necessary for a flourishing

[65] Prov 6:16, 12; 8:7; 13:9; 16:12; 21:27; 24:9; 26:25; 28:9; 29:27.

[66] E. Gerstenberger, *THAT* 2:1054; (*sind mit dem Wesen Jahwes unvereinbar und von ihm abgelehnt*).

human life. By contrast, Prov 16:11 deploys a more positive rhetoric to associate honest scales and balances with YHWH. They belong to him and he is their "maker." Literally they are called "scales and balances of justice" (משפט), and in 11:1 are said to constitute YHWH's pleasure (רצונו).

The primary function of the different sorts of language in these proverbs that have to do with economic practices is, of course, to encourage the hearer who would be wise and righteous to use fair and honest measures in the economic realm.[67] An implication of the rhetoric, however, is that such practices are integral pieces to the establishment of the social justice the book, especially in the prologue (1:3) so highly values, and which for Proverbs is prerequisite for a good life.

4.2.c. *Kindness to the Poor*

The book of Proverbs also presents to its hearers and readers a number of sayings that make clear that the virtue of showing kindness to the poor belongs to the way of wisdom. Such a disposition is an important, perhaps the most important, component of the economic ethic the book puts forward and is too an integral piece of the social justice the book commends. Consider first Prov 14:31:

עשק־דל חרף עשהו ומכבדו חנן אביון

> Whoever oppresses the poor insults his maker, but whoever is kind to the needy honors him. (Prov 14:31)

The first half of the verse speaks of the poor דל, a poverty rhetoric typical of the social justice discourse. The second stich deploys the term אביון, the functional synonym of דל. The proverb, moreover, reveals no indisputable absurdity when read literally and poverty language in the verse is not employed figuratively to a larger instructional end. The verse motivates its claims not with economic rhetoric as the wisdom's virtues discourse does, but similar to the sayings promoting the use of accurate measures, by an explicit appeal to

[67] Proverbs 22:28, which admonishes the hearer: "Do not remove the ancient boundary stone that your ancestors set up" (NJPS) can also be said to belong generally to the set of social justice proverbs that insist on the use of honest and fair weights and measures.

the deity. One's action toward the poor simultaneously constitutes an action toward God. A particular kind of behavior toward the poor person (oppressing) offends, and another kind of behavior toward this one (showing kindness) venerates, the deity. The fundamental concern of the proverb is to discourage abuse of the poor in particular and advocate graciousness toward the same. The line's repeated use of the participle, moreover, hints that the saying is not simply offering an occasional command but is concerned with the formation of the hearer's disposition.[68]

The discourse of social justice in Proverbs also contains a number of sayings that advocate protection of the poor in the legal sphere in particular. Proverbs 22:22 and 29:7, for instance, are succinct in their demands for just treatment of the poor in the forensic realm. The verses read:

אל־תגזל־דל כי דל־הוא ואל־תדכא עני בשער

> Do not rob the poor person because he is a poor person; do not crush the lowly person in the gate.

ידע צדיק דין דלים רשע לא־יבין דעת

> The righteous know the rights of the poor; the wicked have no such understanding.

Proverbs 22:22, which belongs to the opening of the so-called Amenemope section of the book, is cast as a negative admonition. This fact distinguishes it formally from many other social justice sayings, including 29:7. However, as I suggested in Chapter One, indicative statements or observations in Proverbs often function as admonitions. Because the text is persistently concerned with instructing a hearer in virtue, such is likely the case here.

There is also nothing in either 22:22 or 29:7—no absurdity or other maker—to suggest these sayings ought to be understood figuratively.[69] Both verses, moreover, use the same personal terminology for the poor common to the discourse of social justice—the substantivized adjective דל (pl. in 29:7). Proverbs 22:22, however,

---

[68] The participial forms in 14:31 are: *ʿōšēq* ("oppressing"), *ḥōnēn* ("being kind, generous"), *mĕkabbēd* ("honoring").

[69] In Prov 13:23 דכא ("to beat to pieces, crush") is probably best considered a "dead metaphor" that has simply come to mean "oppress."

also introduces a new word, עני, as the parallel to דל. As in 14:31 where דל and its parallel אביון function as like terms, so here דל and עני are essentially equivalents.[70] The latter lexeme (עני) is also a substantivized adjective and likewise belongs to the personal language of poverty. Regardless of the term deployed, the poor in each verse are also grammatical objects.[71]

The language of 22:22 and 29:7, especially the image of the "gate" (שער), and the rhetoric of the "right" (דין), "wicked" (רשע), and "righteous" (צדיק) is drawn from the legal sphere. The demands in 22:22 that the hearer not "rob" specifically the דל nor "crush" specifically the עני are motivated by the claim in v. 23 that YHWH will "plead the case" of the poor and exact punishment on those who perpetrate wrong against them, imagery that likewise points to the legal realm.[72] This cluster of terms, and especially the allusion to the "gate" in 22:22—a term in HB used to describe the locus of judicial activity—indicates that these texts are primarily interested in curbing oppressive activities within a forensic context. Proverbs 22:22, moreover, implies in particular that the wise and righteous person will not use the advantage economic or social position (potentially) brings to judicial proceedings to gain unjustly at the expense of the poor. The legal sphere is thus a particular realm where Proverbs believes the ethical principle of kindness to the poor can be embodied. There is here no split between virtue and law (or legal "rightness"). Rather for Proverbs legal institutions should provide a context for the living of a virtuous life (particularly vis-à-vis the poor).

McKane believes Prov 29:7 is one of the "few examples of a wisdom sentence which is an instrument of prophetic teaching" and that the lexemes "know" and "knowledge" are being deployed in "the prophetic sense."[73] However, it is unnecessary to draw a sharp distinction here between wisdom and prophetic teaching, for both

[70] In the discourse of social justice all three terms—דל, אביון, and עני—are functional synonyms.

[71] Though דל in the second half of 22:22a is employed in a nominal clause.

[72] Proverbs 22:23 reads: כי יהוה יריב ריבם וקבע את־קבעיהם נפש ("For YHWH will plead their case and despoil the ones despoiling them of life;" following NJPS). The meaning of קבע, however, is uncertain. Toy (*Proverbs*, 425–26) notes the word elsewhere in HB appears only in Mal 3:8–9 and suggests a sense of "rob" or "cheat." Cf. Murphy, *Proverbs*, 169.

[73] William McKane, *Proverbs: A New Approach* (Philadelphia: Westminster, 1970), 641.

types of literature draw on larger ancient Near Eastern conceptions of justice. The language of both wisdom and prophetic discourses, in Bakhtin's terms, 'tastes' of its life in a larger ancient Near Eastern discourse of social maintenance. Rather than deploying terms in a prophetic sense, it is better to say that in 29:7, the proverbial discourse of social justice provides a kind of diagnostic case to suggest that the wicked and the righteous stand in different relationship to knowledge, to wisdom. "Knowing" the legal rights of specifically the poor (presumably so that one might act from this knowledge) is the particular virtue this verse wishes to inculcate in the hearer. As von Rad writes: "Wherever the wise men encourage men to practise good behaviour, wherever they try to prevent bad, what is characteristic is the fact that they address themselves to man's ability to think and to his better understanding, in order to reach him by way of reflection."[74] The prologue's highlighting of not only social (and practical) virtues, but also intellectual virtues, together with the book's ordering of certain virtues under the rubric of wisdom (and not only righteousness), also makes clear that the morally "right" person in Proverbs is the one who "knows" rightly. In the legal sphere this means understanding the rights of the poor. The morally wicked person is the one who lacks such understanding. As 28:5 states, though deploying somewhat different terminology:

אנשי־רע לא־יבינו משפט ומבקשי יהוה יבינו כל

> Evil people do not understand judgment; but those who seek the Lord understand all.

4.2.d. *Social Justice and the King*

A number of sayings in Proverbs make mention of the king or a politically elite figure.[75] There is some debate as to whether these proverbs originated in a royal context or find their provenance with

[74] Von Rad, *Wisdom in Israel*, 93. Von Rad's n. 28 reveals that 29:7 is one of the verses he has in mind with such a statement. However, although von Rad recognizes that behind the sages' instruction is a "knowledge of Yahweh's desire for justice" he understands the "law of the act consequence relationship" more literally than I and is more certain than I that the sages' insights are "certainly to be attributed to the experience that they are under the curse of their evil deeds."

[75] For a discussion of the "royal proverbs," see Whybray, *Wealth and Poverty*, 45–59.

the rural folk. Whybray, for example, argues that the "royal proverbs" probably emerged, not in a courtly setting, but in the context of the small farming village.[76] By contrast, Fox suggests, *pace* Whybray, that the language and imagery of the royal proverbs almost certainly emerged from a courtly context.[77] Whatever the origins, or 'genealogies' (see Chapter Two), of the royal proverbs in Proverbs, they are, in the form that we have them in the book, the product of a scribal elite; and several of these utterances belong to the discourse of social justice. Like other sayings belonging to this discourse, these social justice royal proverbs promote the virtue of showing kindness to, and insuring justice for, the poor. A number of the sayings are particularly important, however, for like certain proverbs in the wisdom's virtues discourse treated above, they might be heard on more than one level (cf. 16:19; 17:1; 19:17). Recalling the prologue's invitation to consider wisely the book's tropes and figures is thus also important for understanding fully the social justice discourse, a discourse in which wealth and poverty rhetoric is generally not employed figuratively.

Consider first 28:15, a saying that employs the personal language of דל as the object of the actions of the politically elite figure the text depicts. The saying reads:

ארי־נהם ודב שוקק משל רשע על עם־דל

> A roaring lion and a prowling bear is a wicked man ruling a poor people.

McKane believes proverbs like 28:15 are "a consequence of the careful observation of misrule and its effects."[78] Although a saying like 28:15 could be considered a poetic description of certain kinds of social interaction ("the way things are"), it would be a mistake to assume that it is only an observation. Rather one ought to consider how the verse functions rhetorically and ask what it is "doing" in

[76] Whybray, *Wealth and Poverty*, 45–59.

[77] Fox, "Social Location," 227–239, esp. 232–234. Fox's criticism of a position like Whybray's seems valid, but somewhat overstated. My own view is that although a proverb may employ a particular set of images, it does not necessarily follow that the saying emerged out of the precise milieu from which the images were taken.

[78] McKane, *Proverbs*, 628. McKane is speaking not only of 28:15, but of 28:3 and 16 as well. He writes further that all of these sayings can be "explained as an empirical judgment that probity in politics is the best policy."

the larger moral discourse as well as inquire as to what value or virtue it is recommending or what vice it is disavowing.

The images of the bear prowling and the lion roaring metaphorically define and characterize the actions of the "wicked ruler" toward the דל. Syntactically דל in 28:15 is not required and "people" (עם) might have been modified in another way or not at all. But the adjective's presence provides a degree of specificity for the hearer. The image of the משל רשע ("wicked ruler") is alluding to, if not a royal personage (as 29:14 plainly does; see Chapter Five), then certainly a political figure who does not ensure justice for his עם ("people"). That the following verse (28:16; treated below) deploys the explicit political designation נגיד, describing this person as one who "oppresses," likewise suggests v. 15 is concerned with a political figure and not simply anyone who exercises authority perversely.[79] Because the king in ancient Near Eastern royal ideology has a special duty to ensure the establishment and maintenance of justice, the failure to do so might be viewed as particularly destructive behavior on the part of a political elite so that the images of devouring beasts in 28:15 is especially appropriate.[80]

However deciding whether the imagery in 28:15 was originally concerned to address those in a royal or political context or some other realm is not vital, for it is clear that all Israelites, not just the monarch, had an obligation to act justly toward the poor. Hence, on one level, the didactic end of the verse is not merely or primarily to point out the nature of the *real politick*, but is to discourage a hearer of any standing from acting in unjust ways. The proverb is not so much stating an observation as it is admonishing all hearers to insure the poor דל receives justice. Yet the rhetoric of politics that the proverb employs is more significant as well. Like the rhetoric

[79] Proverbs 28:16 also belongs to the discourse of social justice but will be treated below because its rhetoric follows a more clear act-consequence logic.

[80] Cf. 28:3 which employs analogous images of destruction:

גבר רש ועשק דלים מטר סחף ואין לחם

A pauper who oppresses the poor is a destructive rain that leaves no food.

Although the verse is perfectly comprehensible, the notion of poor persons oppressing other poor persons—an easily verifiable social occurrence—sometimes appears incongruous to interpreters and subsequently different emendations of the line are regularly proposed (e.g., רש to רשע). If "pauper" (רש) in this verse is emended to "prince" (שר), positing a metathesis, it perhaps reflects a similar understanding as 28:15.

of feasting on flesh and sacrifice in 15:17 and 17:1, the terminology in 28:15 is particularly freighted and might be heard in different ways by different hearers. With its negative characterization of the "wicked" ruler, 28:15 is not only a sentence that exhorts any hearer of any social or political rank, it also functions as a declarative speech act. It decrees institutional (royal) abuses of power to be illegitimate (cf. 19:7; 22:9; 28:16; treated in Chapter Five).

Some of the wisdom material attributed to a certain Agur in chapter 30 appears also to concern a political elite and likewise employs a rhetoric of wealth and poverty that belongs to the sub-discourse of social justice.[81] After describing a haughty, impure, and supercilious kind of human in 30:11–13, verse fourteen continues its depiction of such persons. They are:

דור חרבות שניו ומאכלות מתלעתיו
לאכל עניים מארץ ואביונים מאדם

> A breed whose teeth are swords and whose jaws are knives ready to devour the poor of the land, the needy among humans.[82]

Although the lines deploy metaphor, as with other verses belonging to the discourse of social justice, this text does not make use of wealth and poverty language figuratively in order to value virtue and vice. Rather, in keeping with the character of the discourse of social justice, the text employs the personal language of poverty—the substantivized adjectives עני and אביון—as grammatical objects. The violent and vivid language, which similar to 28:15 evokes images of hungry, wild beasts on the prowl, depicts the activity of those who oppress the poor. Although the verse does not explicitly instruct the hearer to avoid such activities, it is clear from the negative imagery that the instructing voice abhors such behavior. In fact, some of the terms and images in the larger pericope describing this "breed of people"—e.g., exultation in one's eyes (30:13)—are elsewhere in Proverbs explicitly associated with the way of folly.[83] As McKane

---

[81] For discussions of the critical issues associated with the Agur collection see Toy, *Proverbs*, 517–18; McKane, *Proverbs*, 643–47.

[82] The final word of v. 14, מאדם ("from/among humans"), might be emended to מאדמה ("from the earth"), which would provide a neater parallelism with the first half of the line. However, the line as it stands is comprehensible.

[83] See, for example, 26:12 and 28:11 where the image (if not identical language) of persons being exalted in their own eyes, is also found.

notes, though the form of the verses hints that they are observations, they function as "denunciatory preaching."[84] Like other sayings belonging to the discourse of social justice, they are not simply a colorful description of the way the world often works, but offer a judgment on certain types of behavior and serve as a kind of admonition. However, although no hearer of the proverb is to oppress the poor, the censure of 30:14 is not merely individualistic. The allusions in the line to sword and knife may also point to those who are invested with the power of the sword—the political elite. For those in the social position to discern it as such, this *mashal*, like 28:15, can function as a censure of institutional political violence.

Finally, Prov 31:2–9 is a further passage belonging to the discourse of social justice that has to do with the role of political elites in maintaining social justice. After Lemuel's mother exhorts him to avoid women and strong drink, neither of which is fitting for princes, in verses five to nine she states her rationale and an alternative:

(5) פן ישתה וישכח מחקק וישנה דין כל־בני־עני
(6) תנו־שכר לאובד ויין למרי נפש
(7) ישתה וישכח רישו ועמלו לא יזכר־עוד
(8) פתח־פיך לאלם אל־דין כל־בני חלוף
(9) פתח־פיך שפט־צדק ודין עני ואביון

5) Lest they [princes] drink and forget what has been ordained, and infringe on the rights of the poor.[85]
6) Give beer to the perishing and wine to the embittered.[86]
7) Let them drink and forget their poverty and put their troubles out of mind.[87]
8) Speak up for the dumb, for the rights of all the unfortunate.[88]
9) Speak up, judge righteously, champion the poor and needy.

---

[84] McKane, *Proverbs*, 652.

[85] The translation of the passage largely follows NJPS. Line five employs singular verbs when plural forms are expected based on v. 4's mention of מלכים ("kings") and רוזנים ("princes"). However, as Murphy notes (*Proverbs*, 240) these forms might be regarded as collectives in v. 5.

[86] The line oddly reverts to the plural in the imperative just at the point one might expect a singular form to begin the Queen Mother's address to Lemuel.

[87] The verbs and pronouns in this line are all in the singular. Plural English forms are deployed for ease of reading in translation.

[88] The final word of the line, חלוף, is difficult. The rendering "unfortunate" follows NJPS. Murphy (*Proverbs*, 240) suggests it may mean "one passed on or over or away." Fichtner's *BHS* notes posit an emendation of the term to חלי ("sickness"), suggesting the final *peh* appears as a result of dittography with the first letter of the next word, v. 9's פתח.

The duty of the king to insure justice for the poor is underscored by these verses. The Queen Mother is plainly drawing on motifs from the ancient Near Eastern ideology of kingship and for the most part the passage reveals the rhetorical features associated with the sub-discourse of social justice. The terminology she uses, for instance, is the personal language of the substantivized adjectives עני and אביון, and these "poor" are again objects of the activity she encourages. The legal language of "rights," "judging," and "advocacy" (דין, שפט, פתח פי) is also prominent. To the extent that any reader or hearer can recognize the call to just dealings with the poor in the lines, they function as a general exhortation for all and not only for a royal figure. However, because the passage's rhetoric has explicitly to do with a king, like other proverbs having to do with the duty of political figures, it articulates a standard by which the legitimacy of political elites can be measured.[89]

4.2.e. *Conclusions*

Acting fairly in the economic sphere by employing honest weights and measures, showing kindness to the economically marginalized, and tending to the rights of the poor in the legal realm are all virtues of wisdom's way. To this extent the discourse of social justice is similar to the wisdom's virtues discourse. The difference is that in the discourse of social justice wealth and poverty rhetoric is not used figuratively to value virtue as it regularly is in the wisdom's virtues discourse. The economic rhetoric of the discourse of social justice rather is concerned specifically with highlighting particular economic virtues for the hearer, i.e., with constructing a particular economic ethic for its addressee.[90] The social justice discourse in large part seeks to minimize the negative social effects that poverty, the manipulation of the legal sphere, the falsifying of weights and measures, or the oppressive execution of royal or political office might produce.

[89] The call for the king to deliver opiates to the poor masses, however, is not a regular aspect of biblical or ancient Near Eastern ideologies of social justice. As Clifford writes in *Proverbs*, 271: "The author transforms traditional warnings to rulers against the abuse of sex and liquor into an exhortation to practice justice."

[90] Proverbs 17:3; 25:4; and 27:21, speak of the purification of precious metals. These sayings are not concerned to value virtue or to construct an economic ethic and hence are not treated in this study.

For Proverbs, such negative activity limits the possibility of human flourishing. By contrast, the acquisition of social virtues and the realization of such values in communal life—e.g., the demonstration of kindness to the poor and fair actions in the market place—contribute to the building of a good and secure life Proverbs assumes humans desire. As 21:15 claims, justice is what those who travel wisdom's path delight in, but not so others whose passions are directed elsewhere:

שמחה לצדיק עשות משפט ומחתה לפעלי און

Justice done is a joy to the righteous, but ruination to the wicked.[91]

[91] The translation follows NJPS.

CHAPTER FIVE

THE GESTALT OF PROVERBS AND THE DISCOURSE OF SOCIAL OBSERVATION IN PROVERBS 10–31

Although thus far I have highlighted the distinct nature and features of the wisdom's virtues discourse and the discourse of social justice in Prov 10–31, occasionally one finds sayings in these chapters where some of the preferred characteristics of one discourse are taken up by the other. This is the case, for instance, in 17:5 (see below) where a social justice proverb, instead of employing one of that discourse's preferred terms for the poor—דל, אביון, or עני—makes use of the term רש, a word common to the wisdom's virtues discourse. As I suggested earlier, however, some overlap between closely related discourses is to be expected and one ought not attempt to force every wealth and poverty saying into procrustean analytical categories.

Yet the overlap of discourse features also suggests more. It points to an interaction, or kind of dialogue, between the sub-discourses of wealth and poverty in Proverbs that is on-going throughout the book. The sayings belonging to the discourse of social justice and the wisdom's virtues discourse that have been considered thus far, both in chapters 1–9 and 10–31, reveal certain patterns of value and usage. In Ricoeur's terms, these patterns, along with the book's prologue, intimate a certain "architecture" to Proverbs' discourse. They suggest, that is, a certain literary and moral Gestalt to the book. It is in relationship to this Gestalt that the remaining wealth and poverty sayings in Proverbs, which employ an act-consequence rhetoric more obviously than most of the verses considered thus far, ought to be assessed and understood. When read against this Gestalt, these remaining sayings can be shown to belong either to the discourse of social justice or the wisdom's virtues discourse. The Gestalt of Proverbs likewise provides the hermeneutical lens for recognizing and analyzing a third sub-discourse of wealth and poverty in Proverbs, the discourse of social observation.

In light of the book's literary and moral Gestalt, this chapter will first consider which of the wealth and poverty sayings in Proverbs that have not yet been considered belong to the wisdom's virtues discourse and which belong to the discourse of social justice. Subsequently the chapter will discuss those remaining sayings in Proverbs that constitute the discourse of social observation. In a final section, I will consider briefly how the final lines in the book, the poem to the woman of worth, also reveals a dialogue of wealth and poverty discourses in Proverbs.

5.1. The Wisdom's Virtues Discourse Revisited

A number of wealth and poverty sayings in Proverbs that have not yet been discussed function essentially in the same manner as the wisdom's virtues proverbs already considered. They serve to value particular virtues and vices via a wealth and poverty rhetoric or related images of material abundance or lack. The language of these remaining sayings, however, makes clearer use of a cause and effect rhetoric than many of the proverbs in the book. Hence to many readers they appear to promise material prosperity almost as an automatic reward to the one who acts in a particular manner. Yet the Gestalt of Proverbs alluded to above—the moral vision and rhetorical and figurative patterns of language use established by sayings already shown to belong to the wisdom's virtues and social justice discourses—indicates that these promises must not be reduced only to literal promises. The act-consequence rhetoric of the sayings to be examined next also functions more symbolically to undergird that larger wisdom mythos I spoke of above. These proverbs offer not merely a literal promise of literal material wealth. They also constitute a symbolic promise of general well being to the one who finds wisdom and function as a motivational device to move and keep the hearer or reader on wisdom's way, pursuing that which is most valuable and that which the cosmos favors, virtue.

5.1.a. *Righteousness and (Wicked) Wealth*

There are a number of wealth sayings in the wisdom's virtues discourse that are concerned primarily with demonstrating the desirability of the particular virtue of righteousness in order to motivate a hearer to acquire this virtue. Each of these lines employs economic terminology with a rhetoric that reflects a wisdom prosperity axiom. However, the book's literary and moral Gestalt demands that their promises of well being not be understood in only, or overly, literal terms. These sayings, moreover, permit one to glimpse more fully what is at stake in the text's "valuing" work through an economic rhetoric.

Consider first three proverbs that deploy a similar rhetoric of economic wages, produce, or reward:

פעלת צדיק לחיים תבואת רשע לחטאת

> The wage of a righteous person leads to life; the produce of a wicked person to sin. (Prov 10:16)[1]

רשע עשה פעלת־שקר וזרע צדקה שכר אמת

> The wicked earn an illusory wage, but the one who sows righteousness has a true reward. (Prov 11:18)[2]

בית צדיק חסן רב ובתבואת רשע נעכרת

> The house of a righteous person is an abundant treasure; but in the produce of a wicked person is something putrid. (Prov 15:6)[3]

---

[1] Rather than rendering לחיים and לחטאת as "[leads] to life" and "to sin," Whybray suggests the *lamed* of each word should be reckoned as the emphatic *lamed*—i.e., "*is* life," etc. In this regard Whybray cites, among others, C. Brockelmann, *Hebräisches Syntax* (Neukirchen: Kreis Moers, 1956), section *31a*, and alludes to Ecc 9:4. See R. N. Whybray, *Proverbs*, (NCBC; Grand Rapids: Eerdmans, 1994), 166.

[2] The translation follows NJPS.

[3] The first half of the line is often translated as "*in* the house of the righteous there is much treasure" (cf. 21:20) and the second half as "*but* trouble befalls the income of the wicked" (cf. NRSV; NJPS). That is, the first half is rendered as if the first word was preceded by the preposition *bet* and the second half as if the preposition connected to the first term was absent. Such renderings are consistent with some MSS, the Syriac, and the Targum (see Fichtner's notes in the *BHS* apparatus), but are likely also an attempt to render the line in a manner more consistent with a wisdom prosperity axiom, literally understood. On v. 15a see W. A. van der Weiden, *Le Livre de Proverbes: Notes philologiques*, (BEO 23; Rome: Biblical Institute Press, 1970), 115. Oesterley writes that the sense of the verb in the second stich "demands the omission of 'in.'" Oesterley rightly recognizes the term נעכרת in the second verse half is somewhat problematic. It is the *niphal* f. sg. part. of ע כ ר and may mean something like "a thing troubled." Oesterley insists that the term "cannot be translated as an abstract noun" and affirms Frankenberg and Toy who emend "so as to read 'is cut off.'" See W. O. E. Oesterley, *The Book of Proverbs with Introduction and Notes* (London: Methuen & Co., 1929), 119; cf. C. H. Toy, *Proverbs. A Critical and Exegetical Commentary on the Book of Proverbs*, (Edinburgh: T&T Clark, 1988), 304–05. Murphy, by contrast, does in fact understand the form as a substantive and renders "disorder, trouble." See Roland E. Murphy, *Proverbs* (WBC; Nashville: Thomas Nelson, 1998), 110. In my view the f. sg. participle must be regarded as a substantive, as Murphy takes it. However, the term here means something like "that which is spoiled, putrid," which fits better with the line's agricultural

The logic of 10:16 is most clear. It discloses its metaphorical structure in its claim that an economic gain ("wage") leads to life for the righteous person, but that another form of economic gain ("produce") leads to "sin" for the wicked person. Any attempt to understand literally how a wage leads to life, and especially how produce leads to sin, ends, in Ricoeur's terms, in an absurdity. A literal understanding of the line is non-sensical. The proverb is comprehensible only if the wage and produce (that which normally accrues to a laborer) of the line are read metaphorically as that which accrues to a person from acting in a righteous or wicked manner.

The nature of the parallelism "life/sin" in 10:16, however, is not as easily grasped as some other pairings in Proverbs (e.g., life/death). Whybray, for instance, is puzzled by the verse since he believes a wisdom prosperity axiom, literally understood, must be at work in the line.[4] He writes: "Sin would naturally be the *cause*, not the result, of the fate of the wicked." Hence he turns to one of the meanings of the cognate verb חטא—"to miss the mark"—to explain that the wicked person "gains nothing."[5] Toy, by contrast, believes that in

imagery. In later Hebrew, the *niphal* of the root ע-כ-ר not only carries the sense of "to be stirred up" (as in HB), but can be extended to mean "to be foul." See Marcus Jastrow, *Dictionary of the Targumim, Talmud Babli, Yerushalmi and Midrashich Literature* (New York: Judaica Press, 1996), 1079; one volume reprint of the two volume 1971 original. A substantive of the f. sg. participle might thus be rendered something like "that which is foul or putrid." If so, the second half of 15:6, which introduces the agricultural image of "produce" with the preposition *bet* (ובתבואת) begins to make sense, the image being of a rotting harvest.

[4] Others who see 10:16 as reflecting a wisdom prosperity axiom include Clifford who, without suggesting the language should be understood other than literally, speaks of "reward and punishment" and envisions "life" to include health, reputation, and children. See Richard J. Clifford, *Proverbs: A Commentary*, (OTL; Louisville: WJK, 1999), 115. Murphy (*Proverbs*, 74) likewise alludes to "the law of retribution" and writes that "the efforts of the just will prosper, in contrast to the wicked who continue on their sinful ways without profit." Cf. Meinhold, who explicitly mentions the *Tun-Ergehen* theory; see Arndt Meinhold, *Die Sprüche* (2 vol.; ZBK; Zürich: Theologischer Verlag, 1991), 2:176. Otto Plöger writes: "If the works of the righteous, which lead to life, are contrasted succinctly with the vain yield of the sinful, which lead even to death, then verse 16 may be seen as conveying a categorical sense." (*So darf dem Vers 16 die Bedeutung einer grundsätzlichen Aussage zugebilligt werden, wenn lapidar dem zum Leben führenden Wirken des Gerechten der nichtige, ja zum Tode führende Ertrag des Frevlers gegenübergestellt wird*). See, *Sprüche Salomos (Proverbia)* (Neukrichen-Vluyn: Neukirchener, 1984), 127. Cf. further Whybray, *Proverbs*, 166; Toy, *Proverbs*, 209; William McKane, *Proverbs: A New Approach* (Philadelphia: Westminster, 1970), 425.

[5] Whybray, *Proverbs*, 166; emphasis in the original.

order to produce a better parallel with the first half of the verse, the term חטאת ("sin") in 10:16 ought to be emended to something like "destruction."[6] Similarly, at least one English translation of the line (NJPS) renders the word ("sin") as "want." Clifford, too, suggests חטאת in this instance, in fact, means something like "want,"" while McKane essentially suggests the term is synecdoche for "death," which may be closer to the mark.[7]

An emendation of לחטאת, however, not only has little textual support (as Toy and Whybray explicitly recognize), it also would obscure an important inter-textual echo.[8] The verse's rhetoric of sin, drawn from the root ח-ט-א, evokes the destructive activities of the robbers in chapter one, who are called חטאים. In 10:16 the benefits that accrue to the righteous person, his "wage" metaphorically speaking, is life. By contrast, that which accumulates to the wicked person, i.e., his metaphorical "produce," is sin. As the sinners' activity in chapter one reminds, however, this kind of "produce" is accompanied by little that is of worth. Rather it is characterized by competitive, brutal conduct that not only undermines the establishment and maintenance of social harmony and equity, but as the father's words in 1:18–19 make clear, ends in death. The parallel life/sin in 10:16 thus does make sense. It is simply a pairing that is more allusively constructed than many.

With its allusion to treasures in the house of the righteous person, Prov 15:6 is reminiscent of 21:20 and 24:3–4 which were discussed in Chapter Four. However, the logic and structure of especially the line's first half can be regarded as more analogous to 10:16. The absurdity produced when one attempts to understand the first stich literally suggests its metaphorical nature. In Ricoeur's terms, the literal reckoning of the line—the righteous person's house "is" a treasure—quickly gives way to the metaphorical understanding—the

[6] Toy, *Proverbs*, 209. Presumably the emendation Toy has in mind is from *ḥaṭṭāt* to *mĕḥittāh*. Cf. Whybray, *Proverbs*, 166.

[7] Clifford, *Proverbs*, 115; McKane, *Proverbs*, 425. Cf. Jutta Hausmann, *Studien zum Menschenbild der älteren Weisheit* (Forschungen zum Alten Testament 7; Tübingen: J. C. B. Mohr, 1995), 52. Commentators like Toy and Hausmann see the verse as concerned with the right and wrong use of wealth. Though such a view is not necessarily wrong, the language is too broad to gain a sense of what this might actually mean—though Hausmann at least links the wrong use of wealth to wrongly trusting in it. See Toy, *Proverbs*, 208–209; Hausmann, *Menschenbild*, 52–53.

[8] Toy, *Proverbs*, 209; Whybray, *Proverbs*, 166.

righteous person's house "is like" a treasure. As with the righteous person's wage in 10:16, the righteous person's house in 15:6, which "is like" abundant treasure, is a figure for that which accrues to him from acting rightly or virtuously. By contrast, the image of the second half of 15:6—of something rotting in the crop of the wicked person—intimates that that which will accrue to the one who acts wickedly may initially appear valuable and desirable, as a gain, but is ultimately not so (cf. 10:16).

Proverbs 11:18 likewise functions in analogous ways to both 10:16 and 15:6. On the one hand, that which accrues to the wicked in this line—a wage—like the produce of the wicked person in the other verses, is not at all valuable. It is labeled "illusory." On the other hand, and similar to the one who acts rightly in 10:16, that which accrues to the one who sows righteousness in 11:18—a reward—is valuable and desirable. It is "true."

The rhetorical strategy deployed by 10:16; 11:18; and 15:6—identifying that which appears desirable as ultimately not so—is one that Proverbs has deployed from the outset of the book. Recall that in chapter one the sinners promise the hearer "all precious wealth," but, according to the instructing voice, can only deliver "unjust gain" which leads to death. Similarly, throughout chapters 1–9 the hearer is warned about the temptations of the strange or foreign woman. On the literal level of the text this woman is likely the wife of another man. However, because she appears to coalesce with Woman Folly and is otherwise described in terms that mirror the description of Woman Wisdom, she is also a cipher for all that belongs to the way of folly. Although the text imagines sex with her will appear desirable to the addressee, the instructing voice insists that this too will lead to death.

That the 'righteousness proverbs' cited above ought to be reckoned metaphorically is revealed as well by a comparison with Ps. 1, especially verses 3–4:

והיה כעץ שתול על־פלגי מים
אשר פריו יתן בעתו ועלהו לא־יבול
וכל אשר־יעשה יצליח
לא־כן הרשעים
כי אם־כמץ אשר־תדפנו רוח

> [The one who delights in Torah] will be like a tree planted by streams of water, which yields its fruit in its season, and its leaves do not

> wither. In all that he does he prospers. Not so the wicked who are like chaff which the wind drives away.[9]

The economic metaphors of productive activity in the proverbial sayings just discussed follow essentially the logical pattern of the metaphor associated with the wicked and those who shun sinful ways in the psalm. In the proverbs, the good and bad things that are said to accrue to the wicked and righteous, their benefits or misfortunes, are called wages and produce. In the psalm, however, the benefits of the one who delights in Torah and the misfortunes of the wicked are described in terms of plant life, a clearly metaphorical description. Those who delight in Torah are likened to flourishing trees while the wicked are said to be like chaff. Each of the righteousness proverbs cited above thus reveal a clear metaphorical structure and this, together with the book's literary and moral Gestalt, points to the symbolic work they do in Proverbs. Their promises cannot be regarded merely in literal terms. Rather their rhetoric undergirds the larger wisdom mythos that insists that even the deep structures of the universe support the primacy and incomparable value of virtue.

Proverbs 10:2; 15:27; and 21:6, which operate by a logic slightly different than the proverbs just considered, allude not to the reward or produce of the wicked person but to wicked wealth. They read:

לא־יועילו אוצרות רשע וצדקה תציל ממות

> Treasures of wickedness do not profit, but righteousness rescues from death.

עכר ביתו בוצע בצע ושונא מתנת יחיה

> Whoever pursues unjust gain makes trouble for his house; whoever hates a bribe will live.

פעל אוצרות בלשון שקר הבל נדף מבקשי־מות

> Treasures gained by a tongue of deception are a driven mist, seekers of death.[10]

---

[9] The translation follows NRSV

[10] The translation is more or less a literal one. The line's sense and syntax, however, are not simple. Whybray (*Proverbs*, 309) and Plöger (*Sprüche Salomos*, 242) suggest that MT's *pōʿal* should be read as *pōʿēl*, "the one getting" (following LXX; ὁ ἐνεργῶν) rather than simply "getting"; or in the translation above, "gained." In regard to the second verse half, Whybray suspects the line is "almost certainly

Whereas in the righteousness proverbs of 10:16; 11:18; and 15:6 (treated above) economic images represent the benefit virtue brings (or the disadvantage of vice), the point of these sayings is simply that wealth acquired by unjust or wicked means is not as valuable as virtue. Proverbs 10:2 is clearest in this regard, contrasting treasures of wickedness that do not profit with righteousness, a virtue that possesses its own worth in that it is able to rescue from death. Proverbs 15:27 is similar. On the one hand, unjust gain doesn't profit, but makes trouble. On the other hand, virtue, specifically the shunning of a bribe, analogous to righteousness in 10:2, leads to life.[11] Proverbs 21:6 does not allude to the value of virtue, but is clear about the limited worth of wealth gained by deception: it is as enduring and valuable as mist or vapor.[12]

That Proverbs should suggest that virtues like righteousness are more valuable than wealth attained in a wicked or unjust manner is not surprising, especially given the text's concern with social justice.[13] Yet the book elsewhere speaks of the value of virtue over wealth with language that is not marked by negative terms. Consider, for example, Prov 11:4 and 11:28:

לא־יועיל הון ביום עברה וצדקה תציל ממות

> Wealth does not profit on the day of wrath, but righteousness rescues from death.[14]

---

corrupt." Instead of "seekers of death," LXX reads "snares of death" (παγίδας θανάτου). The entire Greek verse might be rendered: "He that gathers treasures with a lying tongue pursues vanity on (to) the snares of death." The translation is Whybray's; cf. Toy, *Proverbs*, 400.

[11] The moral status of bribes and gifts in Proverbs needs to be reckoned on a case by case basis through an evaluation of the individual sayings that deploy such language. In some instances, as in 15:27, they are negatively evaluated (cf. 17:23; 28:21) and in other instances they appear to be spoken of positively (cf. 17:8; 18:16; 21:14). A tracing of the common terminology, מתן and שחד, is of little help. Cf., esp., 21:14 where both terms are deployed.

[12] To the extent that 10:2; 15:27; and 21:6 also encourage the hearer to avoid engaging in unjust economic practices, the sayings gesture toward the discourse of social justice, which attempts to construct a concrete economic ethic for the book's addressee.

[13] See Prov 28:20 and 28:22 (cf. 13:11), which are concerned with wealth gained in haste. It appears that for Proverbs wealth gained in haste is suspect and does not belong to wisdom's virtuous way. This is at least the case in 28:22, which links the pursuit of quick gain to the greedy miser.

[14] This line is absent in Rhalf's LXX handbook, which is based on B, S, and A. According to Fichtner's *BHS* apparatus, the line would likewise not be found in the Old Greek.

בוטח בעשרו הוא יפל וכעלה צדיקים יפרחו

> Whoever trusts in their riches will fall, but the righteous will burst forth like a leaf.[15]

The logic of these sayings is virtually the same as those just discussed. The difference, however, is that these proverbs do not speak of wicked wealth, but simply of wealth. Although some, such as Whybray, claim that 11:4, like the nearly identical 10:2, is probably speaking of "ill-gotten wealth," the verse does not restrict its evaluation of wealth's limited worth to wicked wealth.[16] It claims simply that riches (without a modifier) do not profit, at least not in certain contexts—e.g., the day of wrath. This language belongs to moral-religious discourse, for as Meinhold indicates, the phrase likely refers to divine judgment, a sense it carries, for instance, in Zeph 1:18.[17]

Proverbs 11:28 is similar in this regard. As with 11:4, there is no sense that the wealth in this line is tainted, wicked wealth. The verse, moreover, does not name a specific context with which it is concerned, as v. 4 does (the day of wrath). It simply insists, quite generally and boldly, that the one who trusts in riches will metaphorically "fall" (apparently like a leaf from a tree), while the righteous will figuratively burst forth like new foliage (cf. the imagery of Ps 1). The "problem" in 11:28 thus is "trust" in wealth, or, one might say, a misperception of how it does or does not "profit," as 11:4 puts it. This problem, moreover, suggests that there is more to this set of wealth sayings than a simple, though important, moral point about pursuing legitimate rather than illegitimate economic gain. The fundamental issue underlying all of the proverbs under consideration, both those that refer explicitly to wicked wealth and those that do not, is essentially the same—the nature of the value of wealth.

Whether the riches in these wealth sayings is claimed to be illegitimate or not, it is often said that the verses do not violate Proverbs'

[15] As Whybray notes in *Proverbs*, 187–88, there is no need, as Fichtner's *BHS* apparatus proposes, to emend the verse in the direction of Ps 1:3b, which deploys similar images (i.e., יִפֹּל to יִבֹּל; from נבל, "to whither").

[16] Whybray, *Proverbs*, 177.

[17] Meinhold, *Die Sprüche*, 1:187. Cf. McKane, *Proverbs*, 436. The meaning of the phrase, however, may be more circumscribed and refer simply to a legal judgment. Cf. further Meinhold, *Die Sprüche*, 1:187; Plöger, *Sprüche Salomos*, 136; Whybray, *Proverbs*, 177. In light of the parallel term "death" in the second verse half of 11:4, it is likewise possible that any life threatening situation is to be envisioned. Cf. Clifford, *Proverbs*, 122.

basic adherence to a wisdom prosperity axiom. Rather, at most they relativize the value of wealth in relationship to righteousness, or censure an inappropriate trust in wealth.[18] This again is essentially a correct assertion, but such a formulation of the matter does not appreciate fully the way this wealth language is functioning. Several matters become clear when one considers the rhetorical force of the sayings in light of the Proverbs' moral and literary Gestalt.

Notice first that the promises in these lines are not of an economic nature. Yet like the more clearly figurative wealth and poverty sayings already treated, the assurances offered also cannot be reduced to literal promises. This is clear especially in 11:28, where the end of the righteous is compared, by means of a simile, to the leaf of a tree (כעלה). Furthermore, despite the use of the contrastive *waw*, neither 11:4 or 11:28 (or 10:2) sets up "riches" and "righteousness" as absolute opposites in the way wisdom and folly or the righteous and wicked typically are (e.g., as in 11:18 cited above).[19] The comparison is of a different sort. As in other sayings in the wisdom's virtues discourse, riches, the verses assume, are in some sense desirable, valuable. However, if wealth is easily recognizable as desirable because of what it can and should do in its own sphere (i.e., the market place), by underscoring its limited ability to "save" from death (10:2; 11:4) or to keep one from "falling" (11:28), the proverbs imply, by contrast, that what is valuable in the religio-moral or legal sphere(s) are things like righteousness—i.e., wisdom's virtues.[20]

Meinhold is close to the mark when he writes:

[18] Cf. Holger Delkurt, *Ethische Einsichten in der alttestamentlichen Spruchweisheit* (BTS 21; Neukirchen-Vluyn: Neukirchener, 1993), 103 who writes: "11:4 and 28 criticize not riches as such, but rather *trust* in riches" (*kritisieren 11,4.28 nicht den Reichtum als solche, sondern* Vertrauen *auf Reichtum*; emphasis original). Toy, likewise, writes in regard to 11:4: "It is not said that wealth is in itself bad, but it is hinted that some men rely on wealth instead of righteousness to save them from calamity." See *Proverbs*, 222. Whybray likewise states in regard to 11:4 that: "This is not a condemnation of wealth as such." See *Proverbs*, 177; see p. 187 for his remarks regarding 11:28.

[19] Cf. the similar observation by Hausmann, *Menschenbild*, 91.

[20] For other sayings dealing with the ability of "wisdom" to save, see 28:26; 11:9 and cf. Hausmann, *Menschenbild*, 284. I borrow the language of social "spheres" in this context from Michael Walzer, *Spheres of Justice: A Defense of Pluralism and Equality* (New York: Basic Books, 1983).

> The second half of verse four [11:4] is identical with 10:2b, but the first verse half goes further than 10:2a. There, the futility of unrighteous possessions is highlighted; here the uselessness of every possession for a specific situation is asserted. . . . But on the "day of wrath" it [wealth] does not suffice. . . . [Indeed on such a day] even wealth gained in a godly manner would not suffice.[21]

As Meinhold recognizes, for Proverbs riches cannot buy innocence or acquittal before God.[22] However, this proverbial claim (from 10:2 and 11:4) coupled with 11:28's insistence that the righteous (a term also falling under a moral-religious or legal rubric) flourish while those who "trust in wealth" will wither, is quite significant. It intimates that for Proverbs wealth is, or should be, ineffectual in the religio-moral sphere. Moreover, as I suggested in Chapter Two, wealth in Proverbs is a particularly effective symbol for persuasion or motivation. It is what Burke calls a god term. However, if this is so, precisely because it is a god term, it must be distinguished from God. By signaling wealth's limited value in the religious and moral spheres, this is essentially what these sayings do. The sages distinguish wealth from, and do not permit it to compete with, the divine, which for the ancient teachers certainly was the center of religious life, the primary or ultimate locus of value, *and* intimately related to valuable wisdom and its virtues.

Although Prov 10:2; 15:27; and 21:6 are easily understood as censuring the pursuit and acquisition of wicked wealth, these proverbs along with 11:4 and 11:28 (which do not speak of tainted riches) are a further part of the sages' attempt to address a kind of cultural anxiety surrounding wealth and poverty. They attempt to countermand that "unspoken" but real social script that attempts to privilege, unduly as far as Proverbs is concerned, the value of wealth over other goods. In contrast to that script—which perhaps in part over values wealth by intimating riches can and do profit in spheres beyond the market place (e.g., at the temple or "in the gate," where

[21] Meinhold, *Die Spruche*, 1:187. Meinhold's text reads: *V.4 ist in seiner zweiten Halfte identisch mit10,2b, aber der erste Versteil geht über 10,2a hinaus. Dort is die Vergeblichkeit ungerechten Besitizes (vgl. u. a. 3,9; 8,18) für eine bestimmte Situation behauptet. . . . Aber am <<Tag des Zorns>> richtet er nichts aus. . . . Selbst von Gott geschaffener Riechtum (10,3a.22) würde dann nichts ausrichten.*

[22] Or, cannot buy acquittal before humans, e.g. in court, etc., if the phrase "day of wrath" points as well to the human realm.

justice is dispensed)—Proverbs insists that wealth's value ought to be confined to its own realm. Moreover, it insists that that which is of highest worth in any realm is virtue, a view it has championed from the book's outset.

The commentators thus are right to insist that wealth is not being disparaged by the proverbs considered in this section. However, the sayings do not so much relativize wealth's value in relation to a wisdom prosperity axiom conceived in especially literal terms, as they once more exploit the clear value riches possess in the market place to the larger rhetorical and didactic end of valuing wisdom's virtues.[23]

One should note as well that a number of the sayings treated in this section also deploy images that hint more precisely at *why* wealth for Proverbs is not as valuable or desirable as wisdom's virtues. Because the wisdom mythos of Proverbs imagines wisdom to be inherent to the structure of the cosmos, the virtues of wisdom's ways are often associated with that which endures. By contrasts, vice, which finds no genuine place in the deep structures of the universe, is linked with images of that which fades quickly. Proverbs 11:28 is particularly clear in this regard. In this line, as in Ps. 1, images from the realm of plant life highlight the important point. Riches for Proverbs are understood to be fleeting or temporary. They are external to a person and hence subject to the vagaries of fortune and changes in circumstances. If one trusts in wealth, the saying claims, one will not long last but fall like a leaf from a tree. The virtue of righteousness on the other hand endures. It is internal to a person and so not subject to changes in circumstances. Those who possess it will spring forth to life like fresh foliage. Images in other lines also suggest this same point clearly. Proverbs 20:17, for instance, knows that the sweet bread of deception soon turns to gravel in one's mouth. But recall too that Prov 11:18 likewise speaks of the fleeting or

[23] Some—like Clifford (*Proverbs*, 122) and Meinhold (*Die Sprüche*, 1:187)—hint at similar understandings, though their comments are only of a general nature. Clifford, for example, writes simply that: "In mortal danger, riches are of no avail, but only that which assures ultimate protection—righteousness." Certainly this is essentially what the saying literally says, but he does not suggest what exactly Proverbs means by making such a statement. Meinhold's comments are similar: "Before YHWH neither material nor cultic achievements count (Ps. 50:9–13), but [only] the doing of righteousness (21:3)" [*Vor JHWH zählen weder materielle noch kultische Leistungen (Ps. 50, 9–13), aber das Tun der Gerechtigkeit (21, 3)*]. Cf. Plöger, *Sprüche Salomos*, 136.

"illusory" wage of the wicked; 15:6 of their rotting reward; and 21:6 of wicked wealth that vanishes like mist.[24]

5.1.b. *Wealth, Poverty, and the Tropes of the Wise*

Several other sayings in Proverbs function similarly to those just considered but reveal as well further ways how one who is "wise" or "understanding" might interpret Proverbs' tropes and figures (cf. 1:5–6). Consider first Proverbs 28:11. It reads:

חכם בעיניו איש עשיר ודל מבין יחקרנו

> The rich person is wise in his own eyes, but a discerning poor person searches him out.

The line, which contrasts the rich and poor, is sometimes reckoned as an observation.[25] And the proverb, in fact, shares some rhetorical features with sayings that belong to the discourse of social observation (see below). For instance, the rich עשיר here is contrasted with another substantivized adjective—in this case the poor דל. Although דל is a preferred term of the discourse of social justice, in that discourse, recall, the word is always the grammatical object of a verb. The poor person here, however, is a subject who acts, a usage that I will suggest below is typical of the discourse of social observation.

In any case, as with the righteous and wicked in 29:7 (treated in Chapter Four), the דל and the עשיר here in Prov 28:11 stand in different relation to knowledge. The participle מבין reverberates with the meanings of cognate forms like בינה and תבונה, which elsewhere in Proverbs are explicitly linked with the meta-virtue of wisdom. The rich person in 28:11, though confident in his own ability (because of the confidence he places in his wealth?), does not possess knowledge or wisdom or understanding—i.e., virtue. The logic of the proverb is thus similar to the logic of a number of the sayings belonging to the wisdom's virtues discourse. Essentially it indicates that what looks like advantage, e.g., having wealth, often is less than it

[24] Proverbs 20:17 reads in the NRSV: "Bread gained by deceit is sweet, but afterward the mouth will be full of gravel."

[25] Clifford (*Proverbs*, 245), for example, writes: "According to this observation on the effect of wealth and of poverty on wisdom, the social position of the wealthy can mislead them."

appears. Possessing the virtue of understanding or discernment (a moral positive) even though one is poor (an economic negative) is, the verse intimates, more valuable and desirable than being rich (an economic positive) and unduly proud or overestimating one's own ability (a moral negative).[26]

Proverbs 21:17 and 23:20–21 are also interesting examples to consider, for in taking up a wealth and poverty rhetoric they appear largely to be concerned with how the hearer or reader ought to conduct themselves at table. Yet they potentially function in a more sophisticated manner. They read:

איש מחסור אהב שמחה אהב יין־ושמן לא יעשיר

> A person of lack is the one who loves pleasure; whoever loves wine and oil will not be rich.

אל־תהי בסבאי־יין בזללי בשר למו
כי־סבא וזולל יורש וקרעים תלביש נומה

> Do not be among those who guzzle wine or glut themselves on meat. For guzzlers and gluttons will be dispossessed, and drowsing will clothe you in tatters.

On a basic, literal level both texts can be said to be offering advice, if not about table manners, at least about how much food and drink (and presumably in 21:17 other pleasures) one ought or ought not to take.[27] With an impersonal wealth and poverty terminology typical of the wisdom's virtues discourse, 21:17 begins by claiming it is the person of "lack" (מחסור) who loves pleasure. The line ends with

[26] Elsewhere in Proverbs the notion of being "wise in one's own eyes" is said explicitly to belong to the way of folly and wickedness. See, for example, the similar expressions in 26:12 and 30:14.

[27] Proverbs 23:29–35 is similar to 21:17 and 23:20–21 in that the text offers a description of what it views as unpleasant aspects of intoxication. That such behavior does not belong to the way of wisdom is clear from the passage's context. Between 23:20–21 and 23:29–35 one finds exhortations regarding honoring parents, acquiring wisdom, and the dangers of the foreign or strange woman, who like the sinners in ch. 1 "lies in wait" (ערב) and increases transgressions among "men" (באדם). The juxtaposition suggests the text means to make a connection between certain potentially unpleasant effects that one must endure after enjoying alcohol and the temporary, but ultimately harmful pleasures of the foreign woman and the "way" of folly she represents. The text functions both as a warning about what it considers illicit sexual encounters and drunkenness, but both of these also are ciphers for the in part desirable, but ultimately detrimental way of folly.

a reminder that those who indulge themselves will not become rich (לא יעשיר). The admonition of 23:20–21 (part of the so-called Amenemope section of the book) is explicit in asserting that the hearer ought not to indulge in certain kinds of drinking and eating. With a rhetoric analogous to that of 21:17, the line also offers a reason for this advice. Such conduct leads to dispossession (יורש) and, the instructing voice adds, a drowsiness that will also impoverish (literally leave one "in rags").[28]

The rhetorical strategy of both 21:7 and 23:20–21, like many wisdom's virtues sayings, is to pair an economic negative with a moral negative. However, although each text holds out a threat to the glutton, the cause and effect rhetoric in neither unproblematically reflects the common understanding of the wisdom prosperity axiom discussed above. Indeed it is difficult to imagine how enjoyment of wine and oil would lead to literal impoverishment. It is thus sometimes assumed that it is *excessive* indulgence in ("love of") pleasure and *excessive* eating and drinking (guzzling and gluttony) that the text has in mind, as if the cost of such an excessive lifestyle might lead to poverty.[29] This sort of interpretation is imaginable. However, the moral and literary Gestalt of Proverbs makes it clear that Proverbs is preeminently concerned with offering moral instruction and with valuing virtue and vice, and this suggests that the threats inherent to the wisdom prosperity rhetoric of 21:7 and 23:20–21 ought not be reduced simply to the literal level. Rather these assurances serve to underscore the broader wisdom mythos that insists on the preeminent value of virtue and demands that worthless vice be shunned. Although the feasting in the verses sounds desirable, by associating such activity with images of material lack, the proverbs claim it produces well being in the same measure as poverty produces prosperity.

---

[28] Meinhold also understands the sleep of 23:20–21 to be the result of excessive celebration. See *Die Sprüche*, 2:335.

[29] See Clifford, *Proverbs*, 192, 213; Murphy, *Proverbs*, 160, 176; Toy, *Proverbs*, 405; Whybray, *Proverbs*, 312, 338. Cf. Meinhold (*Die Sprüche*, 2:335, 355) who speaks of the poverty in 21:17 as the fault of the individual (*selbsverschuldet*). So too Hans F. Fuhs, *Das Buch der Sprichwörter: Ein Kommentar* (Forschung zur Bibel 95; Wurzburg: Echter Verlag, 2001), 307. See also Plöger, *Sprüche Salomos*, 247; Hausmann, *Menschenbild*, 326, 332. Cf. as well Deut 21:18–21 where participial forms of the same roots that appear in 23:21, זלל and סבא, are employed to describe a rebellious son. In Deuteronomy, however, the precise nuance of the language is not as clear since the forms lack an object (i.e., neither wine or meat is mentioned as that which the rebellious son consumes).

The primary moral concern of both 21:17 and 23:20–21 may be to move the hearer away from what might appear to be a desirable life of pleasure to one which is full of the virtue of moderation. However, the phrase לא יעשיר ("he will not be rich") in 21:17 and the rhetoric of dispossession in 23:21 intimates that for these *meshalim* feasting is the opposite of industriousness, since elsewhere Proverbs has coarsely linked this virtue with economic prospering (cf. 10:4; 12:11, 27; 28:19). The language of guzzling or loving wine and oil, of glutting oneself on meat, and of drowsiness all symbolize non-industrious activity. These particular images of vice function as a kind of synecdoche for the more general vice of slothfulness and, analogous to the relationship between virtue and prosperity, are coarsely linked in the sayings with economic deprivation (cf. 14:23; 24:33–34).

But the lines, cast in the indicative as a kind of observation that over indulgence leads to poverty, may be "doing" more than simply encouraging industriousness. In the context of the ancient Levant, "wine" and "oil" and "meat" are luxury goods—products consumed regularly only by the economic elite. The lines demand the addressee avoid gluttony and practice moderation and so, as 23:21 implies, remain awake and industrious. Yet in so doing the proverbs may gesture toward a critique of those who in fact *do* love oil and wine and meat, those who *do* regularly indulge themselves with such delicacies. Implicit in the rhetoric of moderation is the fact the vices that the text speaks of to make its point are not just any old vices, but specifically (if stereotypically) the vices of the "rich."[30] The sayings thus begin, at least minimally, to locate dangers to a life of wisdom in connection with wealth.

As I argued above, it is best to assume that the collections and the book of Proverbs are the product of an intellectual elite, though not necessarily a political or economic elite. Subsequently I suggested that the interests of the former should not be considered to be identical with the interests of the latter, or the rural folk (see Chapter Two). In such a complex social landscape, the sages who produced and used Proverbs could be certain that sayings such as 21:17 and

[30] Cf. Prov 15:17 and 17:1 discussed above. Whybray, *Proverbs*, 312, recall, regards such sayings as emerging among small farmers who, though not destitute are nonetheless not rich and cannot afford such excessive pleasures.

23:20–21 could be heard "safely" by the political and economic elite to whom they might be in service. That is, on one level, the level of what James C. Scott might call a "public discourse," the call to moderation or industriousness is almost completely innocuous, almost banal—though perhaps nonetheless welcomed by the political and economic elite who may have valued some curbing of the more indulgent ones in their own rank and who would not tolerate such indulgence among those in their midst of inferior status.[31] However, when heard from a somewhat different social location—from the view of a sage whose values and interests would be somewhat different than the political and economic elite—the "hidden transcript" (again borrowing Scott's terminology), or the more stringent critique of the practices of the political and economic elite implicit in the sayings, can be recognized.[32]

Proverbs 11:24–26 and 28:25 are likewise verses that might be heard in different ways by the sages that produced and transmitted Proverbs and others not belonging to their rank. They read:

יש מפזר ונוסף עוד וחושך מישר אך־למחסור
נפש־ברכה תדשן ומרוה גם־הוא יורא
מנע בר יקבהו לאום וברכה לראש משביר

> There is one who scatters and increases more; and one who withholds what is right—only for lack.
> A generous person will grow fat, and one who gives water will also get water.
> The one who withholds grain will be cursed by the people, but blessing is for the head of the one who dispenses it.[33]

רחב־נפש יגרה מדון ובוטח על־יהוה ידשן

> A greedy person provokes a dispute, but the one who trusts in the Lord will grow fat.[34]

---

[31] James C. Scott, *Domination and the Arts of Resistance. Hidden Transcripts* (New Haven: Yale University Press, 1990), 2.

[32] Scott, *Domination*, 4.

[33] The rendering of the lines at points follows NJPS and at points NRSV. The final word of v. 25, יורא, is probably an unusual *hophal* form of the root ר-ו-ה, a *hiphil* form of which begins the second verse half. The interchange between *aleph* and *heh* in III-weak roots is well known. In v. 26 "dispenses" (שבר) may mean simply "sell grain," implying less an act of charity than a refusal to profit by hording or speculation. Cf. Meinhold, *Die Sprüche*, 1:199; Clifford, *Proverbs*, 126; Murphy, *Proverbs*, 84; Toy, *Proverbs*, 235; Whybray, *Proverbs*, 186.

[34] The initial phrase of the verse, רחב־נפש, in all likelihood points to one who is

Nearly all interpreters recognize in these verses some version of the proverbial wisdom prosperity axiom. Yet because Proverbs is regularly regarded as the product of the sages' quasi-empirical observation of the world, the line's cause and effect rhetoric is also often understood in overly literalistic terms. In regard to 11:25 and 28:25, for instance, without offering an indication that the lines should be regarded in a non-literal fashion, Hausmann explicitly alludes to a *Tun-Ergehen* connection. Murphy, similarly without elaboration, states (in regard to 11:25) that: "Blessing (others) leads to prosperity."[35] It is also sometimes claimed that these proverbs recount real, though ironic, occurrences of which the sages took note.[36] Whybray, for example, writes: "Such things do sometimes happen."[37] Toy, too, opines that, "experiences teaches that the man of liberal methods prospers, and such an one, it is probably meant to say, has the blessing of God."[38] Yet it is not clear that empirical observation would bear out the kinds of claims of Whybray and Toy make. The one who hoards and is not generous may well increase his economic status. The well being of the community as a whole, however, depends upon the behavior the verses promote and the act-consequence rhetoric of the text suggests this socially desirable behavior is assumed to be supported by the structure of the cosmos.

Proverbs 11:26 is the most straightforward of the four sayings. Its concern with hoarding and selling grain indicates that it is fundamentally occupied with the question of social responsibility. The 'reward mechanism' it deploys is explicitly social and intuitively on target. The one who does not neglect his social responsibility is viewed favorably by others in the same social formation. The reward mechanism in the other sayings is more hidden than in 11:26, but the structure is the same. Proverbs elsewhere has urged the virtue

"greedy." Cf. Clifford (*Proverbs*, 247) who notes that the versions understood the phrase in this way as well. This figure is essentially the opposite of the נפש־ברכה in 11:25 who, like "the one who trusts the Lord" in 28:25, also will "become fat" (דשן).

35 Hausmann, *Menschenbild*, 232, 271; Murphy, *Proverbs*, 84. Similarly, in relation to 11:25, Toy (*Proverbs*, 235) speaks of certain "social laws."

36 In relation to 11:24, see Murphy, *Proverbs*, 83–84. Clifford, likewise, speaks of the "paradox" in verses such as these. See *Proverbs*, 125.

37 Whybray, *Proverbs*, 186.

38 Toy, *Proverbs*, 235. Toy, however, also recognizes that such sayings can be applied to the moral realm; cf. Murphy, *Proverbs*, 83–84.

of careful and prudent husbandry of goods, as in 21:10 (see Chapter Four). Through the set of sayings cited above, however, the book takes up the corresponding virtue of socially responsible generosity and distribution.

Although the virtue of generosity in 11:24–26 and 28:25 is ascribed value in terms of a broadly economic rhetoric, its desirable aspects are also implicit in the terminology the texts deploy to describe the generous person. This person in 11:25, for instance, is a נפש־ברכה—a person of blessing. The term נפש basically means "throat" and can be used to speak of an appetite, i.e., the "desire" of someone. The person of blessing is thus one whose appetite or desire is for ברכה ("blessing"), a positive and mutually enhancing relationship with one's fellows. This one walks the path of wisdom and does not compete with his companions for gain (e.g., by speculation in grain; cf. 11:26). Nor does he "withhold" what is "right" (ישר), but gives generously (cf. 11:24). All of this, moreover, is consonant with the book's concern with establishing and maintaining social justice and harmony (cf. 1:3).

By contrast, the greedy person is described in 28:25 as רחב־נפש—"wide of throat" or "wide of desire."[39] The language evokes images of the sinners (and Sheol) in chapter one and the wicked in 21:20, both of whom "swallow up" (בלע) what they desire. As Clifford writes, the one who is רחב־נפש is the "voracious man."[40] Similarly, 28:25 hints that confusing the value of the virtue of generosity with the value of material goods or economic gain, and pursuing these with what Plöger describes as *hemminglos zwang* ("unrestrained compulsion"), leads to strife (מדון)—a state of affairs antithetical to the social harmony which, according to the prologue, is most important to wisdom's way.[41]

Although the text motivates what it views as desirable behavior by means of images of material prospering, the figurative and rhetorical patterns of use of wealth and poverty language in Proverbs, the book's Gestalt, again suggests that these images cannot be viewed

[39] Chapter 28 is particularly concerned with the topic of greed (cf. vv. 20, 22, 24).

[40] Clifford, *Proverbs*, 247.

[41] Plöger, *Sprüche Salomos*, 238. See too, Murphy, *Proverbs*, 217, who in regard to 28:25 writes that the greedy person is one who brings about "dissension." Cf. Meinhold, *Die Sprüche* 2:478.

only literally. Certainly the lines' rhetoric contains a promise of material benefit. However, again this promise is not only a literal assurance, but also functions symbolically to reinforce the wisdom mythos, which insists virtue is what is most valuable and that the cosmos is constructed to support the acts of a virtuous life.

It is also significant that the figure of the one who gathers and dispenses grain described in 11:24–26 is reminiscent of the vizier Joseph in Egypt.[42] Indeed the images in this description are appropriated from the world of the economic and political elite. The sayings, as I suggested, underscore the value and desirability of the virtue of generosity and this point would certainly be accessible to a range of hearers. However, by choosing to value generosity via these particular images, the verses also construct a particular expectation that the elite act fairly and responsibly in the economic realm (cf. the social justice discourse). In a sense, one might say the text is attempting to engage in a kind of social control of the wealthy. Against that broader social script which over values material goods, and to which these elite might be particularly vulnerable, Proverbs highlights the value of what is "upright" ישר—scattering, generosity, selling at fair prices, not speculating, rejecting greed. Although, an economic elite would certainly hear the call to generosity, the wise and understanding person who attends to the book's riddles and figures may also hear an implicit critique of any elite that strayed from the *meshalim*'s norms.

5.1.c. *Other Discourses of Desire*

Certain sayings in the sentence collections of Proverbs value wisdom's way with rhetoric that is not properly the language of wealth. Nonetheless, these sayings deploy a rhetoric that is related to the discourse of wealth and poverty in that they too draw on images of that which is desirable. For instance, a number of proverbs already considered deploy food images.[43] Proverbs 13:18, like 3:14–16 (cf.

[42] Plöger, *Sprüche Salomos*, 142; Fuhs, *Das Buch der Sprichwörter*, 201; and Whybray, *Proverbs*, 180, also are reminded of Joseph's activities in Egypt. Cf. Gen 41:37–57.

[43] See 12:11; 15:17; 16:8; 17:1; 20:13, 17; 28:19. The most obvious instance of the sages' expression of the desirability of wisdom's way via food images is perhaps 24:13–14 where the desirability of wisdom (חכמה) is explicitly likened to the sweetness of honey. Honey (or the honeycomb) is likewise deployed to speak of the desir-

8:18) and 4:5–9 (treated in Chapter Three) and 16:19 (treated in Chapter Four), on the other hand, draws both on poverty language and the rhetoric of social status.[44] It reads:

ריש וקלון פורע מוסר ושומר תוכחת יכבד

> Poverty and humiliation are for the one who spurns instruction, but the one who takes reproof to heart gets honor.[45]

The logic of the saying is analogous to the logic of several of the wisdom's virtues proverbs I have already discussed. The verse is attempting to persuade a hearer of the value of heeding instruction and it accomplishes this task rhetorically by promising/threatening poverty to the "one who spurns instruction" (פורע מוסר). In the first half of 13:18, however, a moral negative (spurning instruction) is paired both with an economic negative (poverty) *and* a *social* negative (humiliation); in the second half of the line a moral positive (taking reproof) is also linked to a *social* positive (getting honor). The line thus not only attempts to persuade its hearer of the value of heeding instruction through an economic rhetoric but through the rhetoric of social status. It promises "humiliation" to the one who rejects instruction and "honor" to the one who attends to reproof.[46]

Proverbs 11:16 functions similarly.

אשת־חן תתמך כבוד ועריצים יתמכו־עשר

> A woman of repute obtains honor; ruthless men obtain wealth.[47]

The line is problematic for many. Some have suggested that there is a lacuna in the Hebrew text and have subsequently turned to the

ability of particular values and virtues associated with wisdom's way—e.g., right speech in 16:24 and the proper quest for honor at 25:27, which should be read with 25:16 (cf. 27:7). To these verses one could add 10:3 and 10:21.

[44] Proverbs 19:22 is a further instance of this intermingling of different sorts of rhetoric as well. The saying reads: תאות אדם חסדו וטוב־רש מאיש כזב. The first stich of the line, however, is ambiguous. The term חסד may mean "faithfulness, kindness" as it usually does in HB or it may be the less common "reproach," a term which might be said to belong to a discourse of social status. Hence the proverb might be read as: "What is desirable in a person is loyalty; and it is better to be poor than a liar"; or, "The desire of a person is his reproach; and it is better to be poor than a liar."

[45] The translation follows NJPS.

[46] For the notion of the close relationship between status and wealth in regard to 13:18, cf. especially McKane, *Proverbs*, 456 and Raymond C. Van Leeuwen, "Proverbs: Introduction, Commentary, and Reflections," *NIB* 5:133.

[47] The translation follows NJPS.

LXX and other versions when rendering the line. The appeal to the versions, however, appears largely to be motivated by a desire to have the text conform more neatly to a wisdom prosperity axiom where wealth is the reward of the righteous, not the ruthless. For instance, it is sometimes suggested that עריצים ("ruthless ones") should be emended to חרוצים ("diligent ones").[48] The MT of 11:16, however, is comprehensible. It simply functions in a slightly more nuanced manner than many other wealth and poverty sayings in the book.

The key to understanding the saying is to read it through Proverbs' moral and literary Gestalt, the patterns of value and language usage that other wealth and poverty sayings in the book establish. In the first place it is necessary not to hold to a too rigid view of the wisdom prosperity axiom. Formally the "woman of repute" in the first verse half stands in parallel to "ruthless men" in the second half of the line. The reward of the woman, what she "obtains" or "grasps" is "honor" and this stands in parallel to that which the ruthless strive after, "riches." The first half of the verse thus betrays a logic analogous to several other sayings in the book that belong to the wisdom's virtues discourse: a moral positive ("repute") is paired with, and so valued by means of, a social positive ("honor"). In the second half of the verse, however, the logic is slightly different and to recognize it requires that one both attend to the nuances of the language it deploys and possess a sense of the larger text's developing moral Gestalt.

Within the moral framework that Proverbs develops it is impossible to understand the second half of 11:16 to be suggesting that ruthlessness is that which ought to be rewarded. The wealth that these men obtain is not their reward in the way, say, honor is for the woman of repute in the first verse half. Rather, the line describes not simply what these men "obtain," but what they grasp after or cling to (תמך). The woman in the first half sought repute and is rhetorically promised honor and hence can be symbolically reckoned as traveling the way of wisdom. The ruthless men, by contrast, clutch for riches. The result or reward of this avarice, however, is not

[48] So the NRSV renders 11:16 as: "A gracious woman gets honor, but she who hates virtue is covered with shame. The timid become destitute, but the aggressive gain riches." For a discussion, see Whybray, *Proverbs* 182–83.

explicitly named. The readers are left to draw their own conclusions. And by this point in the instruction the wise and discerning reader imagined by the prologue will be able to understand that wealth does not possess the kind of genuine value many presuppose and that those who ruthlessly purse riches, like the robbers in chapter one, trod not the way of wisdom, but the way of folly and wickedness. A better translation of the line might be one that not only makes clear the nuances of תמך but which also understands the *waw* that introduces the second stich (ועריצים) as a contrastive *waw*: "A woman of repute grasps honor, but ruthless men grasp riches."

Again although in Prov 13:18 and 11:16 an act-consequence rhetoric points to the reward of virtue, this promise cannot be regarded simply or only in terms of literal economic and social status. The literary and moral Gestalt of the book indicates that, like economic rhetoric elsewhere, the images of the non-primary good of social status function as motivational symbols that value virtue and vice. Although the rhetoric hints that the sages believed social status ought to come through the attainment of wisdom, it serves to undergird the larger wisdom mythos that insists the cosmos favors those who attain to the incomparably desirable way of virtue.

A series of other sayings in Proverbs deploy a more general rhetoric of desire than that of food or social status. According to the NRSV renderings, for instance, Prov 13:21; 16:20; and 19:8 speak, respectively, of the righteous person, the one who gains insight, or the one who attains wisdom as *prospering*, a term which in contemporary American English often primarily connotes economic gain.[49]

חטאים תרדף רעה ואת־צדיקים ישלם־טוב

Misfortune pursues sinners, but *prosperity* rewards the righteous. (13:21)[50]

---

[49] *Webster's Ninth New Collegiate Dictionary*, for instance, lists the first definition of "prosper" as "to succeed in an enterprise or activity; *esp.*: to achieve economic success."

[50] Although the use in this verse of abstract nouns as subjects of active verbs may cause confusion, MT is comprehensible as it stands. Fichtner (see the *BHS* apparatus), however, suggests the final two words of the line (ישלם־טוב) should be read as שלום, positing that a dittography with the first word of v. 22 (טוב) produced the present text. A rendering of the second verse half along the lines of, "He (the Lord?) rewards the righteous with good" (see Murphy, *Proverbs*, 95) is unnecessary and destroys the parallelism with the first verse half, which also employs an abstract noun as the subject of an active verb ("misfortune pursues").

משכיל על־דבר ימצא־טוב ובוטח ביהוה אשריו

> Those who are attentive to a matter will *prosper*, and happy are those who trust in the Lord. (16:20)[51]

קנה־לב אהב נפשו שמר תבונה למצא־טוב

> To get wisdom is to love oneself; to keep understanding is to *prosper*. (19:8)[52]

Each of these lines resonates with other lines in Proverbs in significant ways.[53] Each, moreover (particularly 13:21), reflects a wisdom prosperity axiom in some sense.[54] However, these verses also reveal that

[51] Note the end of the first verse half and the beginning of the second plays with the letters ט-ו-ב. To what exactly the דבר in this verse refers—e.g., a human or divine "word" or "affair"—is unclear. The matter is probably undecidable and the text slides between both possibilities, though the second half of the line, which speaks of trust in YHWH, may favor understanding דבר as referring to a divine word.

[52] It is appropriate to emend the infinitive למצא to a finite verb as the versions suggest. See Fichtner's notes in the *BHS* apparatus; Mitchell Dahood, "Congruity of Metaphors," *VTSup* 16 (1967): 40–49, esp. 40; Whybray, *Proverbs*, 278; Murphy, *Proverbs*, 141. An appropriate, though somewhat literal translation of the line based on the emendation might be: "The one who acquires wisdom loves himself; the one guarding understanding will find good."

[53] In 13:21, the image of evil pursuing "sinners" recalls, in ironic fashion, the picture sketched in 1:10–19, where it was sinners who chased after wealth. The משכיל in 16:20, likewise, "finds" (מצא) something valuable just as the robbers in ch. 1 had hoped to "find" (נמצא; "we will find") "all precious wealth" (כל הון יקר; 1:13). This *maśkîl* also might be said to embody the "wise dealing" (*haśkēl*) imagined in the prologue (1:3). Moreover, although he does not "fear the Lord" (cf. the book's motto in 1:7), he nonetheless "trusts in YHWH." In 19:8 the deployment of the verb קנה likewise hearkens back to key verses in chs. 1–9 (e.g., 1:5; 4:5–9; cf. 16:16; 17:16; 23:23). The phrase קנה־לב (lit. "the one who acquires a heart"), which surely means "the one who finds wisdom" (cf. the language of the second verse-half, שמר תבונה, "the one who guards understanding"), also seems to be the opposite of the one who "lacks heart" (חסר־לב)—a common expression throughout Proverbs (see 6:32; 7:7; 9:4, 16; 10:13, 21; 11:12; 12:11; 15:21; 17:18; 24:30; and the similar 28:16).

[54] In the first half of 19:8 "the one who acquires a heart" is said to "love" himself. In the second verse half, however, like the משכיל in 16:20 and the righteous (צדיקים) in 13:21, he is promised something else very valuable (the "good"). Although the first half of 13:21 claims that "evil pursues sinners" (cf. 1:10–19), this may be a description or a prognosis (i.e., hinting as well that sinners pursue evil). The second half of the line, however, like the first half of 16:20, more clearly deploys a cause and effect rhetoric and claims that the righteous will be recompensed (שלם). Regarding the act-consequence notion vis-à-vis 13:21, see Plöger (*Sprüche Salomos*, 163), who alludes to the previous verse and speaks of the *Ergehen* of certain deeds; Whybray (*Proverbs*, 208–09), who approves of the RSV's (and hence the NRSV's) use of the English "prosperity" in the verse and who notes that the verse is a "bare

their act-consequence rhetoric ought not to be conceived of too simplistically as promising automatic material prosperity, for the verses literally deploy the language of the "good" (טוב) to speak of the valuable reward that comes to the righteous person, the insightful one, and the one who "buys a heart."[55] Although טוב in HB can carry economic resonances as the NRSV renderings intimate (in Proverbs see 3:27; discussed in Chapter Three), to what extent one opts for a more or less materialistic reading of the promises of "good" in these sayings is largely a function of how one understands a wisdom prosperity axiom to be at work in Proverbs.

The sayings of 13:21; 16:20; and 19:8 permit readings on multiple levels. The logic of the lines, however, is similar to other wisdom's virtues sayings. Each pairs a moral positive with a promise of "good" (טוב; 13:21b; 16:20; 19:8) or, as in 13:21a, a moral negative (sinners) with a promise of evil (רעה; 13:21). With the possible exception of טוב itself, however, none of the lines uses any economic rhetoric. Rather just as wealth functions in other sayings to value wisdom's way, the more general language of the good articulates the worth of virtue and motivates the hearer to acquire it.

The syntax of 13:21 also suggests that an overly literalistic understanding of the wisdom prosperity rhetoric in this line ought to be

statement about retribution." Murphy (*Proverbs*, 98) also writes in regard to 13:21 and 22 of "the law retribution." Similarly Hausmann (*Menschenbild*, 53, 224, 236) alludes to the *Tun-Ergehen* principle at work in 13:21, as she also seems to in regard to 16:20 and 19:8 (see pp. 271 and 317 respectively). In regard to 19:8, Clifford (*Proverbs*, 176) in mentioning "prosperity" and silver and gold (and alluding to 2.2–4) underscores the material nature of the promise implicit in the verse, for "with wisdom come all other gifts." Toy (*Proverbs*, 371), too, highlights the verse's promise of what is useful in "physical life," though he also more explicitly recognizes the particulars of the promise ought to be more broadly conceived.

[55] In 13:21 NJPS translates טוב with the rhetoric of "reward;" in 16:20 "success;" and in 19:8 "happiness." For the usual, overly literal understanding of the act-consequence schema in relation to the proverbs under discussion, see the citations in the previous note. The statement that all three verses employ language of the good is valid if the MT's text at 13:21 is accepted (cf. n. 50 above). Fichtner's suggestion in the *BHS* apparatus that the final word of the line be perhaps read as שלום and not טוב (postulating the present text reflects a dittography with the beginning of v. 22) would provide a neater parallelism. Yet even if this is so, שלום ("peace," "well being") like the "good" (טוב) is not clearly an economic term, but points to something that throughout HB is typically highly valued. In Proverbs, שלום, like material wealth, is sometimes associated with wisdom's way (e.g., 3:2, 17; cf. 12:20). It, however, more than the rhetoric of wealth, whose value in the economic sphere is clear, more nearly represents the valuable thing promised by the wisdom mythos—human flourishing and well being.

avoided. The idea that an abstract notion such as "misfortune" might pursue anything forces one to a non-literal reckoning of the line's rhetoric. Despite the language of wealth in the previous v. 19, the focus of 16:20 is with the insightful *maskil* who trusts in YHWH.[56] The verse, moreover, may include a kind of pun that hints to the hearer or reader that the "good" which the wise and righteous person will find is in fact not primarily any kind of wealth or riches—עשר—but a reward of another sort. The virtuous person, the text perhaps playfully hints, will not necessarily become an עשיר (a "rich person"), but he will find the contentment of a flourishing life—אשריו ("happy is he"). Similarly 19:8's parallel of the "good" with the phrase אהב נפש ("to love oneself") once more underscores the affective rather than material well being that wisdom is sure to deliver.

These features internal to the sayings together with the patterns of metaphorical and rhetorical use of wealth and poverty language thus far established by the wisdom's virtues discourse suggests that even if טוב in the proverbs cited above can carry an economic sense, it cannot, in the context of the book, be reduced to that single sense. The cause and effect rhetoric of the lines underscores the message of the wisdom mythos that well being awaits those who succeed in the attainment of virtue.

5.2. The Discourse of Social Justice Revisited

As with the sayings belonging to the wisdom's virtues discourse that I just considered, a good number of proverbs belonging to the discourse of social justice deploy an act-consequence rhetoric to motivate the hearer's adherence to their instruction as well. The Gestalt of Proverbs, its moral vision and patterns of figurative and rhetorical use of wealth and poverty language, however, indicates that the reward mechanism articulated by these social justice proverbs also ought not to be regarded merely as literal promises. As with those wisdom's virtues sayings discussed above, the act-consequence language of these social justice proverbs, though motivating adherence

[56] Prov 16:19, recall, speaks of both "poor persons" (עניים) and "spoil" (שלל). The presence of the טוב in the comparative construction of the verse might also be understood as the "catchword" that drew verses 19 and 20 together.

to instruction through the promise of reward (often material reward), reinforces that proverbial wisdom mythos which emphasizes the value of wisdom's way and insists the virtues of social justice are in accord with the genuine fabric of the cosmos.

5.2.a. *Care for the Poor*

Like Prov 14:31; 17:5; and 19:7 discussed in Chapter Four, several other sayings in Proverbs promote the virtue of kindness to the poor. Consider first Prov 21:13; 22:9; and 28:27:

אטם אזנו מזעקת־דל גם־הוא יקרא ולא יענה

> Whoever stops his ears at the cry of the wretched, he too will call and not be answered.

טוב־עין הוא יברך כי־נתן מלחמו לדל

> Those who are generous are blessed, for they share their bread with the poor.

נותן לרש אין מחסור ומעלים עיניו רב־מארות

> The one who gives to the poor will not be in want. But whoever shuts his eyes will have many curses.

Proverbs 21:13 and 22:9 both employ the word דל, one of the terms that the social justice discourse prefers when speaking of the poor person. Proverbs 28:27, however, makes use of the term רש. This word, recall, is common in the wisdom's virtues discourse, and the saying might easily have been grouped with those proverbs advocating a specific virtue, e.g., generosity. However, as in 21:13 and 22:9, the poor person in 28:27 is, grammatically speaking, an object, a feature common to the social justice discourse. Similarly, though the poor person in 21:13 is able to cry, this one is not a subject, but the object of the genitive in the prepositional phrase that forms the predicate of the first clause (מזעקת־דל).[57] Someone else "acts" by turning a deaf ear to this one's cries.

Although each of the sayings cited above employ (to greater and lesser degrees) an act-consequence rhetoric, they do not function

[57] The subject and verb of the clause are expressed by the participle *ʾōṭēm* ("whoever stops").

simply or primarily as observations of a mechanical moral universe where good and wicked deeds are automatically rewarded, though commentators sometimes seem to imply as much.[58] The invocation of the act-consequence schema ought not to suggest that the sages believed an experience of a lack of compassion (21:13), blessedness (22:9), or material security (28:27) follow, literally and inevitably, generous or uncompassionate conduct of every individual's life in some empirically verifiable way. It is, moreover, not simply the case that exceptions to the act-consequence rule occasionally occur. Rather the principle concern of these proverbs lies elsewhere.

As I suggested in Chapter One, in certain contexts even observations and indicative statements in Proverbs can carry the force of admonitions and each of the sayings under consideration function in part as a command.[59] They mean to inculcate in the hearer a particular social virtue. In 22:9 it is the sharing of bread, or more symbolically, acts of generosity on behalf of the poor that is underscored; in 21:13 and 28:27 ignoring or disregarding the plight of the poor (closing one's ears or shutting one's eyes) is disavowed. The latter verse, like 22:9, also advocates generosity to the poor.[60] Moreover each of the proverbs employs participial forms when encouraging

[58] See in regard to 21:13, Murphy (*Proverbs*, 160), who speaks of the "talion law"; Whybray (*Proverbs*, 311), who speaks of "exact retribution." Cf. Clifford, *Proverbs*, 191. In regard to 22:9, see Toy (*Proverbs*, 417), who writes that "blessed" in the verse means "by God, immediately or through natural laws, and by men." Cf. Van Leeuwen, "Proverbs," *NIB* 5:198–99; Delkurt, *Ethische Einsichten*, 124–25; Clifford, *Proverbs*, 248. In regard to 28:27, see McKane (*Proverbs*, 627) who writes that "Yahweh will see to it that only men of character and compassion hold wealth in his community." Cf. Whybray, *Proverbs*, 397. In all three of lines under discussion, Whybray finds evidence that the original speakers of the sayings were agriculturalists who were neither rich or poor, but often in danger of falling into poverty. See *Proverbs*, 311, 320, 397 and Chapter Two.

[59] The comments of several interpreters suggest that they too understand such sayings to be functioning as admonitions or commands. Van Leeuwen ("Proverbs," *NIB* 5:198), for instance, relates 22:9 to Deut 15:9–11 "which forbids stinginess and commands generosity." Whybray's rhetoric (*Proverbs*, 320) in regard to 22:9 is similar: the verse "advocates generosity to the poor." He likewise calls 21:13 "a strongly persuasive variant on the theme of duty to the poor." See *Proverbs*, 311; Clifford (*Proverbs*, 191) calls the verse a concise and challenging statement.

[60] The first half of 28:27 is sometimes read as an ironic observation of a mechanistic moral order similar to the way 11:24–25 sometimes is (see Chapter Four). See, for example, Whybray (*Proverbs*, 397), who alludes to 11:24–25 and writes: "The affirmation that giving away part of one's wealth to the poor will paradoxically lead to an *increase* in one's wealth or prosperity is made in various ways" (italics original).

kindness to the poor, intimating that the sayings, like other social justice proverbs (e.g., 14:31; discussed in Chapter Four) are perhaps concerned more with the hearer's dispositions than the performance of individual acts.[61]

5.2.b. *The Divine Concern for the Poor*

Proverbs 17:5 and 19:17 are both reminiscent of 14:31, which I treated in Chapter Four. Both also speak specifically of the relationship of the deity to the poor. They read:

לעג לרש חרף עשהו שמח לאיד לא ינקה

> Whoever mocks the poor person, insults his maker. Whoever rejoices over another's misfortune will not go unpunished.[62]

מלוה יהוה חונן דל וגמלו ישלם־לו

> Whoever is kind to the poor lends to the Lord and will be repaid in full.

As in 14:31 ("Whoever oppresses the poor insults his maker, but whoever is kind to the needy honors him"), both 17:5 and 19:17 motivate their claims by an appeal to the deity. Each proverb promotes the virtue of kindness to the poor and censures those who would oppress them. In each, moreover, the poor person is the object of the sentence, grammatically speaking. Like 14:31 as well, Prov 19:7 also deploys a term for the poor that is particularly prevalent in the discourse of social justice (דל); Proverbs 17:5 uses רש (cf. 28:27; treated above).

Both 17:5 and 19:17 take up a cause and effect rhetoric and describe the desirable and undesirable consequences of different kinds of conduct. In 17:5 (again like the first half of 14:31) the rhetoric serves to censure a particular kind of behavior—mocking the poor person. In 19:17 (similar to the second half of 14:31) the rhetoric encourages a particular virtue—showing kindness to the poor דל.

---

[61] In regard to 21:13 the participle is: *ʾōṭēm* ("stopping"); in 28:27 *nôtēn* ("giving"), *maʿlîm* ("shutting"). Proverbs 22:9 deploys a perfect form, *nātan* ("he gives").

[62] The translation follows NJPS. The Greek renders לאיד as ἀπολλυμένῳ suggesting a reading of לאבד. However, as Murphy writes (*Proverbs*, 127), perhaps "the abstract is simply rendered as concrete." Cf. further Fichtner's notes in the *BHS* apparatus.

Unlike many sayings that evoke the *Tun-Ergehen* schema, however, in 17:5 and 19:7 cause and effect language is explicitly associated with the deity, which may imply retribution comes directly from the divine rather than as an inevitable consequence of a particular act.[63] The rhetoric associates wise and right conduct less with the true nature of the world, as postulated by the wisdom mythos, than with the one who created the universe by wisdom (cf. Prov 8:22–31). Again as in 14:31, the use of participles also hints that the text's concern is with the formation of the hearer's dispositions.[64]

5.2.c. *Royalty and Justice for the Poor*

Just as Prov 28:15; 30:11–13; and 31:5–9 (all treated in Chapter Four) highlight the role of political elites in maintaining justice for the poor, so too do 28:16 and 29:14. However, these latter verses deploy an act-consequence rhetoric more clearly than the others. They read:

נגיד חסר תבונות ורב מעשקות שנאי בצע יאריך ימים

> A prince who lacks understanding is very oppressive; he who spurns ill-gotten gains will live long. (Prov 28:16)[65]

מלך שופט באמת דלים כסאו לעד יכון

> A king who judges the poor honestly, his throne will be established forever. (Prov 29:14)

Like 29:7 (discussed in Chapter Four), Prov 28:16, although it is cast in negative terms, sets up a close relationship between a social virtue (right social conduct or 'not oppressing') and a broad intellectual virtue—"understanding."[66] With its allusion to the oppressive "prince,"

[63] Cf. Klaus Koch, "Gibt es ein Vergeltungsdogma im Alten Testament?" *Zeitschrift für Theologie und Kirche* 52 (1955): 1–42.

[64] The participles of 17:5 are: *lōʿēg* ("mocking"); of 19:17, *malwēh* ("lending"), *ḥōnēn* ("being generous"). Instead of a participle, the second stich of 17:5 employs the substantivized adjective *śāmēaḥ* ("one who rejoices").

[65] The verse is difficult and the translation follows NJPS. Probably ורב should be emended to ירב so that the first five words might be rendered something like "a prince lacking in understanding increases oppressions." The 3rd pers. sg. impf. verb יאריך appears to take as its subject the m. pl. const. participle שנאי reckoned as a collective. Cf. Murphy, *Proverbs*, 213; Toy, *Proverbs*, 501–02.

[66] As is not uncommon in the wisdom's virtues discourse, the second half of 28:16 also intimates that the injustice of the ruler, like that of the sinners in ch. 1,

Prov 28:16 builds on the imagery of 28:15 (discussed in Chapter Four). This social justice proverb, recall, states: "A roaring lion and a prowling bear is a wicked man ruling a poor people" (ארי־נהם ודב שוקק משל רשע על עם־דל). Proverbs 29:14's use of דל (pl.) as an object of the right legal action of the king intimates that this proverb, too, belongs to the social justice discourse.

The two verses (28:16 and 29:14) promulgate the ancient Near Eastern political or royal ideology, which legitimated political powers to the extent that these insured a minimum standard of justice and protection for society's poor and vulnerable.[67] However, implicit in this promulgation of the ancient codes of social justice is the notion that the monarch's failure to carry out his royal duties as defined by the royal ideology is sufficient grounds for his rule to be declared illegitimate. If, as 29:14 suggests, a king's rule is established through the enactment of justice, it follows that the failure to establish justice would mean that a monarch's position is insecure. Along with sayings like 28:15 and the other royal social justice sayings discussed in Chapter Four, these proverbs thus divest rulers, whose reigns are characterized by injustice, of their authority.

For the sages it is not accumulating wealth through oppression or the arbitrary exercise of power that makes a king, but rather, as 29:14 suggests, the establishment of justice.[68] Proverbs such as 28:16 and 29:14 thus reflect the moral and political values of a caste of intellectual elites. Though ultimately conservative in not actively seeking to undermine traditional political institutions, these scribes are not so uncritically. They formulate moral and political criteria and offer judgments based on these criteria. The assertion that an unjust political figure who seeks unjust gain will not increase his days, and the claim that an honest king's reign will last forever, are obviously

has to do with attempts at acquiring, by unjust means, wealth (בצע) that ultimately will not benefit in that it cannot insure him of life or "length of days."

[67] Cf. Prov 16:12, 20:28; 25:5; 29:4, all of which speak of the proper establishment (i.e., by justice) of a monarch's rule.

[68] Such a moral impulse and critique is reminiscent of the episodes recounted in 1 Kings 21 and Jer 22:13–18. In the former Jezebel encourages Ahab to "act like a king" and seize Naboth's vineyard, an action opposed by the prophet Elijah who, as a representative of more traditional Israelite tribal values, apparently had other notions regarding the nature of kingship. In the latter passage Jeremiah rhetorically inquires of king Jehoiakim as to whether oppressive building projects or the establishment of justice is what establishes royal authority.

not straightforward observations of the world that might be empirically verified. They are a part of Proverbs' construction of a moral universe and identity for its addressees which places a premium both on the individual's attainment of social virtue and the realization of these values in social life. Though one who was immersed in the wisdom mythos might tend to view political realities as corresponding to the act-consequence assertions of lines such as 28:16 and 29:14, whether or not in reality oppressive regimes lasted days or decades is not as significant as the text's implicit *claim* that such a royal house or dynasty *will not* endure.[69]

5.3. The Discourse of Social Observation in Proverbs 10–31

5.3.a. *Characteristics*

Up to this point we have been concentrating attention upon the various sayings in Proverbs that comprise the wisdom's virtues discourse and the discourse of social justice. There is, however, another group sayings in the book that make up a third distinct sub-discourse of wealth and poverty, which I call a *discourse of social observation*. Yet unlike the book's other two wealth and poverty discourses, the sayings belonging to the discourse of social observation do in fact often appear simply to reflect the sages' scrutiny of their social world, including a recognition that the rich, and especially the poor and poverty, are social givens.[70] However, "observations" of socially important categories and groups such as wealth and poverty/rich and poor are, as Bakhtin's insights regarding the social nature of discourse intimate (see Chapter One), never neutral. Though the wealth and poverty sayings we now turn to are regularly cast in the indicative and function, more obviously than many proverbs already treated,

[69] Such a message would prove a particularly forceful, almost prophetic, critique of political or imperial authority in both an 8th century and a post-exilic context. Though perhaps not emerging until the Hellenistic period, the tales in Daniel and Esther explore similar themes of the legitimacy and illegitimacy of political power.

[70] The suggestion that the sages recognized the "given-ness" of social classes and did not respond critically to them is common; see Chapter Three, and cf. further, Murphy, *Proverbs*, 261; T. Donald, "The Semantic Field of Rich and Poor in the Wisdom Literature of Hebrew and Accadian," *OrAnt* 2 (1964): 27–41; R. N. Whybray, *Wealth and Poverty in the Book of Proverbs* (JSOTSup 99; Sheffield: JSOT, 1990), 61.

as observations, they too are "doing" something beyond observing. They present not unfiltered snapshots of brute social fact. Rather, like the photo journalist's art, they are composed and evaluative statements that carry and reflect a particular perspective.[71] They depict "how things are," but only as seen and evaluated within a set of particular assumptions and values.

The moral vision and patterns of language use discernable in the wisdom's virtues and social justice discourses, i.e., the Gestalt of Proverbs, constitutes the set of assumptions and values through which the discourse of social observation views what it observes. This Gestalt, moreover, is the hermeneutical lens for understanding the moral work that the sayings carry out rhetorically. In short, the sayings belonging to the discourse of social observation offer social critique and touch upon a range of topics (e.g., trust in YHWH, the value of social ties, the precarious situation of the poor).[72] On the one hand, sayings belonging to the discourse of social observation often have to do with the same overvaluing of wealth, and confusion of wealth with moral right, that is of concern to the wisdom's virtues discourse. On the other hand, their critique often concerns the negative effects of poverty, which the social justice discourse seeks to redress. In particular, the social observation discourse highlights the adverse social effects produced by excessive lack or wealth and often sets a certain kind of rich person in an unfavorable light.

Besides this common rhetorical thrust, however, the discourse of social observation is also characterized by the fact that, like the discourse of social justice, it employs the personal language of the "poor person," but does not distinguish between the use of the terms רש and דל. It also regularly takes up the personal language of the rich person, notably preferring the substantivized adjective עשיר ("rich

[71] The analogy with photo journalism was suggested to me by Carol A. Newsom (personal communication).

[72] Cf. Pleins' claims that the sages, though promoting charity, offered no such critique. See J. David Pleins, "Poverty in the Social World of the Wise," *JSOT* 37 (1987): 61–78. That they did not offer it in the same way as did the prophets is certain and, in part, to be expected since the sages and individual prophets probably emerged from and flourished in distinct, though not necessarily entirely exclusive, socio historical contexts. Nonetheless, a saying like Prov 21:3 (עשה צדקה ומשפט נבחר ליהוה מזבח; "To do justice and righteousness is more desirable to the Lord than sacrifice") sounds as if it could have been uttered by Amos (cf. Am 4:4–5) or Isaiah of Jerusalem (cf. Is 1:10–20; cf. further 1 Sam 15:22).

person"). Very often, though not exclusively, this discourse will contrast the rich with the poor as well. Yet in distinction to the social justice discourse, the poor person in the discourse of social observation can appear as a grammatical subject. In contrast to the wisdom's virtues discourse, however, this third sub-discourse of wealth and poverty never sets the poor person as a subject in a comparative structure.

5.3.b. *Excessive Wealth, Lack, and the Rich*

On at least nine occasions Proverbs employs the substantivized adjective עשיר.[73] Several of these cases belong to the discourse of social observation where the text contrasts the rich with the poor and is critical of the former. Elsewhere the ill social effects produced by excessive wealth or excessive lack are highlighted. Such lines thus make more explicit the message of those sayings, which one occasionally encounters in the other proverbial wealth and poverty discourses, that begin to locate a danger to the life of virtue with wealth (e.g., 15:17; 16:19; 17:1).

Consider first 10:15; 18:10–11; 18:23; and 22:7. Each text is cast in the indicative, offers a particular perception of social reality, and is in some sense critical of that reality.

הון עשיר קרית עזו מחתת דלים רישם

> The wealth of the rich is their fortress; the ruin of the poor is their poverty. (Prov 10:15)

מגדל־עז שם יהוה בו־ירוץ הצדיק ונשגב
הון עשיר קרית עזו וכחומה נשגבה במשכיתו

> The name of the Lord is a tower of strength to which the righteous person runs and is safe.
> The wealth of the rich person is his fortress; in his fancy it is a protective wall.[74] (Prov 18:10–11)

---

[73] Prov 10:15; 14:20; 18:11, 23; 22:2, 7, 16; 28:6, 11.

[74] On the relatively obscure משכית and its likely meaning, "fancy, imagination," see Plöger, *Sprüche Salomos*, 212 and Whybray, *Proverbs*, 269. Fichtner's *BHS* apparatus proposes an emendation based on the Greek, but the MT is understandable and should be preserved; cf. Murphy, *Proverbs*, 134; Clifford, *Proverbs*, 171.

תחנונים ידבר־רש ועשיר יענה עזות

> The poor person speaks beseechingly. The rich person's answer is harsh. (Prov 18:23)

עשיר ברשים ימשול ועבד לוה לאיש מלוה

> The rich person rules over the poor and the borrower is a slave to the lender. (Prov 22:7)

Verses 10:15; 18:11a; 18:23; and 22:7 each may initially appear to be offering nothing more than an observation of a social reality, namely that wealth secures certain benefits. Delkurt, for instance, associates 10:15 with 13:8 ("Wealth is a ransom for a person's life, but the poor get no threats"; NRSV) and suggests both proverbs underscore the view that wealth can prove an advantage in a variety of circumstances, including a bad harvest (so, his example in regard to 10:15), or even in the legal realm, where one's wealth might free one even from a sentence of death (so, his understanding of 13:8).[75] McKane relates 18:11 to 10:15 and believes the sentiment to be simply that "wealth affords security." The rich person's wealth is "a buffer" protecting him against "the whims and caprice of circumstance."[76] Toy also writes that 18:11 (together with 18:10) "simply states a fact."[77] Similarly Murphy compares 18:11 to 10:15,

---

[75] Delkurt, *Ethische Einsichten*, 101–102. In my view, 13:8 does speak of an advantage that wealth brings its possessor, but questions that value in that its usefulness is found in an adverse situation that the wealth itself may have brought on. Murphy (*Proverbs*, 74) notes: "The point [of 10:15] seems so simple: Riches are a source of strength; poverty is ruinous. There is no intention of communicating here a moral lesson. This is simply a reflection upon reality; that is the way things are." However, relating the line to 18:11 Murphy does indicate that "these sayings have a way of prompting new perspectives." Similarly, Van Leeuwen ("Proverbs," *NIB* 5:111) states the saying has "no moral or spiritual judgments attached (cf. v. 4). But the picture is more complex, as the proverb pair in 18:10–11 shows (cf. 10:29)." Cf. Toy (*Proverbs*, 208) who writes. "There is probably no ethical thought in the proverb the sense is that wealth smoothes one's path in life, bringing supply of bodily needs, guarding against the attacks of the powerful, and giving social consideration . . . while the poor man is exposed to bodily and social privations." See further Friedemann W. Golka, *The Leopard's Spots: Biblical and African Wisdom in Proverbs* (Edinburgh: T&T Clark, 1993), 65 who suggests 10:15 offers a "neutral view of wealth and poverty." Cf. Whybray, *Proverbs*, 165.

[76] McKane, *Proverbs*, 516–17.

[77] Toy, *Proverbs*, 361. Although he suggests too that the verse "appears to say that wealth is a protection not really," Toy believes this sentiment belongs to a redactor and verse 11a would better be read "and like a high wall is his riches."

noting that it "expresses an obvious fact: riches are a protection," though he also recognizes a level of critique or "bite" in the rhetoric of "imagination" or "fancy."[78] Likewise Whybray regards 18:23 as "a 'neutral' comment on a fact of social life and relationships," i.e., as a description of the way things are.[79] Though he rightly believes 22:7 may contain an implicit warning about falling into debt, for him this proverb also "is ostensibly simply a statement about the harsh facts of life."[80] Van Leeuwen, too, recognizes an implicit warning in 22:7 but also characterizes the proverb as "a straightforward observation."[81]

Yet if the wealth verses cited above reflect simple observations of the "way things are," in the context of the book the lines are somewhat incongruous. This apparent incongruity, however, does not necessarily suggest that the proverbial discourse of wealth and poverty is hopelessly ambiguous. It can also be regarded as an invitation to the wise and discerning reader to consider the *meshalim* more closely as sayings which name something that is, but ought not to be. The Gestalt of Proverbs, already established by the wisdom's virtues and social justice sayings treated above, I contend, constitutes a perspective for discerning what sort of observations these Proverbs in fact represent.

For example, just as the wisdom's virtues discourse highlighted the limited value of wealth by evoking the ephemeral nature of riches and subordinating wealth's worth to that of virtue, so too 18:11 critiques a trust in one's wealth by labeling this an "illusion." Moreover, by explicitly naming the עשיר the verse caricatures this "class" or

---

[78] Murphy, *Proverbs*, 136; cf. Whybray, *Proverbs*, 268–69.

[79] Whybray, *Proverbs*, 274. Whether 18:23 is describing a single or typical encounter is not completely clear, though the latter is most likely. Cf. McKane (*Proverbs*, 518), who calls the verse "an acute observation." The line "is factual rather than condemnatory. This is just the way of the world." Delkurt (*Ethische Einsichten*, 117) similarly writes that, "This sentence saying records an observation without drawing out a consequence for any of the participants" (*Dieser Sentenz halt schlicht eine Beobachtung fest, ohne eine Konsequenz für einen der Beteiligten zu ziehen*). Delkurt relates the statement to 22:7 as well. In regard to this latter verse, see McKane (*Proverbs*, 566) who considers the line the product of "a close observer of Israelite society." It is "a frank recognition of the power of wealth" and "must be regarded as a factual statement about the power of money." Cf. Clifford, *Proverbs* 197. Murphy (*Proverbs*, 165) and Whybray (*Proverbs*, 320) regard at least the first half of 22:7 similarly, though these also hint that the line as a whole also may contain a critique.

[80] Whybray, *Proverbs*, 320.

[81] Van Leeuwen, "Proverbs," *NIB* 5:198.

"type" of person as one which typically does trust in wealth. Such a person is one who embodies that implicit but real social script which, as far as Proverbs is concerned, overvalues wealth or wrongly considers it to have significant worth outside the economic realm. Hence the saying in 18:11, at least for one who attempts to discern the book's tropes and figures, also functions more generally as a critique of a certain kind of rich person.[82] This critical function of 18:11 is particularly evident if one reads the line with the immediately preceding verse 10.[83] According to this verse it is not wealth that affords protection, but rather a certain kind of piety that characterizes the virtuous, i.e., the righteous, person. When the two sayings (vv. 10 and 11) are read together, the rich person who trusts in wealth for protection is contrasted with the righteous one who trusts in the Lord. In the context of the book's Gestalt, especially its two ways discourse, this functions not merely to color negatively the rich person, but to associate that person morally and symbolically with the wicked and fool, the entire way of folly and wickedness.

Proverbs 10:15, which shares an identical initial stich with 18:11, is not so explicit in its negative evaluation of the עשיר as is 18:10–11. The wealth of the rich person in 10:15 is not labeled an illusion. The verse appears more as a neutral observation and read in isolation it easily suggests a positive role for riches. The riches of 10:15, like a fortified city, protect their possessor from unforeseen disaster. Riches can offer clear advantages and the rich person in the saying as well as many commentators rightly recognize this. What is not recognized is the value ascribed to material wealth elsewhere in Proverbs. As the wisdom's virtues discourse suggests, wealth holds limited value for the sages outside of the economic realm. It is not an unqualified or universal good. When one recalls this broader valuation of wealth as well as the demands of the discourse of social justice one can also recognize something further about the *mashal* of 10:15. The line clearly contrasts the rich person with the poor person whose lack results in the absence of the same kind of social

[82] Prov 13:23 might likewise be said to belong to those proverbial observations that critique the reality they observe. It reads in the NRSV: "The field of the poor (ראשים) may yield much food, but it is swept away through injustice (בלא משפט)."

[83] As do many commentators. See, for example, Whybray, *Proverbs*, 269; Clifford, *Proverbs*, 171; Meinhold, *Die Sprüche*, 2:303. The similar images of fortifications as well as a shared vocabulary (נשגב in v. 10 and נשגבה in v. 11) suggest reading 18:10 and 18:11 together is warranted.

safety net that the rich person's wealth might be thought to supply. This, however, is not a simple neutral perception of a social given, for the instructing voice calls such a situation "disastrous." The poverty of the poor is evaluated as "their ruin." It may be that the instructing voice of 10:15 knows as well that the overvaluing of wealth, the unbridled quest for economic profit that can make one rich, can also lead to 'ruinous' competitiveness and brutality, creating a human environment that does not embody the social virtues the prologue highlights.

The wisdom's virtues discourse and the social justice discourse also provide a hermeneutical framework for understanding Prov 18:23 and 22:7. Like 10:15, both of these lines also gesture toward a critique of a situation where the poor's lack of economic resources leave them vulnerable. Proverbs 18:23 states that the poor person speaks with petitions and that the rich person answers the poor רש "harshly."[84] The rhetoric here is literally the language of strength. The עשיר replies "strongly" (עזות), and the implication is that the rich person arrogantly does not feel himself bound by the poor person's claim. Excessive lack has put the poor person in a vulnerable social position, and excessive wealth has led the rich person to locate his source of strength or security, not in YHWH or community ties that would oblige him to respond differently, but in riches.

Similarly 22:7 offers a far from neutral observation about the social world of the wise. What the saying "observes" is that significant inequalities in the distribution of wealth are intimately related to particular economic practices. Despite the use of the root מ-ש-ל ("to rule"), the line is not alluding explicitly to a royal or political figure. Rather it highlights simply the unequal social control or power resulting from inequalities in the economic sphere. The verse's second stich is somewhat explicit, not only in regard to how this inequality in power can get played out in economic terms (e.g., one borrows instead of lends), but as regards the larger social effect it can bring about (the borrower becomes slave to the lender). The observation that the "poor" person and "borrower" becomes subject to and

[84] The root ח-נ-ן often, though not exclusively, is taken up by the discourse of social justice and characterizes the wise and righteous person's conduct toward the poor as, e.g., in 14:21, 31; 19:17; 28:8. As here in 18:23, elsewhere in HB (e.g., the Psalms) the term is found on the lips of the one who petitions the divine. It (חנן) is the language of one in need speaking to one who is able, and in some sense, obligated to meet those needs—be it the neighbor, king, or deity.

"slaves" of the "rich" lender, moreover, is constructed from language which, in Bakhtin's terms, led a particularly charged social life in ancient Israel. The rhetoric of slavery in particular would be especially forceful to the Hebrew imagination attuned to the great national narrative of the Exodus.

Although Prov 18:23 and 22:7 may represent "the way the world is," the book's social justice discourse, which has constituted the poor as a class of moral concern, provides a critical perspective for discerning what sort of observation each statement constitutes. They are an articulation of the fact that something 'is,' but ought not to be; and in both verses, the instruction's particularly resonate images, implicitly critiques the reality it observes.[85]

5.3.c. *The Critique of Wealth's Social Ties*

Several other sayings, which do not explicitly contrast the rich person with the poor person, also belong to the wealth and poverty sub-discourse of social observation. These proverbs highlight the nature and kinds of social ties that wealth both produces and severs. However, when one understands these proverbs in dialogue with the other two wealth and poverty discourses in Proverbs, it becomes clear that the observations, which appear to speak positively of wealth's social role, also contain an implicit critique. Consider the following:

גם־לרעהו ישנא רש ואהבי עשיר רבים

> A poor person is despised even by his peers; but a rich person has many friends. (Prov 14:20)[86]

הון יסיף רעים רבים ודל מרעהו יפרד

> Wealth makes many friends, but a poor person looses his last friend. (Prov 19:4)[87]

---

[85] As I suggested above in regard to Prov 21:7 and 23:20–21 and drawing on the work of Scott, these sayings too might be heard on two levels: the level of public discourse accessible to all hearers including the political and economic elite; and the level of the hidden transcript, which might be recognized more easily by the scribes who produced and used Proverbs.

[86] Although the poor person here appears acted upon, a state of affairs which is most typical of the discourse of social justice, the רש is actually the subject of the *niphal* verb.

[87] Although the first stich of 19:4 does not use the substantivized adjective עשיר (which is common in the discourse of social observation), the noun הון ("wealth")

רבים יחלו פני־נדיב וכל־הרע לאיש מתן

> Many court the favor of a great man, and all are the friends of a dispenser of gifts. (Prov 19:6)

כל אחי־רש שנאהו אף כי מרעהו רחקו ממנו [מרדף אמרים לא־המה]

> All the brothers of a poor person despise him. How much more is he shunned by his friends [. . . .]. (Prov 19:7)[88]

Each saying is cast in the indicative and can be said to reflect a genuine scrutiny of social reality.[89] Most commentators, for instance, understand the proverbs as observations of the real social advantages wealth can provide and as a recognition of the 'given-ness' of social-economic stratification.[90] Such a social situation, however, is not immediately or explicitly evaluated as negative.[91] In fact, if one were to read 14:20b, 19:4a, and 19:6b together but in isolation, wealth's social effect might be regarded as exclusively positive (cf. 10:15a).[92] This, for instance, is Meinhold's view. He writes: "That which 10:15a says about the certain security that wealth offers, is not questioned.

---

functions as its equivalent. The term is a favorite of the wisdom's virtues discourse, but is not exclusive to that discourse. As it is contrasted with the poor person (the one experiencing exceptional lack), it appears the text in 19:4 has in mind not simply wealth but "excessive wealth." The word here is essentially metonymy for the person with significant wealth—i.e., the rich person.

[88] The third line of 19:7 is anomalous. Its relation to the first two lines is not clear and it is omitted in the translation given here. The Ketiv reads: מרדף אמרים לא־המה; the Qere is מרדף אמרים לו־המה. If one reads the K the line might be rendered "(one) pursuing words not these" and understood to be modifying, via a m. sg. part., one of the brothers or friends (plural) of the poor person who abandon him. If so, the line would suggest that in their rejection of their poor kin or fellow these brothers or friends are following a way that is not wisdom's. However, there is no agreement in number between the second and third stichs. Cf. Murphy, *Proverbs*, 141; McKane, *Proverbs*, 527; Fuhs, *Das Buch der Sprichwörter*, 274–75; and Fichtner's notes in the *BHS* apparatus.

[89] Proverbs 19:4, 6, and 7 were likely intentionally grouped together by a redactor.

[90] In regard to 14:20, see Murphy, *Proverbs*, 105; Delkurt, *Ethische Einsichten*, 100; Whybray, *Proverbs*, 218–19; McKane, *Proverbs*, 471. On 19:4, see Murphy, *Proverbs*, 142; Delkurt, *Ethische Einsichten*, 100. On 19:6 and 7, see Murphy, *Proverbs*, 143; Delkurt, *Ethische Einsichten*, 100; McKane, *Proverbs*, 526.

[91] The case in 17:8, where a "precious stone" (or perhaps a "bribe") appears to produce positive affects for its bearer, is analogous. It reads: אבן־חן השחד בעיני בעליו אל־כל־אשר יפנה ישכיל; "A precious stone is a charm in the eyes of its possessor; wherever he turns he succeeds."

[92] Proverbs 19:7 tells the same story as the other sayings, but from an opposite social position. The poor person looses his friends because of his poverty.

Also not challenged is what according to 19:4 is an advantage of wealth, namely that it creates friends."[93]

The sayings, however, are not completely neutral statements about the way things are. This set of sayings, which speak of wealth's social benefits, is also explicit regarding the negative social consequences of excessive lack (cf. 20:15b): various social connections are severed—be it friends (14:20; 19:4) or even kin (19:7). In these *meshalim*, moreover, the behavior of the "brothers" and "friends," who "despise" the one in need, transgresses the principles of the social justice discourse that insist one show kindness to the poor. This fact indicates that these observations are functioning simultaneously as social critiques. Indeed 14:20 is immediately followed in v. 21 by a proverb belonging to the discourse of social justice:[94]

בז־לרעהו חוטא ומחונן עניים אשריו

> The one who despises his friend is wrong; the one who shows pity for the poor is happy.[95]

That v. 21 is in some sense intended as a response to v. 20 is clear, for instance, from the fact that the first stich of both verses begin with a one syllable word linked by a *maqqēp* to a following לרעהו while the last word of v. 21, אשריו ("happy is he") plays on the עשיר ("rich") in the second stich of v. 20 (cf. 16:20). Though the verbal terminology of the first half of each of the two verses is not identical (שנא ["to hate"] vs. בוז ["to despise"]), the fact that each root connotes strong negative emotions or affections also ties the two lines together. But if verse 20 states the social observation—the way the world is—and only implicitly critiques that status, verse 21 states wisdom's evaluation more unequivocally. The one who despises a neighbor in verse 20 is said in verse 21 to have simply "missed the mark." That person, like the robbers in chapter one, is a sinner חטא,

[93] Meinhold, *Die Sprüche*, 1.187. The original reads: *Damit wird nicht in Frage gestellt, was 10,15a über die gewisse Sicherheit sagt, die der Reichtum bietet (vgl. aber 18,11). Auch wird nicht bestritten, was nach 19,4 ein Vorzug des Besitzes ist, dass er nämlich Freunde schafft.*

[94] In 14:21 the terminology for the poor, as is typical for the discourse of social justice, is the substantivized (plural) adjective עניים, who are also objects acted upon rather than subjects who act. The verse functions to promote in the hearer the virtue of kindness to the poor by declaring the one who acts graciously (מחונן) to the lowly to be happy or blessed.

[95] Reading the Ketiv *ʿănāyîm* rather than the Qere *ʿănāwîm*.

a characterization which obviously situates this person and such conduct on the way of folly.[96]

The insistence of this set of social observation sayings that excessive lack severs social relationships also ironically calls into question the nature and stability of the social relationships described in the sayings. If the relative lack or excess of material wealth is the operative variable in the *number* of social ties, the *nature* of those social ties is likely uncertain when this variable is in play. The observations, in fact, imply that when this variable is at work, social bonds are likely weak. The rhetorical force of 14:20a, 19:4b, and 19:6 lies in the recognition that "the tie that binds" the "friends" to the rich person is not the rich person's character, nor the values and obligations of community or family, but only the possession of the more ephemeral and unpredictable wealth (cf. 23:4–5). By observing how both excessive wealth and excessive lack produce fragile social ties instead of firm bonds like those based on kinship and friendship, each verse implicitly critiques the economic context that produces such fragile ties.

Proverbs, however, offers not only a critique regarding the weak social ties that wealth produces, it also offers a positive counterpoint in sayings such as 17:17; 18:24; and 27:10a and c:

בכל־עת אהב הרע ואח לצרה יולד

A friend loves at all times; a brother is born for adversity.

איש רעים להתרעע ויש אהב דבק מאח

There are friends who are to appear as friends; but there is one who loves and clings closer than a brother.[97]

[96] For the association of sin and sinners (חטא) with the way of folly and wickedness, see 5:22; 8:36; 10:16; 11:31, etc.

[97] The translation of 18:24 assumes an emendation of the first word of the verse, from MT's איש to יש. Certain LXX MSS, the Syriac, and the Targum follow this reading as well; see Fichtner's *BHS* apparatus; cf. Fuhs, *Das Buch der Sprichwörter*, 274. In the MT the third word of the verse is derived from רעע, "to be bad, displeasing." However, the above translation follows the versions which seem to read instead the *hithpael* of רעה, "appear as friends." The sense is that there are two types of friends: those who seem to be friends, but whose ties to a person are perhaps based on unreliable things such as wealth, and those who are true friends. Cf. Murphy, *Proverbs*, 134; Whybray, *Proverbs*, 274; Toy, *Proverbs*, 366–67.

רעך ורעה אביך אל־תעזב [ובית אחיך אל־תבוא ביום אידך] טוב שכן קרוב מאח רחוק

> Do not abandon your own friend or the friend of your father; [do not go to your kin's house on the day of your disaster;] better is a neighbor nearby than a brother far off.[98]

In each of these sayings the importance of social ties based on something other than material riches is underscored. For Proverbs, it is not wealth that has genuine value in adversity (17:17) or in the day of disaster, as the wisdom's virtues discourse surely also makes clear (e.g., 11:4). Rather it is familial and communal ties; and the wise or virtuous person will attend to these obligations.

5.3.d. *Ironic Wealth and Poverty Sayings*

A number of wealth and poverty sayings that appear as ironic observations also begin to make more sense when understood in light of Proverbs' moral and literary Gestalt. Consider first Prov 13:7:

יש מתעשר ואין כל מתרושש והון רב

> One person shows himself to be rich and has nothing; another shows himself to be poor and has much wealth.[99]

Proverbs 13:7 is precisely the kind of "observation" that it would be difficult to verify in any empirical fashion, since the text itself claims appearances are not always reliable! Murphy, for instance, suggests the saying may be an "observation" that simply states the fact that "appearances are deceiving" so that "no moral issue need be involved." However, he also recognizes that the proverb prompts other legitimate lines of questioning that might have to do, among other things, with whether "the wealth of the poor person consist[s] in another

[98] The middle stich of 27:10 may be a gloss. See Toy, *Proverbs*, 486. The verse nonetheless makes sense. The point perhaps is that the hearer ought not to intrude unduly upon his kin's household. Even if there might be some expectation that kin should assist kin in days of distress, the verse may be suggesting that the one in need ought not to initiate this aspect of the relationship. Yet if the second stich is read with the third, together they may simply underscore the value of a geographically close and reliable friend over a relative who is at some remove. Fichtner's *BHS* notes suggest reading תבוז instead of תבוא in the middle stich so that the demand is that one not "curse" his kin's house in the day of distress. Toy, *Proverbs*, 486, suggests the stich's negative אל should be deleted.

[99] The translation follows NJPS.

order of values, such as dependence upon God." Ultimately however, he seems not to favor such lines of inquiry since they "go beyond the literal sense" of the proverb, which he believes results in one losing sight of the "irony implicit in the literal sense."[100]

However, besides hinting that "one should not judge by appearances," or that one "cannot conceal one's true circumstances," etc., the proverb is also concerned with saying something about the true locus of value in human life.[101] In regard to the first half of 13:7, though one may appear rich in material terms, if this person lacks the virtues of wisdom's ways, he is, in the symbolic world established especially by the wisdom's virtues discourse, in fact "poor." Although he may possess much of value in the market place, in the more significant moral realm he is found wanting. Likewise, and in regard to the second half of 13:7, though one may lack material goods, if this person possesses wisdom's valuable virtues, he might legitimately be declared in possession of much wealth, even if by a certain reckoning of material goods this is not so. Whybray himself recognizes that such a reading, which he associates with Oesterley, in fact "may be in accordance with wisdom teaching." However, he ultimately rejects such broader interpretations because it is "not what the text says."[102] Though 13:7 obviously does not explicitly state its broader meaning, discerning such a meaning is appropriate given both the prologue's invitation to discern the book's tropes and figures and the patterns of language use and values established by other material in the book. Indeed if one does not attempt to discern a fuller meaning to a proverb such as 13:7, it must, in Murphy's language, remain paradoxical and ambiguous.[103]

Consider as well the following ironic sounding sayings:

טוב ינחיל בני־בנים וצפון לצדיק חיל חוטא

> A good person has what to bequeath to his grandchildren; the wealth of sinners is stored up for the righteous. (Prov 13:22)[104]

[100] Murphy, *Proverbs*, 96. Whybray (*Proverbs*, 202) also seems concerned that any interpretation of the verse that considers the line to be more than a "simple observation" is in danger of "overinterpretation."

[101] Whybray, *Proverbs*, 202.

[102] Whybray, *Proverbs*, 202.

[103] Murphy, *Proverbs*, 96.

[104] The translation follows NJPS.

עשק דל להרבות לו נתן לעשיר אך־למחסור

> Oppressing the poor in order to enrich oneself, and giving to the rich, will lead only to loss. (Prov 22:16)[105]

מרבה הונו בנשך ובתרבית לחונן דלים יקבצנו

> The one who increases his wealth by loans at discount or interest amasses it for one who is generous to the poor. (Prov 28:8)[106]

As with several other sayings already considered, the claims of 13:22; 22:16; and 28:8 are problematic for some commentators who understand Proverbs to reflect a wisdom prosperity axiom in a more or less straightforward, literal manner. For example, Van Leeuwen believes 13:22 "extends the act-character-consequence schema . . . to reflect God's generosity over generations" and that "in unexpected ways the good inherit what sinners wrongly took or used." The line, he believes, "provides one solution to apparent failures in the pattern of retribution: Things will be made right in the generations to come."[107] In regard to 22:16, Whybray notes that the first stich might not only suggest that it is the poor דל whose wealth will ironically increase, but that the line "appears to run entirely counter to the spirit of these proverbs and seems even to encourage the oppression of the poor rather than, as would be expected, to promise the ruin of the wicked." He speculates that 22:16 might even be a verse where two "originally unconnected fragments" have been "erroneously set side by side because of their formal parallelism."[108] In regard to 28:8 he suggests the "point of the verse is that while one man may extort money from the poor by usury, his heir may be a generous person who 'pays it back' through gifts to the poor."[109]

However, these proverbial observations need not be understood in such literalistic terms. Indeed, like several sayings treated above, it is not clear that any sort of empirical observation would bear out the kinds of claims the sayings themselves seem to articulate and which the commentators cited seem to reiterate. Rather through their

---

[105] The translation follows NRSV.

[106] The translation follows NJPS. The economic terms in this verse resonate with other texts in HB. Cf., for example, Ex 22:24; Lev 25:36; Deut 23:20. See further, Whybray, *Proverbs*, 391.

[107] Van Leeuwen, "Proverbs," *NIB* 5:134.

[108] Whybray, *Proverbs*, 322.

[109] Whybray, *Proverbs*, 391.

act-consequence rhetoric, the proverbs can be seen to reflect the claim of the wisdom mythos that the deep structures of the universe favor the life of virtue. At the same time the lines highlight the importance of particular social virtues—particularly the notion that justice be shown the poor and that it be embodied in economic practices.

Finally one ought briefly also consider sayings such as Prov 22:2 and 29:13.

These read:

עשיר ורש נפגשו עשה כלם יהוה

A rich person and a poor person meet; the Lord is the maker of them all.[110]

רש ואיש תככים נפגשו מאיר־עיני שניהם יהוה

A poor person and a fraudulent person meet; the Lord gives light to the eyes of both of them.

Proverbs 22:2 contrasts the rich person with the poor person, a feature which is not uncommon to the discourse of social observation. Clearly 29:13 is closely related to 22:2. Both employ the term רש and the verb פגש. Each also relates the poor person and the rich person or fraudulent person to the deity. Certain scholars, such as Kaiser and Pleins intimate that the sayings offer the observation that the sages believed rich and poor are simple social givens and that such social stratification is ordained by God.[111] Others view the proverbs to be underscoring the fundamental equality between rich and poor (or the fraudulent person), which each one's status as YHWH's creatures establishes.[112] This view recognizes the proverb to be offering a kind of critique of contexts where the disparities between rich and poor are great. The two lines also establish a symbolic link between the fraudulent person and the rich person (who are both contrasted with the poor person). Such a pairing serves to characterize at least certain "rich" individuals negatively and is consonant with the fact that Proverbs elsewhere begins to locate in the

[110] The translation follows NRSV.

[111] Walter C. Kaiser, Jr., "The Old Testament Promise of Material Blessings and the Contemporary Believer," *TrinJ* 9 (1998): 151–170; Pleins, "Social World," 69.

[112] Whybray, *Proverbs*, 318; Murphy, *Proverbs*, 165.

pursuit and holding of wealth a danger to the life of virtue. Indeed the fact that in 29:13 the poor person is paired with the fraudulent person and not simply the rich person as in 22:2 indicates as well that the two sayings recognize disparities in wealth may be the result of injustice. The critique the two lines offer is underscored initially when each is read in light of the other and more fundamentally when one reads both in light of the book's developing moral and literary Gestalt.

5.4. The Woman of Worth

A further final, and slightly different, example of the manner in which the various discourses of wealth and poverty in Proverbs interact and stand in mutually interpreting dialogue with one another can be discerned in the acrostic poem of Prov 31:10–31, which describes the אשת חיל ("woman of worth").[113] This poem's wealth and poverty rhetoric might be said at points to belong to any one of the three discourses of wealth and poverty. However the wisdom's virtues discourse and the discourse of social justice are most obviously represented.

Whether the אשת חיל should be understood primarily as a personification of wisdom, the ideal wife of an ancient patriarchal imagination, or in some sense as a description of a particular class of women in Persian or Hellenistic period Syria-Palestine, remains the subject of some debate.[114] Probably the depiction of the figure draws from each possibility and works on all three levels. Yet certainly the description of the "woman of worth" shares a number of characteristics with personified Wisdom in chapters 1–9 and is reminiscent of Proverbs' descriptions of the value of virtue as this picture emerges throughout the wisdom's virtues discourse.[115] The poem, for instance, begins with a series of images that celebrate the woman of worth's

[113] Proverbs 12:4 also alludes to a woman of worth.

[114] Christine Roy Yoder reviews the history of the question in *Wisdom as a Woman of Substance: A Socio-Economic Reading of Proverbs 1–9 and 31:10–31* (BZAW 304; Berlin: W. de Gruyter, 2001), 1–13.

[115] Yoder lists a number of similarities between the woman of valor and personified Wisdom in *Woman of Substance*, 91–93.

diligence—a virtue highly valued by the wisdom's virtues discourse.[116] The text's opening lines also liken her value specifically to material riches. Verses 10–11 read:

אשת־חיל מי ימצא ורחק מפנינים מכרה
בטח בה לב בעלה ושלל לא יחסר

> A woman of worth who can find her? Her worth is far beyond that of rubies.
> Her husband puts his confidence in her and lacks no good thing.[117]

The value of the אשת־חיל here, like the worth of Woman Wisdom in 3:15, is expressed via an economic rhetoric of exchange. Although the terminology of "value" or "worth" is not identical with that of earlier chapters (in 3:15 סחר vs. מכר in 31:10; but cf. 31:18), the imagery is analogous and she is said specifically to be of greater worth than פניים ("rubies"), just as personified Wisdom is in 3:15.[118]

This linguistic link between the description of Wisdom and the woman of worth is striking. However the suggestion that the אשת חיל will bring material prosperity to the one who finds her is also strikingly reminiscent of the rhetoric Proverbs persistently makes use of in order to value wisdom and its virtues. The poem, for instance, proclaims the "possessor" or "husband" of the woman of worth (בעלה; literally "her owner" vs. a possible אישה, "her husband") will lack (חסר) no "good thing" (שלל). Recall that it is at least in part with שלל ("loot") that the sinners in chapter one attempt to lure the son on to their way (1:13). The instructing voice, however, insisted the robbers could not deliver on their promise and later claimed that Wisdom herself possesses her own kind of wealth (הון עתק or "enduring wealth"; see 8:18). Now at the end of the book, the text proclaims the one who is the woman of valor's husband will in fact not lack the valuable things (i.e., שלל) that the sinners promised. Even the designation that this woman is a woman of worth (חיל) reminds the hearer of the manner in which the wisdom's virtues discourse continually insists on wisdom's value in economic terms.

Recall as well that chapters 1–9 also deployed erotic, marriage imagery to persuade the hearer to pursue and acquire desirable

[116] For instance, she sets her hand to wool and flax; she rises early to secure provisions; she acquires an estate; she plants a vineyard.
[117] The translation follows NJPS.
[118] That is, reading the Qere of 3:15; מפנינים.

Wisdom as he might a wife.[119] Like Wisdom in 4:9, who promises to honor the one who acquires or "marries" her, the woman of worth in chapter 31 brings her possessor or husband not only wealth and other material goods (v. 11; cf. 12–19), but also high social status. As v. 23 states: "Her husband is prominent in the gate." The one who acquires or "owns" the woman of Prov 31:10–31, like the one who acquires wisdom elsewhere in Proverbs, indeed "finds" something of great worth.[120]

All these correlations make it likely that on some level the woman of worth of Prov 31:10–31 is to be identified not only with that other woman Proverbs highly values, Woman Wisdom, but with the virtue for which she is a personification. Notice too, however, how the description of the woman of substance proceeds in 31:20:

כפה פרשה לעני וידיה שלחה לאביון

> She opens her hand to the poor. She stretches out her hands to the needy.[121]

Here the poet employs the substantivized adjectives עני and אביון, who are objects of the woman's action, to describe how she acts on behalf of specifically the poor. The vocabulary and syntax of the line is typical of proverbs that belong to the social justice discourse. Among the virtues the woman of worth possesses is kindness to the poor, that integral component of the economic ethic Proverbs attempts to construct for its hearers through the discourse of social justice.

The poem of Prov 31:10–31 thus incorporates at least two of the sub-discourses of wealth and poverty in its description of the woman of worth. On the one hand, the wisdom's virtues discourse underscores the woman's (and hence wisdom's) desirability in terms of wealth images. On the other hand, the rhetoric of v. 20 highlights the fact that the virtue of kindness to the poor—a virtue typical of the social justice discourse, but which also belongs to wisdom's way—

[119] This, recall, is largely Yoder's thesis in *Woman of Substance*. She argues that the description of Woman Wisdom in chapters 1–9 is based on real Persian period women of substance, just as the woman of worth in 31:10–31 is.

[120] Cf. Claudia V. Camp, *Wisdom and the Feminine in the Book of Proverbs* (Sheffield: Almond, 1985), 60, who in discussing Bernhard Lang's *Frau Weisheit* (p. 157), speaks of the personification of wisdom representing "the unlimited value of the wisdom of the school."

[121] The translation follows NRSV.

is also a virtue this woman possesses. Because the woman of worth is at least in part a cipher for Wisdom/wisdom, v. 20 functions to remind the hearer that the truth about wealth and poverty in Proverbs is not only what the wisdom's virtues discourse has to say. This truth also lies with the discourse of social justice, as well as the discourse of social observation. In the midst of a struggle to persuade its hearers that the locus of true value in human life lies with wisdom's virtues rather than any lesser good such as material riches, Proverbs simultaneously insists that the virtues of social justice both belong to wisdom's way and ought to be realized in social life.

Hence, when considered through an examination of its wealth and poverty rhetoric, the book of Proverbs, as many have noted for other theological and literary reasons, appropriately closes with the poem to the Woman of Worth—a figure which imaginatively embodies various aspects of the book's discourse of wealth and poverty.[122]

[122] See, for instance, Camp, *Wisdom and the Feminine*, 255.

CHAPTER SIX

CONCLUSION

6.1. Wealth and Poverty in Proverbs

Although the sages' view of wealth and poverty in Proverbs is generally described as ambiguous, such an evaluation is not entirely accurate. Although complex, being comprised of three distinct subdiscourses, the book's talk of wealth and poverty is more coherent than is usually thought and plays an integral role in the book's construction of a moral vision for its reader or hearer.

The key to recognizing the coherence of Proverbs' discourse of wealth and poverty is an appreciation of the text's figurative interpretive possibilities. The book's prologue, which articulates the primary virtues and goals of Proverbs, itself invites the wise and discerning reader at the outset of the instruction to consider the book's tropes and figures. With various individual *meshalim*, other internal cues, such as the difficulties or absurdities posed by a literal interpretation, likewise point to the text's figurative qualities. Moreover, the literary form which well over half of the book takes—the short, sentence saying—is reminiscent of traditional folk proverbs, which regularly employ metaphor and function metaphorically in the sense that they are generally deployed to say something about human life in some particular context. This fact about folk proverbs ought to encourage the hearer or reader of Proverbs to be attentive to the metaphorical aspects and functions of the formally similar sentence sayings within the literary context of the book. Finally, Proverbs' cause and effect rhetoric, which reveals an act-consequence nexus (or in relation to wealth and poverty language, a wisdom prosperity axiom), likewise is not the kind of language one ought to understand in overly literal fashion, despite the regular efforts of interpreters to read its promises as literal assurances based on the sages' observation of the world. Although the formulation of much of the sages' instruction seems to suggest that the wisdom they proffer was arrived at via observation of social and natural realities, the *Tun-Ergehen Zusammenhang* evident in the book is best regarded as the construction of a symbolic view of the world that is not, and is not meant to be, an empirically verifiable one. Rather it motivates adherence to instruction by offering a particular claim about the true nature of the cosmos, the structure of which favors (or rewards) virtue and opposes (or punishes) vice. This wisdom mythos is the symbolic universe within which adherence to the values and virtues that the book promotes become both meaningful and possible.

Although cause and effect rhetoric can be found in sayings belonging to each of the three sub-discourses of wealth and poverty, it is particularly prevalent in the largest of the three: the wisdom's virtues discourse. This discourse emerges most clearly in chapters 10–31. However, those sayings in Proverbs 1–9 discussed in Chapter Three under the rubric of 'wealth as motivational symbol' likewise belong to the book's wisdom's virtues discourse. This discourse repeatedly employs the language of wealth as a symbol of the positive in order to convince the hearer of the value and desirability of wisdom's way, or particular virtues that belong to that path. This in turn functions to motivate the son to choose that way. Likewise, the instructing voice employs the rhetoric of poverty as a negative motivational symbol to persuade the reader of the undesirability of the way of folly and the vices associated with that way so that the hearer might avoid that path. Distinctively, the sayings that employ wealth and poverty rhetoric in this manner are almost always cast in the indicative and the terminology they use (except in chs. 1–9) is predominantly of an abstract or impersonal nature (either nominal or verbal). The lexemes עשר and הון (along with cognate forms) are the most common words for riches and wealth while מחסור and forms of ר-י-ש dominate the discourse of poverty. Only in the comparative "better than" sayings does the wisdom's virtues discourse employ the more personal language of the rich (but only once), and especially the poor, person. However, unlike other sub-discourses of wealth and poverty, when these comparative sayings speak of the poor they always use the substantivized participle רש and set this figure as a grammatical subject.

Like the wisdom's virtues discourse, the wealth and poverty subdiscourse of social justice in Proverbs can be found throughout the variety of collections that make up the book. It too emerges most clearly in the sayings of chapters 10–31, but also can be discerned in chapters 1–9. The *meshalim* of the early chapters discussed in the section dealing with 'direct instruction' in Chapter Three belong to this sub-discourse. The discourse of social justice, moreover, also possesses its own distinctive characteristics. Unlike the wisdom's virtues discourse, however, the social justice discourse commonly employs a personal vocabulary for the poor. The terms דל, עני, and אביון, who in any particular verse are exclusively grammatical objects acted upon (rather than active subjects), are the preferred vocabulary. Again in distinction to the wisdom's virtues discourse, the discourse of social justice does not employ the rhetoric of wealth and poverty to a larger didactic end. It does not use the language of wealth and poverty as textual symbols of the positive and negative in order to motivate the son to choose the way of wisdom or acquire particular virtues associated with wisdom. It is concerned primarily with constructing for the hearer or reader a particular economic ethic. When it speaks of the poor (it rarely alludes to the rich), it instructs the addressee to act concretely in kind and just ways toward specifically these economically marginalized persons. In so doing, the social justice discourse seeks to instill in this addressee its primary virtue: kindness to the poor. This virtue is of a piece with the book's larger concern with social justice and harmony, as is the discourse's concern that one act fairly and honestly in the market place by employing accurate weights and measures. The sub-discourse of social justice in Proverbs also belongs to a larger biblical and ancient Near Eastern discourse of social maintenance. The vocabulary, imagery, and other linguistic features characteristic of the proverbial discourse of social justice reverberates not only in wisdom texts like Job, but a variety of Psalms as well as a number of the Bible's legal and prophetic passages. Ancient Near Eastern texts as varied as the Aqhat legend, Hammurabi's code, and Amenemope likewise treat similar motifs and employ an analogous rhetoric. One should note as well that this broader biblical and ancient Near Eastern discourse is often concerned not with the welfare of the "poor" alone, but also with other perennially (and stereotypically) vulnerable social groups such as the widow and orphan. For the sake of completeness one should thus include within the sub-discourse of social justice in Proverbs sayings such as 15:25 and 23:10, which promote kindness toward these other social groups or 'types' as well.

Finally there is a group of sayings in Proverbs that make up a third sub-discourse of wealth and poverty: the discourse of social observation. Although many wealth and poverty sayings in the book, which appear to offer straightforward observations of the world, actually function toward larger rhetorical ends, sentences belonging to this third discourse of wealth poverty are in fact largely concerned to offer some kind of comment regarding the "observed" world. These sentences often set the rich and poor person in parallel stichs, but in contrast to the other two discourses, the discourse of social observation prefers to employ the substantivized adjectives עשיר ("rich person") and רש or דל ("poor person") as subjects of simple indicative statements. However, the wealth and poverty sayings belonging to the discourse of social observation do not neutrally "observe" anything. Rather they evaluate the social effects that can result from a person's possession of excessive wealth or experience of lack and are especially critical of a certain kind of "rich" person.

The features of the three sub-discourses of wealth and poverty in Proverbs also occasionally overlap and the discourses themselves stand in a kind of mutually interpreting dialogue with one another. Indeed although the act-consequence rhetoric of many wealth and poverty proverbs may suggest to some that the book promotes a simple retributive moral worldview where the righteous are rewarded with wealth and the wicked with poverty, other proverbs that do not employ a cause and effect rhetoric call this view into question. For many, such a situation implies the existence of a fundamental ambiguity to the book's discourse of wealth and poverty.

However, a critical mass of sayings in Proverbs that belong to the wisdom's virtues discourse and plainly value virtue and vice and motivate adherence to the way of wisdom by means of an economic rhetoric do not employ an act-consequence formula. A number of other sayings that belong to the text's discourse of social justice, which likewise do not employ an act-consequence rhetoric, promote a concrete economic ethic for a hearer. These two sets of proverbs that do not employ a cause and effect rhetoric call into question any claim that Proverbs promotes a retributive moral view of the world in some simple or straightforward manner. This critical mass of proverbs, moreover, reveals a certain moral vision and certain patterns of figurative use of wealth and poverty language in Proverbs. It constitutes, that is, a kind of moral and literary Gestalt to the book that functions as an interpretive lens to understand other wealth and poverty sayings in the text. Some of these other wealth and poverty sayings belong to either the wisdom's virtues discourse or the discourse of social justice, or to the book's third sub-discourse of wealth and poverty, the discourse of social observation.

The various wealth and poverty sayings in Proverbs thus complement one another and form a complex view of wealth and poverty. Of course, occasionally one encounters economic sayings that do not fit seamlessly into the scheme I have articulated. Proverbs 14:24 and 15:15, for instance, represent exceptions one would expect to discover in such a large and complex discourse as the discourse of wealth and poverty in Proverbs. My claim, however, is certainly not that the book's discourse of wealth and poverty is completely univocal, only that it is less equivocal than is usually thought. Essentially the discourse of wealth and poverty in Proverbs recognizes the worth riches hold in the market place, seeks to limit wealth's worth to the economic realm, and describes the desirability of wisdom and its virtues by means of wealth, and other desirable, imagery (the wisdom's virtues discourse).[1] The book, however, is also critical of the adverse social effects of excessive riches and lack, and of an economic elite with whom the text associates these adverse effects (the discourse of social observation). Correspondingly, the text seeks to limit the adverse social effects of excessive lack by insisting that kindness be shown to the poor and that some minimum standards of social justice be maintained (the discourse of social justice). For sages who know the value and dangers of wealth, and who put a premium on the life of virtue, the saying of Prov 30:8–9 makes good sense:

> Give me neither poverty (ראש) nor riches (עשר), but provide me with my daily bread, lest being sated, I renounce, saying "Who is the Lord?" Or, being impoverished (אורש), I take to theft and profane the name of my God.[2]

Such is the moral vision Proverbs promotes and hopes, through its instruction in virtue, to instill in the character of the reader of the book.

Wealth and poverty for Proverbs is more than a simple sapiential *topos* or wisdom commonplace. Rather it is central to the sages' project and fundamental to the book's overall goals or end—the promotion of wisdom's virtuous way. Indeed the fact that much of Proverb's

[1] Hence for the sages of Proverbs both the literal and symbolic promises of well being in a saying like Prov 22:4—"The effect of humility is fear of the Lord, wealth (עשר), honor (כבוד), and life"—would be clear.

[2] The translation follows NJPS. Verse eight begins with the words: "Keep lies and false words far from me."

wealth and poverty language (e.g., הון, forms of רוש/ריש, and עשר) does not show up much in HB outside of the wisdom corpus, or is particularly prevalent in Proverbs (e.g., דל) is likewise suggestive. Wisdom voices concerned with questions of value in human life have laid a strong claim to this rhetoric and in Proverbs have dictated its symbolic usage in a quite particular way. Though not uncomplicated, the sages' views on wealth and poverty are not incompatible with one another and essentially represent the outlook of a caste of intellectually elite scribes in ancient Israel and Judah (Yehud). These scribes would have at least in part served the economic and political elite and likely drew on the traditional proverbial wisdom of their people. However, due to their unique skills and social position, their interests and values would not have been identical to either those of the economic and political elite or the rural folk. Indeed on the one hand, the fact that the sages formulate moral criteria by which they evaluate and critique the economic and political elite suggest some social distance from these sovereigns. On the other hand, the persistent claim that virtue is better than wealth and poverty is not as reproachable as vice, hints that the sages were also at some remove from the poorest strata of their society.

6.2. Evaluating Wealth and Poverty in Proverbs

How one evaluates the moral vision of Proverbs as it emerges from the text's discourse of wealth and poverty is, of course, a further, vital question for students of the book. Although such an evaluation deserves more consideration than I can offer here, some preliminary thoughts regarding the book's understanding of wealth and poverty are in order.

Likely many contemporary readers will find aspects of the proverbial-scribal moral vision appealing—e.g., its insistence on the value of virtue over material wealth, its highlighting of social virtue, and its assumption that political elites have an obligation to insure minimal standards of justice be enacted in the social realm. Nonetheless, despite these aspects of Proverbs' moral vision, which might in various contemporary contexts be worthy of emulation or at least consideration, other components of the book's ethical horizon that emerge from a study of its wealth and poverty rhetoric will also give many pause. For instance, Proverbs values virtue for its imagined male and heterosexual audience not merely in terms of material wealth, but in terms of the sexual desirability of women; and it addresses poverty not through the restructuring of institutions that perhaps contribute to acute and perennial social and economic stratification, but through the mechanism of charitable giving. Despite its worthy and appealing moral impulses, Proverbs remains a deeply patriarchal, paternalistic, and inherently conservative text. These aspects of the book ought not to be ignored or uncritically glossed over, but included in any serious consideration of Proverbs' value for, and ability to contribute to, contemporary ethical discourse.

6.3. The Social-Historical Setting

My re-evaluation of the discourse of wealth and poverty in Proverbs has primarily been concerned to demonstrate that the book's wealth and poverty talk is both vital to the book's construction of a moral vision and identity for its hearer and is not as "ambiguous" as it usually is said to be. Along the way, however, other important conclusions were reached. One of the most important of these conclusions, for instance, is the need to attend to the book's figurative interpretive possibilities. It is also possible at the end of this study, to say something, though likely not as much as one would like, about a possible socio-historical context from which the book of Proverbs likely emerged.

Negotiating the value of various goods is, of course, a perennial task for all communities and societies. However, there are also periods in the history of any society when this task takes on greater urgency. Proverbs' strong claim to, and rhetorical manipulation of, wealth and poverty language implies that its moral discourse on wealth and poverty is not a randomly constructed set of notions, but is one formulated in, and in response to, an environment where the negotiation of the worth of different social goods, particularly but not only that of material wealth, was acutely problematic.

In particular the discourse of wealth and poverty in the various collections of Proverbs reflects an economic environment where, for example, a variety of economic practices were widely known and where material wealth carried clear value. It suggests as well a milieu where the plight of the economically marginalized was plainly visible. It also suggests an environment where the sages were concerned that the worth of wealth might be transgressing beyond its proper realm, the economic sphere, and was intruding upon arenas, such as the moral and judicial realms, where they believed it ought not to have any currency. It reflects a context where, in the sages' view, wealth was overvalued at the expense of other social goods. Moreover it reflects a context where, on the one hand, the composers and compilers of Proverbs began to contest what they perceived to be a false reckoning of where the key to human flourishing is to be located and where, on the other hand, these sages attempted to redress certain ill social effects that such a false reckoning might have produced. The discourse of wealth and poverty in Proverbs, that is, reflects a context in which the sages grappled with an implicit but real social script that suggested a good and flourishing life is to be secured in the attainment of one or another lesser good, including especially material prosperity. Against this diffuse but real social script the sages insisted that it is the way of wisdom, with its emphasis on intellectual, practical and especially social virtue, which would produce the flourishing life they believed humans desire. Although this social script was not necessarily well-established in any particular competing discourse when Proverbs was produced, the book reflects a context where the sages anxiety concerning economic matters was itself beginning to emerge in a discernable set of discourse practices and patterns.

Though it is impossible to discern precisely when any particular wealth and poverty saying or passage in Proverbs might be best placed in the history of ancient Israel and Judah (Yehud), some plausible, general suggestions regarding the date and socio-historical context of the book can be offered. As I suggested in Chapter Two, the preconditions for the formation of a scribal caste able to produce a book like Proverbs would not have been in place in Israel or Judah before the 8th century BCE. Subsequently the precise socio-economic environment that the discourse of wealth and poverty in Proverbs assumes and to which it responds would not have existed before the 8th century BCE. The texts of Amos, Micah, Isaiah of Jerusalem, and even Hosea all provide evidence that the level and kinds of economic activity and problems Proverbs assumes, was present in at least segments of pre-exilic Israelite and Judean culture as early as the 8th century.[3] It is thus possible that some of the col-

[3] Cf. Friedemann W. Golka, *The Leopard's Spots: Biblical and African Wisdom in*

lections of chapters 10–31, together with their wealth and poverty sayings, received initial shape in this period. Indeed Prov 25:1—"These too are proverbs of Solomon, which the men of King Hezekiah of Judah transmitted"—suggests as much; and Prov 21:3—"To do justice and righteousness is more desirable to the Lord than sacrifice"—sounds as if it could have been spoken by Amos (cf. Am 4:4–5) or Isaiah of Jerusalem (cf. Is 1:10–20; cf. further 1 Sam 15:22).

Yet surely all of the collections in the book of Proverbs, in particular chapters 1–9, did not reach their final form until some time after the exile. As I intimated above, scholars are divided when it comes to the question of the date of the formation of the text as a whole. Some favor the Persian period; others look to the Hellenistic era. It is possible that most of the collections in Proverbs and the individual sayings making up these collections were brought together in the late Persian period. Of course a Hellenistic date for the culmination of the tradition process cannot be excluded. The LXX of Proverbs, in which one can discern "differences in order, minuses, and pluses all differing from" MT, may attest to the fact that the final form of the book was still somewhat contested in the Greek period.[4] It is thus possible that the Hellenistic period was the age when the Hebrew collections of proverbs were consolidated.

The evidence for significant economic activity in the Persian period marshaled by Seow and Yoder likewise suggests the sages' anxiety regarding economic matters, as revealed through Proverbs' discourse of wealth and poverty, could well have emerged in the age of Persian imperial domination.[5] Yet as is well known the Hellenistic era in Syria-Palestine seems to have witnessed an even greater increase in economic activity than the Persian period and the sorts of economic practices and concerns that Proverbs alludes to would perhaps have been better known in the Greek period than in the Persian age. The

Proverbs (Edinburgh: T&T Clark, 1993), 54. See further Marvin L. Chaney's description of the 8th century political economy, "Bitter Bounty: The Dynamics of Political Economy Critiqued by the Eight-Century Prophets," in *Reformed Faith and Economics* (ed. Robert L. Stivers; Lanham, Md.: University Press of America, 1989), 15–30.

[4] Emmanuel Tov, *Textual Criticism of the Hebrew Bible* (Minneapolis: Fortress: 1992) 337; Hebrew original 1989. Of course, these differences, pluses, and minuses may also be problems of the inner Greek tradition process.

[5] See C. L. Seow, *Ecclesiastes: A New Translation with Introduction and Commentary* (AB 18c; New York: Doubleday, 1997), 21–36; Christine Roy Yoder, *Wisdom as a Woman of Substance: A Socio-Economic Reading of Proverbs 1–9 and 31:10–31* (BZAW 304; Berlin: W. de Gruyter, 2001), 39–72.

matter is perhaps finally not decidable and Proverbs' discourse of wealth and poverty would not necessarily contradict a Persian period or Hellenistic period dating of the book.

Whether one prefers a Persian period or Hellenistic date for Proverbs, it is certain that the increase in economic activity in the Hellenistic period would have spawned an anxiety vis-à-vis the economic sphere that was at least as acute as that of any earlier age. It is likely that such a situation would have evoked further responses from wisdom voices at home in Yehud.[6] The wisdom instruction found at Qumran called 4QInstruction, which makes considerable use of especially poverty rhetoric, witnesses to one such response. The Wisdom of Ben Sira, which also deploys extensive economic rhetoric, witnesses to another.[7] Although these texts appear to have negotiated matters in a manner somewhat different from what one finds in Proverbs' discourse of wealth and poverty, they are nonetheless deeply influenced by Proverbs and adopt much from Proverbs. A consideration of the discourse of wealth and poverty in these wisdom texts, however, is another project.

[6] Besides the new economic realities, other particularities of the Jewish-Hellenistic environment in Palestine, including the rise of an authoritative body of texts (Torah and the Prophets, at least; cf. Sirach's "Prologue"), would have made this all but inevitable.

[7] The LXX of Proverbs itself might attest to such a response outside of Syria-Palestine. See Ronald L. Giese, "Qualifying Wealth in the Septuagint of Proverbs," *JBL* 111 (1992): 409–25.

SELECT BIBLIOGRAPHY

Alonso Schöckel, L., and J. Vilchez. *Proverbios*. Nueva Biblia Española. Sapienciales I. Madrid: Ediciones Cristiandad, 1984.

Austin, J. L. *How to Do Things with Words*. Oxford: Oxford University Press, 1962.

Bakhtin, M. M. "Discourse in the Novel." *The Dialogic Imagination: Four Essays*. Ed. Michael Holquist. University of Texas Press Slavic Series 1. Austin: University of Texas Press, 1981.

Bakhtin, M. M. *Problems of Dostoevsky's Poetics*. Theory and History of Literature 8. Manchester: Manchester University Press, 1984.

Barr, James. *The Semantics of Biblical Language*. London: Oxford University Press, 1961.

Barton, John. *Understanding Old Testament Ethics: Approaches and Explorations*. Louisville, Ky.: Westminster/John Knox Press, 2003.

Baudissin, W. G. "Die alttestamentliche Religion und die Armen." *Preussische Jahrbücher* 149 (1912): 193–231.

Beentjes, Pancratius C. *The Book of Ben Sira in Hebrew: A Text Edition of All Extant Hebrew Manuscripts and a Synopsis of All Parallel Hebrew Ben Sira Texts*. Supplements to Vetus Testamentum 68. Leiden: E. J. Brill, 1997.

Bergant, Dianne. *Israel's Wisdom Literature: A Liberation-Critical Reading*. Minneapolis: Fortress Press, 1997.

Birch, Bruce C., and Larry L. Rasmussen. *Bible and Ethics in the Christian Life*. Expanded and revised edition. Minneapolis: Augsburg Fortress, 1989.

Birkeland, Harris. "'Ani Und 'Anaw In Den Psalmen." *Skrifter utgitt av Det Norske Videnskaps-Akademi i Oslo* 4 (1932): 1–118.

Blenkinsopp, Joseph. "The Social Context of the 'Outsider Woman' in Proverbs 1–9." *Biblica* 72 (1991): 457–73.

Bodine, Walter Ray, ed. *Discourse Analysis of Biblical Literature: What It Is and What It Offers*. Atlanta: Scholars Press, 1995.

Botterweck, G. Johannes, ed. *Theological Dictionary of the Old Testament*. Grand Rapids: Eerdmans, 1974.

Bové, Paul A. "Discourse." *Critical Terms for Literary Study*. Ed. Frank Lentricchia and Thomas McLaughlin. Chicago: University of Chicago Press, 1990.

Brockelmann, Carl. *Hebräische Syntax*. Neukirchen: Kreis Moers, 1956.

Brown, Gillian, and George Yule. *Discourse Analysis*. Cambridge Textbooks in Linguistics. Cambridge; New York: Cambridge University Press, 1983.

Brown, William P. *Character in Crisis: A Fresh Approach to the Wisdom Literature of the Old Testament*. Grand Rapids: Eerdmans, 1996.

Bruppacher, Hans. *Die Beurteilung der Armut im alten Testament*. Zürich: Verlag Seldwyla, 1924.

Burke, Kenneth. *A Rhetoric of Motives*. Berkeley: University of California Press, 1969.

Camp, Claudia V. "What's So Strange about the Strange Woman?" *The Bible and the Politics of Exegesis*. Ed. David Jobling et al. Cleveland: Pilgrim Press, 1991

———. *Wisdom and the Feminine in the Book of Proverbs*. Bible and Literature 11. Sheffield: Almond Press, 1985.

Carasik, Michael, "Who were the 'Men of Hezekiah' (Proverbs xxv 1)?" *Vetus Testamentum* 44 (1994): 289–300.

Causse, Antonin. *Les "pauvres" d'Israël (Prophètes, Psalmistes, Messianistes)*. Strasbourg: Librairie Istra, 1922.

Ceresko, Anthony R. *Introduction to Old Testament Wisdom: A Spirituality for Liberation*. Maryknoll, N.Y.: Orbis Books, 1999.

Chaney, Marvin L. "Bitter Bounty: The Dynamics of Political Economy Critiqued by the Eight-Century Prophets," in *Reformed Faith and Economics*. Ed. Robert L. Stivers; Lanham, Md.: University Press of America, 1989.

Clifford, Richard J. *Proverbs: A Commentary*. Old Testament Library. Louisville, Ky.: Westminster/John Knox Press, 1999.

——. "Introduction to Wisdom Literature." *The New Interpreter's Bible. Volume V: Introduction to Wisdom Literature, the Book of Proverbs, the Book of Ecclesiastes, the Song of Songs, the Book of Wisdom, the Book of Sirach*. Nashville: Abingdon, 1997.

Cohen, Haim. "Two Misunderstood Verses in the Book of Proverbs." *Shnaton* 11 (1997): 139–52.

Cowley, A. E., and E. Kautzsch, eds. *Gesenius' Hebrew Grammar*. Oxford: Clarendon Press, 1988.

Crenshaw, James L. "The Book of Sirach: Introduction, Commentary, and Reflections." *The New Interpreter's Bible. Volume V: Introduction to Wisdom Literature, the Book of Proverbs, the Book of Ecclesiastes, the Song of Songs, the Book of Wisdom, the Book of Sirach*. Nashville: Abingdon, 1997.

——. "Poverty and Punishment in the Book of Proverbs." *Quarterly Review* 9 (1989): 30–43.

Crenshaw, James L., and John T. Willis. *Essays in Old Testament Ethics: J. Philip Hyatt, in Memoriam*. New York: KTAV, 1974.

Culler, Jonathan. *Structuralist Poetics: Structuralism, Linguistics and the Study of Literature*. Ithaca: Cornell University Press, 1975.

Curran, Charles E., and Richard A. McCormick. *The Use of Scripture in Moral Theology*. Readings in Moral Theology 4. New York: Paulist Press, 1984.

Dahood, Mitchell. "Congruity of Metaphors." *Hebräische Wortforschung: Festschrift Zum 80. Geburtstag von Walter Baumgartner*. Supplements to Vetus Testamentum 16. Leiden: E. J. Brill, 1967.

——. "The Phoenician Background of Qoheleth." *Biblica* 47 (1966): 264–82.

——. *Proverbs and Northwest Semitic Philology*. Scripta Pontificii Instituti Biblici 113. Rome: Pontifical Biblical Institute, 1963.

Davies, Philip R. *Scribes and Schools: The Canonization of the Hebrew Scriptures*. Library of Ancient Israel. Louisville, Ky.: Westminster/John Knox Press, 1998.

Delkurt, Holger. *Ethische Einsichten in der alttestamentlichen Spruchweisheit*. Biblisch-Theologische Studien 21. Neukirchen-Vluyn: Neukirchener Verlag, 1993.

Di Lella, Alexander A., and Patrick W. Skehan. *The Wisdom of Ben Sira: A New Translation with Notes, Introduction, and Commentary*. Anchor Bible 39. Garden City, N.Y.: Doubleday, 1987.

Donald, T. "The Semantic Field of Rich and Poor in the Wisdom Literature of Hebrew and Accadian." *Oriens Antiquus* 2 (1964): 27–41.

Donner, Herbert, and Wolfgang Röllig. *Kanaanäische und Aramäische Inschriften*. 2. durchgesehene und erw. Aufl. Wiesbaden: Harrassowitz, 1966.

Driver, G. R. "Problems in the Hebrew Text of Proverbs." *Biblica* 32 (1951): 173–97.

Eagleton, Terry. *Ideology: An Introduction*. London; New York: Verso, 1991.

Erman, Adolf. "Eine Ägyptische Quelle der 'Spruch Salomos'." *Sitzungberichte der preussischen Akademie der Wissenschaften* (1924): 86–93.

Eskenazi, Tamara C., and Kent Harold Richards. *Second Temple Studies, 2: Temple and Community in the Persian Period*. Journal for the Study of the Old Testament Supplement 175. Sheffield: JSOT Press, 1994.

Fairclough, Norman. *Discourse and Social Change*. Cambridge, UK; Cambridge, Mass.: Polity Press, 1992.

Fensham, F. Charles. "Widow, Orphan, and the Poor in Ancient Near Eastern Legal and Wisdom Literature." *Journal of Near Eastern Studies* 21 (1962): 129–39.

Finnegan, Ruth. "Proverbs in Africa." *The Wisdom of Many: Essays on the Proverb*. Ed. Wolfgang Mieder and Alan Dundes. New York: Garland, 1981.
Fishbane, Michael. *Biblical Interpretation in Ancient Israel*. Oxford; New York: Clarendon Press, 1985.
Fontaine, Carole R. "Proverbs." *Women's Bible Commentary*. Expanded edition. Ed. Carol A. Newsom and Sharon H. Ringe. Louisville, Ky.: Westminster/John Knox Press, 1998.
——. *Traditional Sayings in the Old Testament*. Bible and Literature 5. Sheffield: Almond Press, 1982.
Foucault, Michel. *The History of Sexuality, Volume I: An Introduction*. Harmondsworth: Penguin Books, 1981.
——. *Discipline and Punish: The Birth of the Prison*. Harmondsworth: Penguin Books, 1979.
——. *The Archaeology of Knowledge*. London: Tavistock Publications, 1972.
——. *The Order of Things: An Archaeology of the Human Sciences*. New York: Pantheon Books, 1971.
Fowler, Roger. "Discourse." *A Dictionary of Modern Critical Terms*. Revised and enlarged edition. Ed. Roger Fowler. London: Routledge & Kegan Paul, 1987.
——. *Linguistic Criticism*. Oxford; New York: Oxford University Press, 1986.
Fox, Michael V. *Proverbs 1–9: A New Translation with Introduction and Commentary*. Anchor Bible 18a. New York: Doubleday, 2000.
——. *A Time to Tear Down and a Time to Build Up: A Rereading of Ecclesiastes*. Grand Rapids: Eerdmans, 1999.
——. "The Social Location of the Book of Proverbs." *Texts, Temples, and Traditions: A Tribute to Menahem Haran*. Ed. Michael V. Fox, et al. Winona Lake, Ind.: Eisenbrauns, 1996.
——. "World Order and Ma'at: A Crooked Parallel." *Journal of the Ancient Near Eastern Society* 23 (1995): 37–48.
Fuhs, Hans Ferdinand. *Das Buch der Sprichwörter: Ein Kommentar*. Forschung zur Bibel Bd. 95. Würzburg: Echter Verlag, 2001.
Gadamer, Hans-Georg. *Truth and Method*. 2nd revised edition. New York: Continuum, 1994.
Garrett, Duane A. *Proverbs, Ecclesiastes, Song of Songs*. The New American Commentary 14. Nashville: Broadman Press, 1993.
Giese, Ronald L., Jr. "Qualifying Wealth in the Septuagint of Proverbs." *Journal of Biblical Literature* 111 (1992): 409–25.
Gillingham, Susan. "The Poor in the Psalms." *Expository Times* 100 (1988): 15–19.
Goff, Matthew J. *The Worldly and Heavenly Wisdom of 4QInstruction*. Studies on the Texts of the Desert of Judah 50. Leiden: E.J. Brill, 2003.
Golka, Friedemann W. *The Leopard's Spots: Biblical and African Wisdom in Proverbs*. Edinburgh: T&T Clark, 1993.
Gottwald, Norman K. *The Hebrew Bible: A Socio-Literary Introduction*. Philadelphia: Fortress Press, 1985.
Gottwald, Norman K., and Richard A. Horsley, eds. *The Bible and Liberation: Political and Social Hermeneutics*. Revised edition. Maryknoll, N.Y.: Orbis Books, 1993.
Grant, C. David. *God the Center of Value: Value Theory in the Theology of H. Richard Niebuhr*. Fort Worth: Texas Christian University Press, 1984.
Green, Barbara. *Mikhail Bakhtin and Biblical Scholarship: An Introduction*. Society of Biblical Literature Semeia Studies 38. Atlanta: Society of Biblical Literature, 2000.
Gutiérrez, Gustavo. *On Job: God-Talk and the Suffering of the Innocent*. Maryknoll, N.Y.: Orbis Books, 1987.
——. *A Theology of Liberation: History, Politics, and Salvation*. Maryknoll, N.Y.: Orbis Books, 1973.
Harland, P. J. "בצע: Bribe, Extortion or Profit?" *Vetus Testamentum* 50 (2000): 310–22.
Harnish, Robert M. "Communicating with Proverbs." *Communication & Cognition* 26 (1993): 265–90.

Harrington, Daniel J. *Wisdom Texts from Qumran*. Literature of the Dead Sea Scrolls. London: Routledge, 1996.
Hausmann, Jutta. *Studien zum Menschenbild der älteren Weisheit*. Forschungen zum alten Testament 7. Tübingen: J. C. B. Mohr, 1995.
Heim, Knut Martin. *Like Grapes of Gold Set in Silver: An Interpretation of Proverbial Clusters in Proverbs 10:1–22:16*. Beiheft zur Zeitschrift für die alttestamentliche Wissenschaft 273. Berlin: Walter de Gruyter, 2001.
Hermisson, Hans Jürgen. *Studien zur Israelitischen Spruchweisheit*. Wissenschaftliche Monographien zum alten und neuen Testament 28. Neukirchen-Vluyn: Neukirchener Verlag, 1968.
Jamieson-Drake, David W. *Scribes and Schools in Monarchic Judah: A Socio-Archeological Approach*. Journal for the Study of the Old Testament Supplement 109. Sheffield: Almond Press, 1991.
Janzen, Waldemar. *Old Testament Ethics: A Paradigmatic Approach*. Louisville, Ky.: Westminster/John Knox Press, 1994.
Jastrow, Marcus. *A Dictionary of the Targumim, Talmud Babli, Yerushalmi, and Midrashic Literature*. New York: Judaica Press, 1996.
Jaworski, Adam, and Nikolas Coupland. *The Discourse Reader*. London; New York: Routledge, 1999.
Jenni, Ernst, ed. *Theologisches Handwörterbuch zum alten Testament*. 2 Vols. Munich: Chr. Kaiser Verlag, 1971.
Kaiser, Walter C., Jr. "The Old Testament Promise of Material Blessings and the Contemporary Believer." *Trinity Journal* (1988): 151–70.
Kayatz, Christa. *Studien zu Proverbien 1–9: Eine Form- und Motivgeschichtliche Untersuchung unter Einbeziehung Ägyptischen Vergleichsmaterials*. Wissenschaftliche Monographien zum alten und neuen Testament 22. Neukirchen-Vluyn: Neukirchener Verlag, 1966.
Kirshenblatt-Gimblett, Barbara. "Toward a Theory of Proverb Meaning." *The Wisdom of Many: Essays on the Proverb*. Ed. Wolfgang Mieder and Alan Dundes. New York: Garland, 1981.
Koch, Klaus. "Gibt es ein Vergeltungsdogma im Alten Testament?" *Zeitschrift für Theologie und Kirche* 52 (1955): 1–42.
Kovaks, Brian W. "Is There a Class-Ethic in Proverbs?" *Essays in Old Testament Ethics*. Ed. James L. Crenshaw and John T. Willis. New York: KTAV, 1974.
Kugel, James L. *The Idea of Biblical Poetry: Parallelism and Its History*. New Haven: Yale University Press, 1981.
Kuschke, A. "Arm und Reich im Alten Testament mit besonderer Berücksichtigung der nachexilischen Zeit." *Zeitschrift fur die alttestamentliche Wissenschaft* 57 (1939): 31–57.
Lakoff, George, and Mark Johnson. *Metaphors We Live by*. Chicago: University of Chicago Press, 1980.
Lakoff, George, and Mark Turner. *More Than Cool Reason: A Field Guide to Poetic Metaphor*. Chicago: University of Chicago Press, 1989.
Lang, Bernhard. *Wisdom and the Book of Proverbs: An Israelite Goddess Redefined*. New York: Pilgrim Press, 1986.
Lelièvre, André, and Alphonse Maillot. *Commentaire des proverbes, chapitres 1–9*. 3 vols. Lectio Divina, Commentaires 8. Paris: Editions du Cerf, 2000.
——. *Commentaire des proverbes: Les proverbes de Salomon, chapitres 10–18*, Lectio Divina, Commentaires 1. Paris: Editions du Cerf, 1993.
Lentricchia, Frank, and Thomas McLaughlin. *Critical Terms for Literary Study*. Chicago: University of Chicago Press, 1990.
Lichtheim, Miriam. *Ancient Egyptian Literature: A Book of Readings*. 3 vols. Berkeley: University of California Press, 1973.
Linafelt, Tod. *Ruth*. Berit Olam. Collegeville, Minn.: Liturgical Press, 1999.
Lohfink, Norbert. "Poverty in the Laws of the Ancient Near East and of the Bible." *Theological Studies* 52 (1991): 34–50.

——. *Option for the Poor: The Basic Principle of Liberation Theology in the Light of the Bible.* Berkeley: BIBAL Press, 1987.
——. "Gottes Reich und die Wirtschaft in der Bibel." *Internationale katholische Zeitschrift "Communio"* 15 (1986): 110–23.
Maier, Christl. *Die Fremde Frau in Proverbien 1–9: Eine Exegetische und Sozialgeschichtliche Studie.* Biblicus et Orientalis 144. Fribourg, Switzerland: Universitätsverlag; Gottingen: Vandenhoeck & Ruprecht, 1995.
Malchow, Bruce V. "Social Justice in the Wisdom Literature." *Biblical Theology Bulletin* 12 (1982): 120–24.
Matthews, Victor H., and Don C. Benjamin, eds. "*Honor and Shame in the World of the Bible.*" *Semeia* 68 (1994): 1–61.
McKane, William. *Proverbs: A New Approach.* Old Testament Library. Philadelphia: Westminster Press, 1970.
Meinhold, Arndt. *Die Sprüche, Bd 1: Kapitel 1–15; Bd 2: Kapitel 16–31.* Zürcher Bibelkommentare, Altes Testament 16. Zürich: Theologischer Verlag, 1991.
Mieder, Wolfgang. *Proverbs Are Never out of Season: Popular Wisdom in the Modern Age.* New York: Oxford University Press, 1993.
Mieder, Wolfgang, and Alan Dundes. *The Wisdom of Many: Essays on the Proverb.* New York: Garland, 1981.
Mills, Mary E. *Biblical Morality: Moral Perspectives in Old Testament Narratives.* Aldershot: Ashgate, 2001.
Mills, Sara. *Discourse.* New Critical Idiom. London; New York: Routledge, 1997.
Morson, Gary Saul, and Caryl Emerson. *Mikhail Bakhtin: Creation of a Prosaics.* Stanford: Stanford University Press, 1990.
Munch, P. A. "Einige Bemerkungen zu den ʿAnawim und den resaʾim in den Psalmen." *Le Monde Oriental* 30 (1936): 13–26.
Murphy, Catherine M. *Wealth in the Dead Sea Scrolls and in the Qumran Community.* Studies on the Texts of the Desert of Judah 40. Leiden: E. J. Brill, 2002.
Murphy, Roland E. *Proverbs.* Word Biblical Commentary 22. Nashville: Thomas Nelson, 1998.
——. *The Tree of Life: An Exploration of Biblical Wisdom Literature.* Anchor Bible Reference Library. New York: Doubleday, 1990.
Naré, Laurent. *Proverbes salomoniens et Proverbes mossi: Étude comparative à partir d'une nouvelle analyse de Pr 25–29.* Publications Universitaires Européennes. Série 23, Theologié v. 283. Frankfurt am Main: Peter Lang, 1986.
Newsom, Carol A. *The Self As Symbolic Space: Constructing Identity and Community at Qumran.* Studies on the Texts of the Desert of Judah 52. Leiden: E. J. Brill, 2004.
——. *The Book of Job: A Contest of Moral Imaginations.* Oxford; New York: Oxford University Press, 2003.
——. "Bakhtin, the Bible, and Dialogic Truth." *Journal of Religion* 76 (1996): 290–306.
——. "Knowing as Doing: The Social Symbolics of Knowledge at Qumran." *Semeia* (1992): 139–53.
——. "Woman and the Discourse of Patriarchal Wisdom: A Study of Proverbs 1–9." *Gender and Difference in Ancient Israel.* Ed. Peggy L. Day. Minneapolis: Fortress Press, 1989.
Nickelsburg, George W. E. "Revisiting the Rich and the Poor in 1 Enoch 92–105 and the Gospel According to Luke." *Society of Biblical Literature Seminar Papers* (1998): 579–605.
Nielsen, Kirsten. *There Is Hope for a Tree: The Tree as Metaphor in Isaiah.* Journal for the Study of the Old Testament Supplement 65. Sheffield: JSOT Press, 1989.
Nussbaum, Martha C. *The Therapy of Desire: Theory and Practice in Hellenistic Ethics.* Princeton: Princeton University Press, 1994.
Oesterley, W. O. E. *The Book of Proverbs with Introduction and Notes.* London: Methuen & Co., 1929.

Ogletree, Thomas W. *The Use of the Bible in Christian Ethics.* Philadelphia: Fortress Press, 1983.
Perdue, Leo G. *Proverbs.* Interpretation Bible Commentary. Louisville, Ky.: John Knox, 2000.
——. *Wisdom and Cult: A Critical Analysis of the Views of Cult in the Wisdom Literature of Israel and the Ancient Near East.* Missoula, Mont.: Scholars Press, 1977.
Peristiany, John G., ed. *Honour and Shame: The Values of Mediterranean Society.* Chicago: University of Chicago Press, 1966.
Pitt-Rivers, Julian. "Honour and Social Status." *Honour and Shame: The Values of Mediterranean Society.* Ed. John G. Peristiany. Chicago: University of Chicago Press, 1966.
Pleins, J. David. *The Social Visions of the Hebrew Bible: A Theological Introduction.* Louisville, Ky.: Westminster/John Knox Press, 2001.
——. "Poor, Poverty." *Anchor Bible Dictionary* 5:402–412. 6 vol. Ed. David Noel Freedman. New York. Doubleday, 1992.
——. "Poverty in the Social World of the Wise." *Journal for the Study of the Old Testament* (1987): 61–78.
Plöger, Otto. *Sprüche Salomos (Proverbia).* Biblischer Kommentar, Altes Testament 17. Neukirchen-Vluyn: Neukirchener Verlag, 1984.
Rahlfs, Alfred. *'Ani Und 'Anaw in den Psalmen.* Göttingen: Dieterich, 1892.
Ricoeur, Paul. *Time and Narrative, Vol. 3.* Chicago: University of Chicago Press, 1988.
——. *The Rule of Metaphor: Multi-Disciplinary Studies of the Creation of Meaning in Language.* University of Toronto Romance Series 37. Toronto: University of Toronto Press, 1977.
——. *Interpretation Theory: Discourse and the Surplus of Meaning.* Texas Christian University Press, 1976.
——. "Biblical Hermeneutics." *Paul Ricoeur on Biblical Hermeneutics. Semeia* 4. Ed. John Dominic Crossan. Missoula, Mont.: Scholars Press, 1975.
Ringgren, Helmer, and Walther Zimmerli. *Sprüche/Prediger.* Göttingen: Vandenhoeck & Ruprecht, 1962.
Schams, Christine. *Jewish Scribes in the Second-Temple Period.* Journal for the Study of the Old Testament Supplement 291. Sheffield: Sheffield Academic Press, 1998.
Schroer, Silvia. *Die Weisheit hat ihr Haus gebaut: Studien zur Gestalt Sophia in den biblischen Schriften.* Mainz: Grünewald, 1996.
Schwantes, Milton. *Das Recht der Armen.* Beiträge zur biblischen Exegese und Theologie. Frankfurt: Peter Lang, 1977.
Scott, James C. *Domination and the Arts of Resistance: Hidden Transcripts.* New Haven: Yale University Press, 1990.
Scott, R. B. Y. *Proverbs and Ecclesiastes: Introduction, Translation, and Notes.* Anchor Bible 18. Garden City, N.Y.: Doubleday, 1965.
Searle, John R. *Speech Acts: An Essay in the Philosophy of Language.* London: Cambridge University Press, 1969.
Seitel, Peter. "Proverbs: A Social Use of Metaphor." *The Wisdom of Many: Essays on the Proverb.* Ed. Wolfgang Mieder and Alan Dundes. New York: Garland, 1981.
Seow, C. L. *Ecclesiastes: A New Translation with Introduction and Commentary.* Anchor Bible 18c. New York: Doubleday, 1997.
Shumway, David R. *Michel Foucault.* Boston: Twayne Publishers, 1989.
Simms, Karl. *Paul Ricoeur.* Routledge Critical Thinkers. London; New York: Routledge, 2003.
Simpson, J. A., E. S. C. Weiner, and Oxford University Press. *The Oxford English Dictionary.* 2nd ed. Oxford; New York: Oxford University Press; Clarendon Press, 1989.
Spohn, William C. *What Are They Saying about Scripture and Ethics.* Revised and expanded edition. New York: Paulist Press, 1995.
Steiert, Franz-Josef. *Die Weisheit Israels: Ein Fremdkörper im alten Testament? Eine Untersuchung*

zum Buch der Sprüche auf dem Hintergrund der ägyptischen Weisheitslehren. Freiburger Theologische Studien, 143; Freiburg im Breisgau: Herder, 1990.

Stone, Ken. *Practicing Safer Texts: Food, Sex, and Bible in Queer Perspective.* London and New York: T&T Clark, 2005.

Strugnell, John, and Daniel J. Harrington and Torleif Elgvin, in consultation with Joseph A. Fitzmyer, *Sapiential Texts, Part 2: Cave 4. XXIV.* DJD XXXIV. Oxford: Clarendon Press, 1999.

Tamez, Elsa. *When the Horizons Close: Rereading Ecclesiastes.* Maryknoll, N.Y.: Orbis Books, 2000.

Tanner, Kathryn. *Theories of Culture: A New Agenda for Theology.* Guides to Theological Inquiry. Minneapolis: Fortress Press, 1997.

Taylor, Archie. "The Wisdom of Many and the Wit of One." *The Wisdom of Many: Essays on the Proverb.* Ed. Wolfgang Mieder and Alan Dundes. New York: Garland, 1981.

Terdiman, Richard. *Discourse/Counter-Discourse: The Theory and Practice of Symbolic Resistance in Nineteenth-Century France.* Ithaca: Cornell University Press, 1985.

Tov, Emanuel. *Textual Criticism of the Hebrew Bible.* Minneapolis: Augsburg Fortress, 1992.

Toy, C. H. *Proverbs: A Critical and Exegetical Commentary on the Book of Proverbs.* International Critical Commentary 16. Reprint. Edinburgh: T&T Clark, 1988.

Van den Berghe, P. "'Ani Und 'Anaw Dans Les Psaumes." *Le Psautier: Ses origines, ses problèmes littéraires, son influence: Études présentées au 12e journées Bibliques Orientalia et Biblica Lovaniensia 4.* Ed. Robert de Langhe. Louvain: Université de Louvain, 1962.

Van Leeuwen, Raymond C. "The Book of Proverbs: Introduction, Commentary, and Reflections." *The New Interpreter's Bible. Volume V: Introduction to Wisdom Literature, the Book of Proverbs, the Book of Ecclesiastes, the Song of Songs, the Book of Wisdom, the Book of Sirach.* Nashville: Abingdon, 1997.

——. "Wealth and Poverty: System and Contradiction in Proverbs." *Hebrew Studies* 33 (1992): 25–36.

——. *Context and Meaning in Proverbs 25–27.* Society of Biblical Literature Dissertation Series 96. Atlanta: Scholars Press, 1988.

Voloshinov, V. N. *Marxism and the Philosophy of Language.* 6th edition. Cambridge, Mass.: Harvard University Press, 1996.

Von Rad, Gerhard. *Wisdom in Israel.* London: SCM, 1972.

——. "The Beginnings of Historical Writing in Ancient Israel." *The Problem of the Hexateuch and Other Essays.* New York: McGraw-Hill, 1966.

Walzer, Michael. *Spheres of Justice: A Defense of Pluralism and Equality.* New York: Basic Books, 1983.

Washington, Harold C. *Wealth and Poverty in the Instruction of Amenemope and the Hebrew Proverbs.* Society of Biblical Literature Dissertation Series 142. Atlanta: Scholars Press, 1994.

——. "The Strange Woman (אשה זרה/נכריה) of Proverbs 1–9 and Post Exilic Judaean Society." *Second Temple Studies, 2: Temple and Community in the Persian Period.* Ed. Tamara C. Eskenazi and Kent Harold Richards. Journal for the Study of the Old Testament Supplement 175. Sheffield: JSOT Press, 1994.

Watson, Wilfred G. E. *Classical Hebrew Poetry: A Guide to Its Techniques.* 2nd edition reprint with corrections. Sheffield: JSOT Press, 1984

Weiden, W. A. van der. *Le livre des Proverbes. Notes philologiques.* Biblica et Orientalia 23. Rome: Biblical Institute Press, 1970.

Weinfeld, Moshe. *Social Justice in Ancient Israel and in the Ancient Near East.* Jerusalem: Magnes Press, 1995.

Weinsheimer, Joel C. *Gadamer's Hermeneutics: A Reading of Truth and Method.* New Haven: Yale University Press, 1985.

Westermann, Claus. *Roots of Wisdom: The Oldest Proverbs of Israel and Other Peoples.* Louisville, Ky.: Westminster/John Knox Press, 1995.

——. *Forschung am alten Testament: Gesammelte Studien II.* München: Kaiser, 1974.

——. "Weisheit im Sprichwort." *Schalom. Studien zu Glaube und Geschichte Israels.* Ed. K.-H. Bernhardt. Stuttgart: Calwer, 1971.

Whybray, Roger N. *The Book of Proverbs: A Survey of Modern Study.* History of Biblical Interpretation 1. Leiden: E. J. Brill, 1995.

——. *The Composition of the Book of Proverbs.* Journal for the Study of the Old Testament Supplement 168. Sheffield: JSOT Press, 1994.

——. *Proverbs.* New Century Bible Commentary. Grand Rapids: Eerdmans, 1994.

——. *Wealth and Poverty in the Book of Proverbs.* Journal for the Study of the Old Testament Supplement 99. Sheffield: JSOT Press, 1990.

Winston, David. *The Wisdom of Solomon: A New Translation with Introduction and Commentary.* Anchor Bible 43. Garden City, N.Y.: Doubleday, 1980.

Wischmeyer, Oda. *Die Kultur des Buches Jesus Sirach.* Beiheft zur Zeitschrift für die neutestamentliche Wissenschaft 77. Berlin: Walter de Gruyter, 1995.

Wittenberg, G. H. "The Lexical Context of the Terminology for 'Poor' in the Book of Proverbs." *Scriptura* (1986): 40–85.

Wright, Benjamin G., III. "The Discourse of Riches and Poverty in the Book of Ben Sira." *Society of Biblical Literature Seminar Papers* (1998): 559–78.

Wright, Benjamin G., III, and Claudia V. Camp. "Who Has Been Tested by Gold and Found Perfect? Ben Sira's Discourse of Riches and Poverty." *Henoch* 23 (2001): 153–74.

Yoder, Christine Roy. *Wisdom as a Woman of Substance: A Socioeconomic Reading of Proverbs 1–9 and 31:10–31.* Beiheft zur Zeitschrift für die alttestamentliche Wissenschaft 304. Berlin: Walter de Gruyter, 2001.

INDEX OF ANCIENT SOURCES

INDEX OF MODERN AUTHORS

SUBJECT INDEX